Inclusion without Representation in Latin America

This book analyzes why and how fifteen Latin American countries modified their political institutions to promote the inclusion of women, Afrodescendants, and indigenous peoples. Through analysis and comparison of experiences in Argentina, Bolivia, Brazil, Chile, Colombia, and Mexico, the book accounts for the origins of quotas and reserved seats in international norms and civic mobilization. It shows how the configuration of political institutions and the structure of excluded groups set the terms and processes of inclusion. Arguing that the new mechanisms have delivered inclusion but not representation, the book demonstrates that quotas and reserved seats increased the presence in power of excluded groups but did not create constituencies or generate civic movements able to authorize or hold accountable their representatives.

Mala Htun is Professor of Political Science at the University of New Mexico. She is the author of *Sex and the State: Abortion, Divorce, and the Family under Latin American Dictatorships and Democracies* (2003). Her work has appeared in *American Political Science Review*; *Perspectives on Politics*; *Politics, Groups, and Identities*; *Latin American Research Review*; *Latin American Politics and Society*; and *Politics & Gender*, among other journals and edited volumes. In 2015, Htun was selected as an Andrew Carnegie Fellow. She has held the Council on Foreign Relations International Affairs Fellowship in Japan and was a fellow at the Kellogg Institute of the University of Notre Dame and the Radcliffe Institute of Harvard. Her work has been supported by grants and fellowships from the National Institutes of Health, National Science Foundation, Social Science Research Council, and National Security Education Program.

CAMBRIDGE STUDIES IN GENDER AND POLITICS

Cambridge Studies in Gender and Politics (CSGP) publishes empirical and theoretical research on gender and politics. The Series advances work that addresses key theoretical, normative, and empirical puzzles concerning sex and gender, and their mutual impacts, constructions, and consequences regarding the political, comprehensively understood.

General Editors

Karen Beckwith   *Case Western Reserve University (Lead)*
Lisa Baldez   *Dartmouth College*
Christina Wolbrecht   *University of Notre Dame*

Editorial Advisory Board

Nancy Burns, *University of Michigan*
Matthew Evangelista, *Cornell University*
Nancy Hirschmann, *University of Pennsylvania*
Sarah Song, *University of California at Berkeley*
Ann Towns, *University of Gothenburg*
Aili Mari Tripp, *University of Wisconsin at Madison*
Georgina Waylen, *University of Manchester*

Aili Mari Tripp, *Women and Power in Postconflict Africa*

Inclusion without Representation in Latin America

Gender Quotas and Ethnic Reservations

MALA HTUN

University of New Mexico

CAMBRIDGE
UNIVERSITY PRESS

CAMBRIDGE
UNIVERSITY PRESS

32 Avenue of the Americas, New York, NY 10013-2473, USA

Cambridge University Press is part of the University of Cambridge.

It furthers the University's mission by disseminating knowledge in the pursuit of education, learning, and research at the highest international levels of excellence.

www.cambridge.org
Information on this title: www.cambridge.org/9780521690836

© Mala Htun 2016

First published 2016

Printed in the United States of America by Sheridan Books, Inc.

A catalog record for this publication is available from the British Library.

Library of Congress Cataloging in Publication Data
Names: Htun, Mala, 1969– author
Title: Inclusion without representation in Latin America : gender quotas and ethnic reservations / Mala Htun.
Description: Cambridge, UK; New York, NY : Cambridge University Press, 2015. |
Series: Cambridge studies in gender and politics | Includes bibliographical references and index.
Identifiers: LCCN 2015029268| ISBN 9780521870566 (hardback) |
ISBN 9780521690836 (paperback)
Subjects: LCSH: Political participation – Social aspects – Latin America. | Women – Political activity – Latin America. | Minorities – Political activity – Latin America. | Democracy – Social aspects – Latin America. | Representative government and representation – Latin America. | Political culture – Latin America. | Latin America – Politics and goverment – 21st century.
Classification: LCC JL966.H78 2015 | DDC 320.98082–dc23
LC record available at http://lccn.loc.gov/2015029268

ISBN 978-0-521-87056-6 Hardback
ISBN 978-0-521-69083-6 Paperback

For Doug

Contents

Tables and Figures

Tables

Figures

Preface and Acknowledgments

I began to observe inclusion without representation in the mid-1990s. I was consulting for the Inter-American Dialogue and participating in meetings with women politicians, government officials, and activists from all over the Americas. At those events, I witnessed disagreements about the objective of women's inclusion in power. Some believed that the point of women's presence was to advance the representation of women's interests and other democratic values. Others simply wanted women there, regardless of their views or behavior. As one very senior government official put it: "If there are going to be dictators, we want women dictators too."

In light of these experiences, I had little faith in the hypothesis that the presence of more women in power would lead to better representation of women's interests and policy changes. I didn't believe that women and other disadvantaged groups had inherent interests. I had seen too much diversity among women, even among those from an elite political class willing to participate in women's meetings, to believe they would act collectively to pursue a political agenda without a great deal of prior work. Some women I met were committed feminists; others were more like Margaret Thatcher. Some had spent their careers fighting for human rights; others were relatives of *golpistas*.

Part of my early work involved identifying and analyzing various governmental initiatives to expand women's rights. States were creating new agencies for women, adopting national action plans and gender-sensitive budgets, modifying laws to combat violence, creating women's health programs, protecting rights of domestic workers, improving access to child care, and expanding services for victims of violence. These programs were not always well implemented or adequately funded, but their mere existence marked a dramatic change over the past.

I did not see greater government attention to women's rights as causally linked to women's greater numbers in power. Instead, I attributed policy changes to the influence of international norms and agreements, pressure from civic movements, and the autonomous action of highly placed and committed individuals. If anything, women's greater access to power was occurring simultaneously with other policy changes. In some places, there was representation without inclusion.

I came later to the study of Afrodescendants and indigenous peoples. Except in the case of Brazil – in which I had a longstanding interest and passion – my motivation was primarily comparative. I wanted to know why more countries had adopted quotas for women than quotas for groups marked by ethnic and racial disadvantages. I had spent time studying ethnic politics, and the relative lack of ethnic- and race-based public policies in Latin America was puzzling.

Over time, this question became less relevant, as racial and ethnic politics became more salient in the 1990s and 2000s. Yet the "race making" of Latin American states is unique, and patterns of racial and ethnic formation differ from those in other regions. The politics of inclusion and representation offers a lens to analyze these processes. By exploring claims for inclusion, state responses, and the implementation of quotas and reserved seats, this book draws out the lessons of Latin American experiences for the comparative politics of race and ethnicity.

This book improved thanks to comments from Lisa Baldez, Francesca Refsum Jensenius, Courtney Jung, Yu-Ming Liou, Vicky Murillo, Tianna Paschel, Jennifer Piscopo, Michelle Taylor-Robinson, Mateo Villamizar, and anonymous reviewers. Jorge Domínguez, Kent Eaton, Christina Ewig, Bret Gustafson, Raul Madrid, Laurel Weldon, and Kurt Weyland made constructive suggestions on earlier versions of chapters. I appreciate the feedback from members of the comparative historical analysis study group at the University of New Mexico, including Tamara Kay, Kendra Koivu, Sara Niedzwiecki, Mark Peceny, Bill Stanley, and Richard Wood.

I am grateful to Fernando Botero Zea and his father, Fernando Botero, for permission to use the image on the cover of this book. Rafael Archondo, Fernando Cepeda, Juan Enríquez, Mark Jones, René Mayorga, and Gina Parody helped me with contacts. Anna Calasanti, Colin Hannigan, Melina Juarez, and Juana Perez provided research assistance.

Juan Pablo Ossa, Marina Lacalle, and Juan Carlos Micozzi collaborated with me on parts of this work. Papers those authors and I published in 2013 in *Politics, Groups, and Identities* and the *Journal of Politics in Latin America* are updated in this book as Chapters 4 and 7, respectively. Earlier versions of this project were developed when I was a fellow at the Radcliffe Institute for Advanced Study at Harvard and at the Kellogg Institute of International Studies at the University of Notre Dame. Over the years, my research benefitted from collaboration with colleagues at the Inter-American Dialogue – Joan Caivano, Peter Hakim, and Michael Shifter – and at the Inter-American Development Bank–Vivian Roza, Gabriela Vega, Judith Morrison, and Ana Maria Brasileiro.

I presented portions of this book in seminars and workshops at different institutions, including Georgetown, University of Arizona, University of Texas at Austin, Purdue, Texas A&M, University of Toronto, Dartmouth, Princeton, the New School, MIT, University of Pittsburgh, Harvard, and University of Chicago. Participants at those events contributed important perspectives.

Between the time I began this project and the time I finished it, I got married, gave birth to three children, and lived in three different cities. Without the support and encouragement of my husband, Doug Turner, I would not have finished this project (and countless others). I dedicate this book to him.

List of Acronyms

ADN	National Democratic Alliance (Alianza Democrática Nacional)	Colombia
AICO	Movement of Indigenous Authorities (Autoridades Indígenas de Colombia)	Colombia
ASI	Indigenous Social Alliance (Alianza Social Indígena)	Colombia
CEDAW	Convention on the Elimination of All Forms of Discrimination Against Women	
CEO	Chief Executive Officer	
CIDOB	Confederation of Indigenous Peoples of Bolivia (Confederación de Pueblos Indígenas de Bolivia)	Bolivia
CM	Citizen's Movement (Movimiento Ciudadano)	Mexico
CNMCIOB-BS	Bartolina Sisa National Confederation of Campesino, Indigenous, and Native Women of Bolivia (Confederación Nacional de Mujeres Campesinas Indígenas Originarias de Bolivia "Bartolina Sisa")	Bolivia
CONAMAQ	National Council of Ayllus and Markas of Qullasuyu (Consejo Nacional de Ayllus y Markas del Qullasuyu)	Bolivia
CONIVE	National Council of Venezuelan Indians (Consejo Nacional Indio de Venezuela)	Venezuela
CRSUCIR	Central Regional Sindical Única de Campesinos Indígenas de Raqaypampa	Bolivia
CSCB	Syndicalist Confederation of Intercultural Communities of Bolivia (Confederación Sindical de Comunidades Interculturales de Bolivia)	Bolivia
CSUTCB	United Confederation of Peasant Workers of Bolivia (Confederación Sindical Única de Trabajadores Campesinos de Bolivia)	Bolivia
DC	Christian Democratic Party (Partido Demócrata Cristiano)	Chile

DEM	Democrats (Democratas)	Brazil
EDUCAFRO	Citizenship and Education of Afrodescendants and Poor People (Educação e Cidadania de Afrodescendentes e Carentes)	Brazil
ETIs	Indigenous Territorial Units (Entidades Territoriales Indígenas)	Colombia
EU	European Union	
FA	Broad Front (Frente Amplio)	Uruguay
FAP	Broad Progressive Front (Frente Amplio Progresista)	Argentina
FIES	Financiamento Estudantil (tuition program)	Brazil
FNMCB	National Federation of Peasant Women of Bolivia (Federación Nacional de Mujeres Campesinas de Bolivia)	
FUNECO	Ebony Foundation of Colombia (Fundación Ébano de Colombia)	Colombia
ILO	International Labor Organization	
IPU	Inter-Parliamentary Union	
KMT	Chinese Nationalist Party (Kuomintang)	Taiwan
LAESER	Laboratory for Economic, Historical, Social, and Statistical Analysis of Race Relations (Laboratorio de Analises Economicas, Historicas, Socais e Estatisticas das Relações Raciais)	Brazil
LAPOP	Latin American Public Opinion Project	
MAS	Movement toward Socialism (Movimiento al Socialismo)	Bolivia
MIP	Pachakuti Indigenous Movement (Movimiento Indígena Pachakuti)	Bolivia
MIRA	Movimiento Independiente de Renovación Absoluta	Colombia
MNR	Revolutionary Nationalist Movement (Movimiento Nacionalista Revolucionario)	Bolivia
MP	Member of Parliament	
MPU	United Popular Movement (Movimiento Popular Unido)	Colombia
MSI	Indigenous Social Movement (Movimiento Social Indígena)	Colombia
NGO	Nongovernmental Organization	
PAIS	Proud and Sovereign Fatherland (Patria Altiva y Soberana)	Ecuador
PAN	National Action Party (Partido Acción Nacional)	Mexico
PC do B	Communist Party of Brazil (Partido Comunista do Brasil)	Brazil
PDA	Alternative Democratic Pole (Polo Democrático Alternativo)	Colombia
PERLA	Project on Race and Ethnicity in Latin America	
PIN	National Integration Party (Partido de Integración Nacional)	Colombia
PJ	Peronist Party/Justicialist Party (Partido Justicialista)	Argentina

PLN	National Liberation Party (Partido Liberación Nacional)	Costa Rica
PODEMOS	Social and Democratic Power (Poder Democrático y Social)	Bolivia
PPB	Progressive Party of Brazil (Partido Progressista)	Brazil
PPD	Democratic Party (Partido Por la Democracia)	Chile
PR	Proportional Representation	
PRD	Party of the Democratic Revolution (Partido de la Revolución Democrática)	Mexico
PRI	Institutional Revolutionary Party (Partido Revolucionario Institucional)	Mexico
PROUNI	University for All Program (Programa Universidade para Todos)	Brazil
PS	Socialist Party (Partido Socialista)	Argentina
PS	Socialist Party (Partido Socialista de Chile)	Chile
PSDB	Brazilian Social Democratic Party (Partido da Social Democracia Brasileira)	Brazil
PSUV	United Socialist Party of Venezuela (Partido Socialista Unido de Venezuela)	Venezuela
PT	Workers' Party (Partido dos Trabalhadores)	Brazil
PDT	Democratic Labor Party (Partido Democrático Trabalhista)	Brazil / Brazil
PMDB	Brazilian Democratic Movement Party (Partido do Movimento Democrático Brasileiro)	Brazil / Brazil
PP	Progressive Party (Partido Progressista)	Brazil
PSB	Brazilian Socialist Party (Partido Socialista Brasileiro)	Brazil
PSDB	Brazilian Social Democracy Party (Partido da Social Democracia Brasileira)	
PTB	Brazilian Labor Party (Partido Trabalhista Brasileiro)	
RN	National Renewal Party (Renovación Nacional)	
SC	Scheduled Castes	India
SEPPIR	State Secretariat for the Promotion of Racial Equality (Secretaria de Políticas de Promoção da Igualdade Racial)	Brazil
SERNAM	National Women's Service (Servicio Nacional de la Mujer)	Chile
SMD	Single-Member District	
ST	Scheduled Tribes	India
TIPINIS	Isiboro Secure National Park and Indigenous Territory (Territorio Indígena Parque Nacional Isiboro)	Bolivia
UCR	Radical Civic Union (Unión Cívica Radical)	Argentina
UDI	Independent Democratic Union (Unión Democrática Independiente)	Chile
UERJ	State University of Rio de Janeiro (Universidade Estadual do Rio de Janeiro)	Brazil

UFMG	Federal University of Minas Gerais	Brazil
UN	United Nations	
UNDP	United Nations Development Programme	
UNE	Christian Democratic Party (Unidad Nacional de la Esperanza)	Guatemala
UNICAMP	State University of Campinas	Brazil
UNIFEM	United Nations Development Fund for Women	
URNG	Guatemalan National Revolutionary Unity (Unidad Revolucionaria Nacional Guatemalteca)	Guatemala
US	United States	
USP	University of São Paolo	Brazil
WINAQ	K'iche'ean People's Party	Guatemala

Introduction: Politics of Inclusion in Latin America

Political exclusion has been pervasive in Latin America. Portraits of fair-skinned men cover the walls of government buildings. Women, Afrodescendants, and indigenous peoples are scarcely seen in these portraits and barely present in the diplomatic corps, heads of government agencies, and, until recently, in national legislative chambers. Beginning in the last decade of the twentieth century, governments in more than a dozen countries modified political institutions to promote greater inclusion of members of social groups defined by gender, race, ethnicity, or a combination of these criteria (see Table 1.1). Between 1991 and 2013, fifteen Latin American governments approved national laws requiring political parties to nominate a minimum number of women as candidates in popular elections.[1] Bolivia, Colombia, and Venezuela created small numbers of reserved legislative seats for indigenous peoples (and Colombia did the same for "black communities"), Peru required parties to include indigenous candidates on their lists in local elections in the Amazonian region, and Mexico engineered some two dozen single-member districts around areas where indigenous voters were a majority. Meanwhile, scores of Brazilian universities introduced admissions quotas by race and class, prompting the government to adopt a national law in 2012 imposing such quotas on the entire federal university system.

Official efforts to promote inclusion were informed by claims of organizations advocating the rights of historically excluded groups. The second wave of feminist movements mobilized across the region in the 1970s, 1980s, and 1990s to demand an end to violence and discrimination, an expansion of social policies, and access to political power (Alvarez, 1990; Baldez, 2002; Jaquette, 1994). In the Andes, Mexico, and Central America, groups foregrounded an

---

[1] A sixteenth country, Venezuela, repealed its gender quota law in 2000, but then introduced quotas for regional and municipal elections in 2008 (Piscopo, 2015).

indigenous political identity to demand recognition, autonomy, land, and presence in political decision making (Jung, 2008; Lucero, 2008; Yashar, 2005). Black movements challenged racism, entrenched inequalities, and the ways that national ideologies of mixture hid, and diluted, Afrodescendant identity (Caldwell, 2007; Hanchard, 1994; Paschel, 2010; Rahier, 2012).

At the same time, an emerging global discourse connected democratic legitimacy to social diversity in decision-making bodies. The Beijing Platform for Action, endorsed by 150 world governments in 1995, including 19 in Latin America, recommended that states take "positive action" to achieve equal representation of women and men in all governmental and public administration positions (United Nations, *Report of the Fourth World Conference on Women*, 1996). Adopted at the 2001 World Conference Against Racism, The Durban Declaration and Program of Action – endorsed by all seventeen Latin American countries that participated in the meeting – similarly called for the full participation of Afrodescendants in politics.[2] The United Nations Declaration on the Rights of Indigenous Peoples, similarly affirmed by nineteen Latin American governments, codifies their "right to participate in decision making on matters which would affect their rights" (Article 18, adopted in 2007).[3] The Inter-American Development Bank sees affirmative action and quotas in politics as a mechanism to promote its broader goal of social inclusion and as an important tool to combat discrimination and stigma suffered by excluded groups (Buvinić, 2004).

Political theorists supplied the intellectual foundation for these trends by arguing that the political presence of social groups defined by gender, race, and ethnicity improves democratic governance. In diverse societies, different groups have distinct positions, experiences, and perspectives (Young, 2000, p. 136). Their inclusion in the political process informs deliberation and decision making with the special, situated knowledge of each element of society and improves participation and engagement (Kymlicka, 1995; Mansbridge, 1999a; Phillips, 1995; Young, 2000). When marginalized groups are present in decision making, policy outputs are more likely to combat, rather than reproduce, historical patterns reinforcing structural inequalities (Williams, 1998). Political inclusion builds trust and promotes a more egalitarian society.

Scores of countries outside of Latin America have taken explicit action to promote inclusion. In 2014, some seventy-eight countries across the globe had gender quotas or reservations, ethnic quotas or reservations, or both. Informal strategies to promote inclusion have appeared in dozens more, such as gender quotas used voluntarily by political parties in more than thirty countries; ethno- or race-conscious districting practiced in Ukraine and the United States; exemption from electoral thresholds for ethnic minority political organizations in Germany, Denmark, and Poland; and the overrepresentation of

---

[2] www.un.org/News/Press/docs/2002/GA10012.doc.htm.
[3] Colombia initially abstained and then, in 2009, endorsed the Declaration.

ethnic territories in the United Kingdom, Denmark, Tanzania, and Finland (Central Intelligence Agency, 2011; Htun, 2004b; Paxton & Hughes, 2013; Quotaproject, 2011; Reynolds, 2005). Some of these mechanisms of political inclusion stem from historical arrangements intended to make democracy possible in a plural society – such as the consociational model popularized by Arend Lijphart (Lijphart, 1977) – or to forge peace after civil conflict. Yet the vast majority of these institutional arrangements reflect attempts to improve actually existing democracies by making them more inclusive and legitimate (Dryzek, 1996).

Not everyone agrees that guarantees of inclusion and other affirmative action mechanisms advance democratic governance. Liberals criticize the focus on groups, rather than individuals; civic republicans lament the emphasis on differences rather than common projects. Libertarians allege that policies to promote inclusion, and affirmative action mechanisms more generally, produce greater social inequality (for more analysis see Htun, 2004b; Towns, 2010). In principle, quotas and reservations violate citizens' democratic rights to stand for office and to enjoy a free choice of representatives (Rehfeld, 2009a). Especially in the context of Latin America's racial and ethnic fluidity, codifying "race" in law and policy runs the risk of fixing racial identities and inciting conflict (Fry et al., 2007).

Historically, guarantees of political inclusion were used to restrict popular rule and entrench elite privileges. The French Estates-General allocated power by social rank (clergy, nobility, and everyone else) and voting typically occurred not by member but by estate. The Lancaster House Constitution, product of the 1980 agreement between Zimbabwean liberation armies, white Rhodesian settlers, and British colonial authorities, guaranteed whites 20 percent of the seats in the new Zimbabwean parliament, even though they made up only two percent of the population. South Africa's tricameral parliament of the 1980s included separate chambers for whites, coloreds, and Indians (but not for the black majority, who were excluded). The use of quotas, reservations, and other qualifications on electoral candidates to advance democracy is thus not without a certain irony.

How did guarantees of political inclusion evolve from an obstacle to an instrument of democracy? Why have a growing number of governments institutionalized inclusion, and what policies did they adopt? How do mechanisms of inclusion vary across countries and social groups? Have they improved the presence in power of members of disadvantaged groups and the representation of their interests?

This book focuses on Latin America to begin to answer some of these questions. Through analysis and comparison of experiences in Argentina, Bolivia, Brazil, Chile, Colombia, and Mexico, I account for the origins of quotas and reserved seats in international norms, domestic political coalitions, and moments of political opening forged by democratization and constitution making. I show that the existing configuration of political institutions (electoral rules and party systems), combined with the structure of excluded groups, set the terms and processes of inclusion. Institutions and group structures constrained the strategies available to excluded groups, the extent to which new constituencies could be engineered, and the means through which group members were able to gain access to decision making. I argue that quotas in political parties and reserved seats in parliament have delivered inclusion but not representation. Policies of inclusion have increased the presence in power of some members of excluded groups but not generated the formal and informal processes through which groups can authorize and hold accountable their designated representatives and the political class as a whole.

Inclusion versus Representation

This book defines inclusion in a minimal way as the presence in decision making of members of historically excluded groups. My notion of political inclusion presupposes formal enfranchisement, which depended on struggles for suffrage and citizenship waged by disadvantaged groups. Yet even decades after they gained full political rights, including the right to cast votes and stand for election, women, Afrodescendants, and indigenous peoples in elected office were scarce. The presumed injustice of this enduring discrepancy between their political participation as citizens and their presence in decision making constituted the impetus for the claims making analyzed in this book. As Williams puts it, "The chronic underrepresentation of historically marginalized groups is intrinsically unfair" (Williams, 1998, p. 19).

Other scholars define political inclusion more broadly to encompass not just presence but also representative behavior, power, policy influence, and even socioeconomic parity (Hero & Wolbrecht, 2005; Schmidt et al., 2010; Weldon, 2011). To understand the potential and limitations of institutional engineering, however, we must disaggregate and more precisely specify the concept of inclusion (cf. Rehfeld, 2009a). The linkages among presence, representative behavior, policy influence, and policy outputs are complex (cf. Goetz, 2003; Hassim, 2009).

Representation – defined here as an activity or behavior – is a complex, multidimensional concept, which Hanna Pitkin likened to a convoluted object in a dark room. Any single theory of representation, she wrote, is analogous to the part of the object illuminated by a flash bulb photograph, and reveals as much about the motives and worldview of the theorist as it does about what representation actually means. From one angle, representation can simply mean a resemblance or accurate reflection. From another, it can refer to a principal authorizing an agent to act on her or his behalf. Representation can occur when one agent is held to account for her actions by a group of principals, or it can be a process wherein one thing evokes emotions or attitudes normally invested in another. Finally, representation may mean acting on behalf of or in a manner responsive to the interests of citizens (Pitkin, 1967).

Pitkin's own preference is for this last view, which she calls "liberal" or "substantive" representation. She argues that representation must be thought about as a creative activity: "the forging of consensus, the formulating of policy, the activity we roughly designate by 'governing' " (Pitkin, 1967, p. 90). The activity of representation is bounded on the front side by the authorization to act (election) on the part of voters and on the back end when the representative is held to account retrospectively (reelection). These two bookends – authorization and accountability (the "two purposes of the vote"[Przeworski, Stokes, & Manin, 1999]) – are what distinguish *democratic* representation from other forms of representative politics (Rehfeld, 2006).

Though representation is an activity engaged in primarily by elected officials, it depends crucially on political processes involving civil society. For representatives to act on the behalf of interests of others, those others – we, citizens – must organize, deliberate, articulate interests, and communicate. Political representation activates a "communicative current" between civil and political society (Urbinati, 2006, p. 24). It is a process of mediation between the concerns and preferences of citizens and the decisions and policies on the government (Williams, 1998, p. 25). The organization of citizens around collective projects and the formation of public opinion make representation possible.

Origins of Quotas and Reserved Seats

For a long time, exclusion had the status of a problem no one noticed. In the 1980s and 1990s, this changed. The transition to democratic governance, the mobilization of social movements advocating rights of marginalized groups, and the consolidation of international norms of human rights (including women's rights, the rights of indigenous peoples, and the rights of Afrodescendants) raised global awareness that large sectors of the citizenry were unjustly excluded from political decision making. By seeking to include them, governments could promote a variety of desirable goals. Activists and advocates claimed that inclusion would improve the representation of the interests of marginalized groups, enhance democratic legitimacy, and change public policy outcomes.

At the same time, international organizations and scholars began to use parliamentary presence as a measure to gauge a country's progress toward greater equality. The Inter-Parliamentary Union, the United Nations Development Program, and the World Economic Forum rank ordered countries based at least in part on the proportion of parliamentary seats held by women (Inter-Parliamentary Union, 2013; United Nations Development Program, 1995; World Economic Forum, 2013). The Catalyst Census rated Fortune 500 companies according to the number of women on their boards (Catalyst, 2013). These rankings and other "performance measures" published by international organizations helped establish standards of democracy, progress, and modernity, creating the impression that country X was ahead of or behind country Y on these criteria.[4] To look better on the global stage by ascending in the ranking, national governments felt pressure to diversify decision making.

An anecdote will help to illustrate this point. In the early 2000s, the Inter-American Dialogue and International Center for Research on Women published a "report card" on women and power in Latin America and the Caribbean, which I prepared. At that time, Uruguay occupied second-to-last place in rankings of numbers of women in power (taking into account ministers, senators, deputies, and mayors). (Brazil occupied the last place.) We sent the report card to governments throughout the region. In response, the president of Uruguay sent the Dialogue a personal letter acknowledging receipt of the report card and declaring his intention to take measures to remedy the country's shortcoming in the future. He did not want Uruguay to continue to look bad on regional rankings.

The emergence of global incentives to promote inclusion did not mean that the achievement of government consensus was automatic. Some, but not all, countries adopted quotas and reserved seats. What made the difference? In the case of gender quotas, multipartisan and multisectoral coalitions of women politicians, which formed in some countries but not others, were the decisive factor. Male allies, presidents who for reasons of conviction or opportunism gave the decision nod to pro-quota coalitions, played an often-unacknowledged but important role in the adoption of quota laws. Broad-based coalitions were similarly important for the introduction of reserved seats by ethnicity and race, which took advantage of political opportunities created during constituent assemblies and other processes of reform. For example, the Colombian Constituent Assembly of 1990–1991 created a climate of participatory democracy, which made all actors more accepting of indigenous demands for guarantees of inclusion (later extended to groups of Afrodescendants) (Van Cott, 2000). Constitutional reform in Bolivia created a window of opportunity for coalitions of women to demand codification of gender parity and for indigenous groups to gain recognition of the right to inclusion.

Terms and Processes of Inclusion

Global experiences offer many examples of the different ways that institutions have been engineered to promote the inclusion of disadvantaged or minority groups. Some governments have introduced candidate quotas in parties, separate voter rolls, reserved parliamentary seats, special districts, and unique appointment procedures. Others opted for more general measures such as lower proportional representation (PR) thresholds, exceptions to PR thresholds, multimember districts, and overrepresentation of targeted geographical

---

[4] Rankings provoke changes in behavior and in the way people think. Experimental research shows that rankings may induce people to perceive qualitative differences as hierarchical relationships of superiority and inferiority (Espeland & Sauder, 2007).

regions (Htun, 2004b; Lijphart, 1999; Reynolds, 2005, 2011). Not all options are viable or desirable in every country. Different inclusion mechanisms do different types of work and relate to political institutions in distinct ways (Htun, 2004b; Bjarnegård and Zetterberg, 2014). Features of preexisting political institutions – such as whether a country has a majoritarian electoral system or uses PR, is federal or unitary, and the size of electoral districts – impose practical constraints on institutional engineering and condition the interests of actors vis-à-vis new policies. Majoritarian systems may introduce reserved seats instead of changing rules to PR (Lijphart, 1986a). PR systems, unable to switch to majority-rule single-member districts (SMDs), may create virtual districts or separate voter rolls. Party leaders will be likely to oppose policies that have the potential to harm their electoral prospects and to prefer policies that alter only minimally those rules from which they have benefitted.

Structural characteristics of excluded groups, such as the nature and stability of group boundaries, shape the terms and processes of inclusion.[5] When group boundaries are self-evident, it is relatively simple for political institutions to target benefits and sort voters by group (though such moves may still be contested). When group boundaries are more ambiguous, the application of group-specific policies – whether on political inclusion or access to higher education – poses practical difficulties. The government's conception of the targeted group may not match the self-perceptions of disadvantaged citizens. There may be confusion about whom the new policies are meant to benefit. The introduction of categorical distinctions among citizens may seem like a novelty and provoke principled opposition.

As we see in this book, gender quotas were a struggle to achieve, but once on the books, they were simple to implement. Women and men were easily identified (though not every human being conforms to a gender binary) and few people contested the classification. It was easy for parties to figure out which people, when placed on party lists, would help them fulfill the quota. Monitoring compliance was facilitated by the fact that most names indicate the sex of the bearer.

Racial and ethnic boundaries are less clear cut, particularly in Latin America. Ideologies of nationhood celebrated mixing and unity, and deemphasized status group differences. Though people refer to one another with racial and ethnic categories all the time, their use of labels varies and follows a plurality of criteria (Harris, 1964; Sheriff, 2001; Wade, 1993, 1997). Until the 2000s, most censuses did not even count by race or ethnicity (Loveman, 2014). In these

---

[5] Many scholars may question the utility of the notion of "group structure." Brubaker, for example, argues that ethnic, racial and/or national groups are not "things" but "ways of seeing" (2004). Jung's work documents how the formation of groups is a product of politics, rather than a precondition for politics (Jung, 2008). I agree that over the long haul, group structure is not fixed but flexible. In the shorter term, group structure is stable enough to inform the decisions of activists and governments about inclusion strategies and policies.

respects, the region differs from the United States, India, and South Africa, where ethnic and racial categories, membership in those categories, and criteria for classification were codified by the state over decades (Degler, 1971; Harris, 1964; Hoetink & Hooykaas, 1971; Marx, 1998; Tannenbaum, 1946). Since Latin American states did not "make race" in a consistent way, contemporary efforts to promote inclusion and representation through group-based policies face hurdles. Electoral agencies purporting to sort candidates and voters by race and ethnicity confront societies that are not explicitly and consistently organized along these lines. Unlike in the United States, where people identify themselves by race when applying for jobs, arriving at the doctor's office, answering surveys, soliciting welfare benefits, and in virtually any encounter with a public or private organization, most Latin Americans have lived their entire lives without ever answering a question about their race (Loveman, 2014, p. xi). It is an enterprise many citizens view as ethically abhorrent and advocates of group-based policies are frequently accused of importing a U.S. model of race relations (Bourdieu & Wacquant, 1999).

Group Representation

Excluded groups can achieve representation in two ways. Formally, they can be organized into constituencies, the building blocks of a system of representative democracy. Constituencies are defined as the "group in which a citizen's vote is counted for the purpose of electing a political representative" (Rehfeld, 2005, pp. 36–44). In the traditional, principal–agent model of representation, constituencies (principals) authorize representatives (agents) to engage in behavior that advocates their interests or opinions. Periodic elections induce responsiveness and accountability of the agents (Mansbridge, 2003; Pitkin, 1967; Przeworski et al., 1999; Rehfeld, 2009b; Urbinati & Warren, 2008, p. 389). Constituencies may be drawn in many ways, such as by territory, number of votes cast, profession, social class, or ethnicity. Electoral constituencies vary on other dimensions, including their degree of voluntariness, permanence, and homogeneity, as well as the manner in which they are justified (Rehfeld, 2005, pp. 36–44).

Among existing electoral systems, the major distinction in constituency definition lies between SMD plurality and PR systems. In the former, where constituencies are circumscribed by territory, district lines can be drawn around areas where disadvantaged groups cluster geographically, enabling them to constitute a majority and thus elect a "candidate of their choice." Such a practice has been in use for decades in India, where special districts are used to elect members of Scheduled Castes and Scheduled Tribes to parliament, and in the United States' majority–minority districts created to elect African-Americans and Latinos. In a proportional representation system, constituencies are formed by the group of voters that support a particular political party on election day. In this context, the vehicle for group representation is the political party whose candidates and voters belong to historically excluded groups. By self-constituting an electoral constituency, the group may collectively authorize and hold accountable its own representatives (cf. Guinier, 1994).

The second way excluded groups achieve representation is by organizing themselves into an informal constituency and relying on other modalities of representative behavior. As Mansbridge points out, representatives do not act merely as agents responsive to the principals of their district but also as gyroscopes following internal convictions and personal judgments; surrogates championing the rights of voters with whom they have no electoral relationship; and in an anticipatory fashion, acting in a way pleasing to voters at the next election (Mansbridge, 2003). Once these other modes of representation are taken into account, the proper unit of analysis for the study of representation is not just the formal constituent–representative dyad. Rather, the appropriate unit of analysis is parliament as a whole (Weissberg, 1978). What is more, quality is not determined only by the extent to which representatives fulfill the promises they made to voters at election time and by the correspondence between voter preferences and representatives' behavior (Mansbridge, 2003; Pitkin, 1967; Przeworski et al., 1999; Rehfeld, 2009b). Rather, the quality of representation should be evaluated by systemic criteria such as the character of deliberation in the polity, communication, mutual education, the accuracy of information, whether all relevant perspectives are present, and whether salient interests have a voice (Mansbridge, 2003).

Excluded groups can induce representation by introducing issues to the political agenda, shaping national public opinion, forging coalitions, sharing information, and building organizations. By contacting and communicating across the political spectrum, excluded groups can potentially compel *any* elected official to represent their opinions, interests, and perspectives. As Young puts it, an important measure of democracy is the degree to which people are connected "to a plurality of representatives who relate to different aspects of their lives" (Young, 2000, p. 133). If a group is able to engage in a collective project of formulating positions and advancing interests, it can potentially impose a mandate on, and hold accountable, the entire political system.

Inclusion, Not Representation

The new institutions engineered by Latin American governments, including quotas in political parties, reserved parliamentary seats, and special districts, have delivered inclusion but not representation. For the most part, they have increased access to decision making by members of marginalized groups. But the way institutions were engineered precluded group representation along the lines of the principal–agent model. With few exceptions, Latin America's marginalized groups did not correspond to those formal constituencies able to authorize and hold accountable their designated representatives in the ways anticipated by classical democratic theory. Women, Afrodescendant, and indigenous representatives tended to be elected by voters as a whole, not by disadvantaged groups. As a result, the same forces that fought for political inclusion often had little say over which group members ended up gaining power as their representatives, and little control over such individuals once they were in office. Sometimes, women nominated to comply with gender quotas had little interest in advocating women's rights, while indigenous and Afrodescendant "representatives" lacked connections to movements advocating the rights of these groups. As Anne Phillips predicted in the mid-1990s, the problem with the "politics of presence" is the failure of most electoral institutions to engineer linkages of authorization and accountability between legislators from excluded groups and the constituencies they purportedly represent (Phillips, 1995).

Nor have excluded groups consistently formed political parties to take advantage of reserved seats or the chance for representation under PR systems. Echoing global trends, Latin America lacks women's parties.[6] Ethnic parties, the subject of considerable research in comparative politics (see, e.g., Chandra, 2004, 2005; Horowitz, 1985; Ishiyama, 2009; Ishiyama & Breuning, 2011; Rabushka & Shepsle, 1972), and the dominant vehicle for the representation of minority groups in much of the world (Krook & Moser, 2013), have historically been absent in Latin America. Though parties deemed "ethnic" by scholars began to *emerge* in the last few decades of the twentieth century (Madrid, 2008; Rice & Van Cott, 2006; Van Cott, 2005), most have not *lasted* as ethnic parties.[7] In fact, the more "ethnic" the party, the less successful it has tended to be. As Raul Madrid has argued, parties such as the Movimiento al Socialismo (MAS) in Bolivia and Pachachutik in Ecuador succeeded precisely by becoming nonethnic parties – that is, by appealing to diverse sectors of people and espousing a populist discourse (Madrid, 2012). Other parties that began as ethnic parties later became more inclusive, such as Consejo Nacional Indio de Venezuela (CONIVE) in Venezuela and the Alianza Social Indígena (ASI) in Colombia (Angosto Ferrández, 2011; Laurent, 2012a).

The factors that shape political representation are not as susceptible to institutional engineering as those that determine the degree of political inclusion. Modifications of electoral regulations – such as the introduction of quotas and reserved seats – can improve political inclusion relatively independently of contextual factors (Krook & Moser, 2013). By contrast, the dynamics of political representation – including the accountability of individual legislators, the emergence of political parties, their programmatic or patronage orientation, the formation of governments, and the ideological congruence between voters

---

[6] There is one exception: a feminist party contested Paraguay's 2013 elections, advocating the legalization of abortion and other women's rights. Retrieved from www.worldcrunch.com/world-affairs/paraguay-039-s-first-woman-presidential-candidate-tries-to-crack-macho-culture/feminism-election-women-rights-lilian-soto/c1s11468/#.Vb1S_ngqdUQ (accessed April 20, 2013).

[7] Following Chandra, I consider an ethnic party to be a party that presents itself as the champion of one particular group or set of groups (Chandra, 2004, p. 2).

and legislators – respond to entrenched institutional rules and to the specificities of local contexts shaped by history, economic development, and social structure (Ferree, Powell, & Scheiner, 2013; Shugart, 2013). In Latin America, as in many newer democracies, the dominant logic of constituency formation among disadvantaged voters is patronage: political bosses and brokers forge constituencies of voters by offering material goods and favors (Ames, 1995; Auyero, 2001; Brusco, Nazareno, & Stokes, 2004; Calvo & Murillo, 2004; Chandra, 2004; Levitsky, 2003; Mainwaring, 1999; Wilkinson, 2007).[8] These representational dynamics are not as easily altered as the terms of political inclusion, at least in the short term.

As argued previously, excluded groups seeking representation may involve the entire political system. This requires work. A group must formulate perspectives and project interests; these cannot simply be read off the mere existence of the category (cf. Weldon, 2011, p. 14). Though simply being a woman is enough to fill a party list position mandated by a candidate quota, simply being a woman is not enough to engender representation. (The same holds for simply being indigenous, or simply being black.)[9] No individual can represent the perspective of a group. Developing group perspectives, opinions, and interests is a process involving intragroup communication and organization. "The group perspective is created when individual members of the group interact with other members of the group to define their priorities" (Weldon, 2002, p. 1156). Often, the group perspective is reflected in collective products, such as websites, pamphlets, and magazines where the group or movement presents and justifies its concerns (Ibid., p. 1157). To be good representatives, elected officials ideally should be connected to these processes (Dovi, 2002).

Mutual deliberation and communication are important to ensure that the group's interests and perspectives are truly representative of the whole, rather than merely reflective of powerful subsectors. As theories of intersectionality point out, marginalized groups are riven with differences and inequalities. Neither "women," nor "Afrodescendant," nor "indigenous" is a *single* group: they are *collections of groups*.[10] Far from the *premise* of politics, the

---

[8] In other parts of the world, ethnic parties are patronage parties. Promises of reward are directed exclusively toward a particular group (or groups). Voters vote for ethnic parties because they expect their co-ethnics more reliably to deliver material benefits (Chandra, 2004). Most of Latin America's "ethnic" parties, however, project clear political programs and have explicitly attempted to distinguish themselves from clientelism, corruption, and other traditional features of politics in the region (Van Cott, 2005, p. 12). They are explicitly *anti*-patronage.

[9] Much of contemporary feminist theory rejects the notion that women have a set of identifiable experiences, needs, or interests that a representative can act on behalf of (Fraser, 2007; Htun, 2005; Weldon, 2011; Young, 1994). Women are too large and diverse a category to have a shared identity or shared interests. Their experiences and needs are shaped not just by gender but also by other axes of social differentiation (race, class, ethnicity, sexual orientation, and so forth). The same holds for Afrodescendants and indigenous peoples.

[10] "Women" includes white women, mestiza women, rich women, poor women, old women, lesbian women, and so forth. "Indigenous" is a diverse category encompassing thousands of

existence of common interests and perspectives across diverse members of these groups is a political *achievement*. When disadvantaged groups are able to defend common positions, it is because of their prior political work, which usually involves explicit attempts to incorporate more disadvantaged subsectors (cf. Weldon, 2006, 2011).

Groups that are able to organize across lines of intersectional difference often succeed in advancing compelling demands for inclusion. Since they can communicate and project common projects, such groups are also better positioned to induce processes of representation. As this suggests, inclusion and representation should not be conceptualized as the beginning and the end of a single causal process. Rather, inclusion and representation should be seen as *joint* products of processes of group mobilization and deliberation in civil society.

Contributions of the Book

This book analyzes the responses of Latin American countries to pressures for political inclusion posed by transitions to democracy; the mobilization of new social movements; and the expansion of international norms on women's rights, indigenous rights, human rights, and antiracism. These forces combined in the last decade of the twentieth century and the first decade of the twenty-first to produce a historically unique politically opening. Other democratic moments, such as the struggle for independence from Spain (Domínguez, 1980), achievement of male suffrage (Valenzuela 1985), or the incorporation of the labor movement (Collier & Collier, 1991), included some sectors of the citizenry while excluding others. "Universal" male suffrage, for example, coexisted with restrictions on woman suffrage and literacy requirements that disenfranchised many indigenous peoples. Not until the late twentieth century did Latin America confront the challenge to include *all* citizens.

My arguments about the origins, processes, and consequences of mechanisms to promote the inclusion of marginalized groups in Latin America offer several contributions to broader literature on comparative politics and to our understanding of the challenges and possibilities for deepening democracy and achieving social justice. First, the book identifies the social, historical, and institutional factors that shape and constrain processes of inclusion, factors that are likely to be relevant in other countries and regions. These include the configuration of preexisting electoral and party systems, the structures of excluded groups, and the availability of models of inclusion being applied to other groups in the same country, regionally, and globally. In addition,

distinct groups, which in Latin America include speakers of a few hundred different languages, highland and lowland dwellers, rural and urban residents, people of different class backgrounds, and people with varying identities (Htun & Ossa, 2013). As discussed in Chapter 6, 62 percent of Bolivia's population identifies with one of the country's indigenous groups (thirty-six are recognized in the Constitution). Far fewer identify with the generic category of "indigenous."

the book highlights the interests of salient political actors vis-à-vis excluded sectors, such as party leaders seeking to maintain their share of seats and build a caucus of compliant legislators, as well as politicians reluctant to give up their seats. These institutions and interests forged the mezzo-level context in which inclusion occurred, furnishing elements for a polity-centered analysis of claims making from below and responses from elites at the top (cf. Skocpol, 1992).

Second, the book offers tests and empirical demonstrations of claims made in the literature on normative political theory. Many of the arguments I make here – particularly concerning the difficulty of establishing links of accountability between representatives and constituencies of voters from excluded groups – bear resemblance to problems flagged by political theorists (Dovi, 2002; Phillips, 1995; Williams, 1998). Yet many of the claims of normative theorists rest on conceptual logic and not the actual experiences of countries attempting to promote inclusion. To the extent that normative democratic theory relies on empirical evidence, it tends to be drawn from the United States (see, e.g., Guinier, 1994; Mansbridge, 1999b, 2003, 2011; Rehfeld, 2005; Williams, 1998). The United States is an inherently important case, but offers few examples of state-constructed inclusion beyond the majority–minority districts authorized by the Voting Rights Act. The SMD system used for the vast majority of congressional and state legislative elections is different from Latin America's electoral regimes.

Third, the book informs comparative analysis of identity politics. Latin America's racial and ethnic formation differs in key respects from that of countries where the majority of approaches to comparative ethnic politics were developed and reveal the limitations of concepts such as "ethnicity," "ethnic group," and "ethnic party." Ethnicity, race, and nation, and the social groups they define, are not "things in the world." They are "ways of seeing" or "perspectives on the world" (Brubaker, 2004; Brubaker, Loveman, & Stamatov, 2004). The history of these "ways of seeing" evolved differently across regions. Dominant theories of ethnicity and race in comparative politics were based not on Latin America, but on the experiences of Africa, Asia, and the United States, where racial and ethnic perspectives on the world developed in historically specific ways.

Latin American experiences showcase attempts to institutionalize inclusion in a context of fluid, ambiguous, and non-state-sanctioned group identities. Given the direction the world is heading – toward greater recognition of fluidity and mixity, even in countries with historic legal segregation (Prewitt, 2005; Skidmore, 1993a) – the region's experiences are instructive for all democracies. How can the state recognize status groups for political inclusion without cementing identities as principles of representation? The challenge of institutional recognition without reification is broadly relevant, and other countries can learn from the ways that Latin American countries succeeded and failed. By analyzing how marginalized groups seek and achieve inclusion policies, as well as how countries implement them, we can gain a better sense of what types of institutional arrangements to promote diversity in elected office are feasible, practical, and desirable.

Fourth, the book compares the inclusion and representation of women, indigenous peoples, and Afrodescendants. It identifies similarities and differences in claims making and state responses, at least in the cases analyzed. I propose reasons for the greater prevalence of mechanisms to promote women's inclusion than those explicitly targeting other groups. I attribute differences to the ways these groups are historically and contingently constructed, not to immutable features of gender, race, or ethnicity.

Finally, the book reveals the possibilities and limitations of the formal rights granted under democratic regimes. Though rights to political inclusion are important on their own, they do not generate the processes required for the representation of interests of marginalized groups and policy changes to promote equality. Especially in the weak states of much of the global south, progressive laws and policies on the books are not always enforced or implemented, and thus do not always translate into improvements in the situation of disadvantaged social groups on the ground (cf. Levitsky & Murillo, 2009). Across multiple sectors, there is a giant gap between formal rights – such as to political presence – and the ancillary, lateral, and infrastructural power needed to make those rights effective (Brinks & Botero, 2014). Political inclusion is just one aspect of a much larger process of achieving justice for marginalized groups.

Methodology

Latin American experiences constitute a critical case to explore the mechanisms and consequences of inclusion. They are representative of a new form of inclusion intended to deepen and enhance already existing democracy, not make it viable in a postconflict or "divided" society. No other region has a comparable density of countries with statutory policies that have been applied to different types of groups within varying institutional configurations. Some Latin American countries have more than twenty years of experience applying mechanisms to secure group inclusion: Argentina's gender quota law dates from 1991 and was first applied in 1993; Colombia's reserved seats for indigenous peoples were adopted and implemented in 1991. Between 1996 and 2009, fourteen other countries introduced policies to promote inclusion (Table 1.1) and by 2014, three-quarters (78 percent) of countries in the region (fifteen of a total of nineteen) had a statutory inclusion policy, though the target group and details of the policies varied. Policies directed at women were by far the most common, followed by indigenous peoples. To date, only Colombia has attempted to guarantee the political inclusion of Afrodescendants.[11]

---

[11] Bolivia's legislative reservations also apply to Afrodescendants, insofar as Afro-Bolivians share the same rights as other constitutionally recognized "originary peoples" and share a congressional seat with several indigenous groups in the province of La Paz (see Chapter 6).

TABLE I.I. *Mechanisms to Promote Political Inclusion in Latin America*

Country	Date of Original Law	Details
By gender at the national level[a]		
Argentina	1991	30% of candidates for lower and upper house
Bolivia	1997	50% of candidates for lower and upper house
Brazil	1997	30% of candidates for lower house
Colombia	2000	30% of appointed executive posts
	2011	30% of candidates for lower and upper house
Costa Rica	1996	50% of candidates for unicameral parliament
Dominican Republic	1997	33% of candidates for lower house
Ecuador	1997	50% of candidates for unicameral parliament
El Salvador	2013	30% of candidates for unicameral parliament
Honduras	2000	40% of candidates for unicameral parliament
Mexico	1996	50% of candidates for lower and upper house
Nicaragua	2012	50% of candidates for unicameral parliament
Panama	1997	50% of candidates in primary elections for unicameral parliament
Paraguay	1996	20% of candidates in primary elections for lower and upper house
Peru	1997	30% of candidates for unicameral parliament
Uruguay	2009	33% of candidates for lower and upper house (applies to 2014 elections only)
By race or ethnicity		
Bolivia	2009	Seven lower house seats reserved for "originary peoples"
Colombia	1991	Two Senate seats reserved for indigenous peoples; two house seats for "black communities"; one house seat for indigenous peoples

(*continued*)

TABLE I.I (*continued*)

Country	Date of Original Law	Details
Mexico	2001	Indigenous populations must be taken into account in redistricting (2006 and 2009 redistricting rounds created twenty-eight districts with high indigenous populations)
Peru	2002	"Native communities" must occupy 15% of slots on party lists in regional elections in Amazonian region
Venezuela	1999 Constitution; 2005 law	Three congressional seats reserved for indigenous peoples; one seat reserved in eight state legislatures; one seat reserved on municipal councils in indigenous areas

[a] Several countries also apply gender quotas in local elections and have modified quota provisions since the laws were adopted. For more information see Chapter 2.

This book presents the results of a multimethod research project designed to answer the questions of why policies of inclusion were adopted, what they look like, whether they worked, and what their consequences have been. I began to work on the project in 1996, initially with the intention of influencing public policy on women's rights and leadership. My focus expanded later to include the social and political inclusion and representation of other marginalized groups such as indigenous peoples and Afrodescendants. Since the early 1990s, I have made over 20 trips to Latin America (which includes the countries studied in this book, as well as Costa Rica, Peru, Venezuela, and Nicaragua), and interviewed politicians, government officials, judges, lawyers, activists, academics, and journalists, as well as representatives of international organizations (See Appendix 1 for a list of research trips and a partial list of people I interviewed). I worked as an advisor and consultant on women's leadership and social inclusion to the Inter-American Dialogue and the Inter-American Development Bank, which facilitated my access to political and intellectual elites. I participated in and observed events including conferences, seminars, and workshops, meetings of politicians and activists, election rallies, and plenary and committee sessions in national legislatures. Being present in these contexts enabled me to engage in informal conversations and group discussions about the topics of this book. In addition, I presented my research at meetings in Washington, D.C. and several Latin American countries where the subjects of this study discussed and often challenged my findings.

The book considers events that occurred through 2014. It draws on diverse sources of data, including personal interviews; participant observation; analysis of primary source data such as bill introduction and voting records, legislative debates, and discussions in constituent assemblies; laws, decrees, constitutions, and policy statements; and secondary literature. I use data on the racial and ethnic composition of the population from national censuses and PERLA headed by Edward Telles, and include information on Afrodescendants and indigenous peoples in national parliaments collected by me, LASER in Rio de Janeiro, and various secondary sources. Jennifer Piscopo provided data on quota laws; Piscopo and I assembled data on women's presence in elected and appointed office.

The empirical chapters adopt different methodologies to answer the specific question posed. In Chapter 3, I conduct a comparative historical analysis of political processes unfolding over time to answer the question of why quotas were adopted in Mexico and Argentina but not in Chile. Other chapters engage in historical, comparative analysis of the struggles of different disadvantaged groups within single countries. Chapter 4 compares the political claims of, and state responses to, women and indigenous peoples in Bolivia. Chapter 5 compares the evolution and consequences of inclusion policies for indigenous peoples and Afrodescendants in Colombia. Chapter 7 draws on a large database of bills introduced in the Argentine parliament and the fates of these bills. The chapter relies on electronic coding of bill content according to their emphasis on women's rights and gender issues. My coauthors and I used multivariate regression analysis to test hypotheses about trends in bill submission and approval across the large sample.

Plan of the Book

Chapter 2 analyzes the participation of women, Afrodescendants, and indigenous peoples in elected office. The chapter also discusses the challenges involved in collecting such information, in light of the history of census practices in the region. After defining what I mean with key terms used in the rest of the book (such as "Afrodescendant," "race," and "ethnicity"), I show that in most countries, women, blacks, and indigenous peoples are underrepresented in office relative to their population size. The data reveal that Latin America's disadvantaged groups tend not to cluster by party but to get elected from parties across the political spectrum. In addition, the chapter describes the mechanisms of inclusion that have been adopted across the region.

In Chapter 3, I account for the adoption of gender quotas across Latin America. I argue that the decisive factor behind quota adoption was the collective action of women politicians and activists. Such action cannot be assumed; it must be explained. Based on the intersectional approach, which presumes differences and conflicts among women, I describe how common experiences of exclusion within parties, frustration with masculinized norms, and the failure of gradualist policies to promote equality helped to bridge ideological differences between Left and Right. Case studies reveal how multipartisan coalitions of women helped get quotas approved in Argentina and Mexico, and how the absence of multipartisan cooperation precluded adoption of quotas in Chile.[12] One factor enabling women to agree was a self-limiting perspective on quotas: they were seen as a mechanism for *inclusion* only, not as a vehicle to achieve *representation*. Achievement of quotas was not tied to a common agenda of broader women's rights reform.

Chapter 4 (written with Juan Pablo Ossa) addresses the puzzle of why Bolivia endorsed a gender parity law but only a token number of reserved legislative seats for indigenous peoples. The country's first indigenous-led government, led by a president who was no feminist, was seemingly more responsive to women's demands than to the claims of indigenous movements. Adopting an intersectional perspective, the chapter analyzes the internal differences and power struggles among women and indigenous peoples. The chapter reveals how preexisting political institutions – namely, parties – shape the terms of inclusion. I argue that parties are likely to be more favorable to candidate quotas than to large numbers of reserved legislative seats. Whereas the former affect only individual men within the party, the latter have the potential to alter the interpartisan balance of power. The chapter describes how white urban feminists and indigenous women united to demand parity while sectors of the indigenous movement divided over whether and how the indigenous majority should be included in politics. Though quotas had the potential to benefit the majority of women, reserved seats were seen largely as a matter of concern to a disadvantaged subgroup of indigenous peoples. In line with Strolovitch's findings from the United States (Strolovitch, 2007), the chapter confirms that advocates for marginalized groups tend to foreground the interests of their most advantaged sectors.

Chapter 5 analyzes the rise and fall of mechanisms of political inclusion in Colombia. The Constitution of 1991, designed to introduce an inclusive, participatory democratic regime, envisioned reserved seats for indigenous peoples and "black communities." Adoption of the seats responded to the broader embrace of multiculturalism by Latin American governments, societal mobilization, and the "ethnicization" of Afrodescendant rights. More than twenty years later, in the 2014 elections, the two politicians who won the "black community" seats were not black. What happened? The chapter describes aspects of institutional design – constituency definition, ballot access, and ballot structure – which offered some inclusion but no guarantee of representation. Institutions set the stage for opportunistic political behavior, which ultimately undermined the legitimacy of the seats and enabled the perverse outcomes of 2014.

---

[12] By the time this book was going to press in 2015, Chile had adopted a gender quota law as part of a broader package of electoral reforms (April of 2015). The quota will be applied for the first time in 2017.

Chapter 6 illustrates the challenges faced by Latin American states seeking to use racial categories as the basis of public policy. I explore why Brazil, Latin America's largest country (where nonwhites make up more than half the population), opted to promote racial equality through quotas in higher education and not political inclusion. Marking a watershed change in the state's historic approach to race (which had been to deny its salience), quotas had been installed in the vast majority of public universities and were mandated by law for all federal universities in 2012. The meaning of race was contested at the level of implementation: the ways policymakers understood racial categories did not match how they were experienced by intended quota beneficiaries (Schwartzman, 2009). What is more, quota policies gradually evolved from a mechanism to reverse the status hierarchy privileging whiteness into a tool to combat class inequality (Peria & Bailey, 2014). The national law subsumed racial status to class criteria. The chapter concludes by arguing that Brazil stands to learn from Cuba's attempts to combat racism through socioeconomic redistribution, which have succeeded in some respects but failed in others.

Through analysis of legislative behavior in the Argentine Congress, Chapter 7 (written with Marina Lacalle and Juan Pablo Micozzi) explores what happens after women enter power as the result of quotas. Our analysis of patterns of bill introduction shows that many – but not all, or even a majority – of women legislators desired to advocate women's rights, and that women's advocacy increased as their numbers grew. But the likelihood that women's rights bills would be approved declined, suggesting that formal and informal norms marginalizing women and reducing their legislative efficacy persisted. At the same time, there is evidence that women's presence was associated with changes in the behavior of parliament as a whole: the more women were present, the more likely it became that *men* would author bills related to women's rights.

The conclusion reminds us why we should not expect too much from mechanisms of inclusion. They may bring anti-feminists and party hacks to power. They may rely on racial and ethnic categories crafted by elites, and, sometimes, on assumptions imported from other regions. They may not deliver good representation (and may make things worse). They may distract attention from enduring gender disadvantages. But quotas and reserved seats are still valuable. By putting members of marginalized groups in positions of power, they weaken discriminatory stereotypes, promote recognition, and communicate a message of inclusiveness. Diversity in leadership transforms the face of the polity. And in the long run, a democracy that looks better may end up working better.

2

Women, Afrodescendants, and Indigenous Peoples in Elected Office

In Latin America's history, women, Afrodescendants, and indigenous peoples were juridically excluded from full citizenship rights and politically disenfranchised (see, e.g., Andrews, 2004; Graham et al., 1990; Harris, 1964; Miller, 1991; Mörner, 1967; Wade, 1997). Over time, legal discrimination was reformed (at variable rates across countries and groups), but the patterns it forged remained. Inter-group differences in well-being today show a remarkable parallel to the *sistema de castas* created under the Spanish empire. Education, income levels, and experience of discrimination largely track skin color, with whites at the top and people with the darkest skin at the bottom (Telles, 2014b). Latin America's homosocial elite has anchored a status hierarchy privileging whiteness and maleness. Almost nowhere are women, Afrodescendants and indigenous people present in elected office in proportion to their overall numbers in the population. The political exclusion of disadvantaged groups reflects, and perpetuates, their subordinate social positions. Women, Afrodescendants, and indigenous peoples suffer lower wages; discrimination; a higher probability of being poor, unemployed, and living in inadequate conditions; and a greater likelihood of victimization and violence. These social and status inequalities are at odds with an inclusive, democratic society.

This chapter describes patterns of exclusion in Latin America by presenting data on the presence of women, Afrodescendants, and indigenous peoples in elected office. Women's numbers have grown in several countries, in some places dramatically, as a result of the introduction of gender quota laws. Indigenous peoples and Afrodescendants tend to be scarce in elected office, though their presence has risen in some countries. None of these excluded groups tend to cluster in their own party or set of parties. All tend to be elected from parties throughout the political spectrum. This chapter also describes the different mechanisms countries have adopted to promote inclusion, including candidate quotas in parties and reserved parliamentary seats. Appendix 2 presents a list of inclusion mechanisms used worldwide.

Terminology

In general, I use the term "Afrodescendant" to refer to people not currently living in Africa, or born there, but with ancestors originating from the region. The term was not very common as recently as ten years ago. Many scholars referred instead to "Afro-Latins" or more specifically to "Afro-Colombians," "Afro-Brazilians," "Afro-Cubans," and the like, and also to "blacks" (see, e.g., Andrews, 2004; Sawyer, 2006; Telles, 2004; Wade, 1993). Scholarship published since 2010, however, has used the term "Afrodescendant" almost exclusively (see, e.g., Loveman, 2014; Telles, 2014b). This book uses the term "Afrodescendant" interchangeably with "black."

Contemporary use of the word "Afrodescendant" by scholars, international organizations, and development practitioners has its origins in the Durban Declaration and Programme of Action adopted at the World Conference against Racism in 2001. The Declaration referred to "peoples of African descent" as people neither born nor living in an African country, but who had ancestors from the region.[1] The term gained broad purchase for its use by the Inter-Agency Consultation on Race in Latin America (IAC), formed in 2000. Coordinated by the Inter-American Dialogue, the IAC was a network of development organizations with projects intended to combat social exclusion and racism suffered by Afrodescendants.[2] In their official documents, organizations such as the Organization of American States, the Inter-American Development Bank, and the World Bank have similarly used the term "Afrodescendant" to refer to these groups (though the IADB's website uses the term "African descendants").

In the case of Brazil, I refer to people who declare their race/color on the census and other instruments as "pardo" or "preto" as black. In doing so, I conform to recent official discourse, as the government considers *pretos* and *pardos* to form the *população negra*, or the black population (Government of Brazil, 2010). This practice marks a change from the past, as historically, *pardo* was a category specifically intended to denote people who were neither *preto* (the word in the census to denote black) nor *branco* (white). In spite of the government's efforts to tell them otherwise, many people who declare themselves

---

[1] It also called specifically on countries of the Americas to recognize the existence of Afrodescendant populations, the racism they suffer, and historically entrenched inequalities in access to health care, education, and housing (United Nations, 2001).

[2] Member organizations of the IAC included the World Bank, the Inter-American Development Bank, the British Government's Department for International Development, the Pan-American Health Organization, the Ford Foundation, the Inter-American Foundation, and the Inter-American Commission on Human Rights.

as *pardo* do not consider themselves to be *negro* or Afrodescendant (Campos, 2013; Schwartzman, 2009; Feres Júnior, 2008). Though my terminology suggests that *pardo* → black → Afrodescendant, this is not always the case in lived reality.

Race and Ethnicity

It is important to clarify what I mean by race, ethnicity, and color. These terms do not have an *inherent* meaning. They have *historical* meanings shaped by the distinct ways that states, international organizations, and scientific and intellectual discourses have classified, categorized, and identified people. As Brubaker, Loveman, and Samatov point out, race, ethnicity, color, nation, and other categories are "not things in the world but ways of seeing the world" (Brubaker et al., 2004, p. 47). "Racial," "ethnic," or "national" groups do not exist independently of their identification, classification, and demarcation: they are created in and through such acts (Ibid.).

Racial and ethnic "ways of seeing" evolved differently in Latin America than in other areas of the world. Colonial powers in Africa and Asia, particularly the British, invented ethnic identities and then codified ethnic boundaries in laws and public policies (Anderson, 1991; Mamdani, 1996, 2001; Ranger, 1983; Vail, 1989). This does not imply that intergroup differences were absent prior to colonial rule. But they were not institutionalized and enforced by the power of the modern state, nor known as "ethnic." State practices of naming, labeling, and classifying, through the census as well as other instruments, formed part of a technology of rule. They made subject populations legible and facilitated the allocation of jobs and educational opportunities, while enabling official discrimination, reifying social divisions, and laying the groundwork for ethnic conflict and even genocidal violence (Horowitz, 1985; Mamdani, 2001; Montville, 1990; Scott, 1998). Official categorizations helped manufacture and maintain inequalities.

Though colonial Latin American states engaged in ethnic and racial classification, and used these categories to allocate rights and privileges, such practices were rejected and abandoned by Independent states (Cope, 1994; Graham et al., 1990; Mörner, 1967; Seed, 1982). Latin American countries forged models of the nation based not on racial or ethnic pluralism but on mixing and miscegenation. Ideologies of *mestizaje* (mixity), the *raza cosmica* (the cosmic race), and *blanqueamiento* (whitening), combined with administrative practices (such as the failure to count citizens by race and ethnicity, and the absence of segregation or official discrimination), upheld a different "way of seeing." Latin American societies were multihued, with different social classes and cultural practices. They were not multiethnic, in the sense of being composed of distinct descent-based groupings.[3] Yet stratification and inequality

---

[3] The growing popularity of ethnic idioms in the region, particularly after the 1990s, has shifted this panorama, but not for everyone.

based on color, language, culture, and other characteristics has persisted. The coexistence of flexibility on the one hand with racism and discrimination on the other marks Latin America's uniqueness in the study of comparative ethnic politics (cf. Wade, 1997).

Since the 1990s, many Latin American governments have introduced new policies to combat racism, inequality, exclusion, and discrimination, including the quotas and reservations studied in this book. The conceptualization and implementation of such policies depend on a good diagnosis of the problem, which requires social and economic data disaggregated by race and ethnicity. Such data were widely unavailable until very recently. Today, virtually every Latin American country attempts to enumerate its Afrodescendant and indigenous populations, permitting analysis of the racialization of social inequality. Yet as we see later in this chapter, different methods of classifying and counting groups yield dramatically different pictures of the racial and ethnic composition of the citizenry. What you choose to see determines what you get. And different people may see different things, even viewed through the same lens.

As there is no single underlying racial or ethnic reality to depict, but rather multiple dimensions, there is little point in hewing to precise terminology. To make my writing less tedious, I use the terms "race" and "color" interchangeably. Often, however, I use the term "ethnicity" for different purposes. As Wade points out, Latin America's racial identifications and categorizations historically were based on physical characteristics, whereas ethnic labels derived from perceptions of cultural differences, including language use (Wade, 1997). In practice, the groups denoted by such terms overlap (indigenous peoples, for example, are marked both racially and ethnically, as are some Afrodescendant groups). This overlap has only grown in the recent round of censuses, as questions about Afrodescendancy and indigeneity often use the same referents (ancestry, traditions, physical appearance, and so forth).

The ways Latin Americanists use the terms "race" and "ethnicity" differs from the practice in mainstream comparative politics. Dominant approaches define ethnicity and race as an attribute of individuals and groups that is based on descent (Chandra, 2004, 2006; Fearon, 2003; Horowitz, 1985). The descent-oriented nature of race and ethnicity implies that, though identities and groups can change, the extent of change is limited (sticky), at least in the short term (Chandra, 2006).

In Latin America, everyday practices of ethnic and racial identification and classification are usually not based on descent. Criteria for classification tend to revolve around perceived phenotype and perceived social status. As a result, siblings (of the same parents) can belong to different "races." And a person's ethnic or racial category can change as she or he acquires an education, earns more income, or changes neighborhoods (Graham et al., 1990; Harris, 1964; Telles, 2004, 2014b; Wade, 1997). In a nationally representative study of Peruvians conducted by the Project on Ethnicity and Race in Latin America (PERLA), for example, only 61 percent of respondents who reported that they had indigenous ancestry actually identified with the indigenous category (Sulmont & Callirgos, 2014). In Mexico, people jettison their indigenous identity by learning Spanish, wearing Western clothes, and moving out of indigenous communities (Martínez Casas et al., 2014).

Patterns of Exclusion in Latin America

Rigorous analysis of the political presence of excluded groups is thwarted by a lack of data. Though women are easy to count, Afrodescendants and indigenous peoples are not. Until 2014, when the Brazilian electoral court began to include a question about race/color when candidates declared their intention to run for office, no country had collected such information about elected officials and international organizations, such as the Inter-American Development Bank and the World Bank, did not gather it on a regular basis.[4]

Statistical data on race and ethnicity in all spheres have been historically scarce, especially for Afrodescendants. Though Brazil and Cuba had collected data on race/color for many decades, only in the 1990s did an additional country – Colombia – begin to collect data on Afrodescendancy. And that year – 1993 – the Colombian census dramatically undercounted numbers of blacks by asking a question about whether or not respondents were members of a "black community."[5] In the 2000s, a total of nine countries inquired about Afrodescendancy. By the 2010s, this number had grown to sixteen. Only Chile, the Dominican Republic, and El Salvador neglected to enumerate Afrodescendants in their national censuses in that decade (Del Popolo et al., 2009; Loveman, 2014). More countries historically collected data on indigeneity, and those that did not do so began to enumerate indigenous peoples in the 1990s and 2000s. By the 2010 round, every Latin American country except for the Dominican Republic asked questions intended to measure the size of the indigenous population (Loveman, 2014).

For both groups, criteria for counting differed across countries and over time within the same country. In the 2010 round, for example, ways of measuring Afrodescendancy or blackness varied. Questions or inquiries could be about race/color, culture, traditions, group membership, physical appearance, individual self-identity, or ancestry. Ways of naming blackness included Afrodescendant, *negro*, *pardo*, *moreno*, *mulato*, Afro-Colombian/ Afro-Ecuadorian, and so on. Methods of enumerating the indigenous populations also differed: questions could refer to self-identification; membership

---

[4] Other countries have opted not to gather such data. When the Costa Rican electoral court considered including a space on registration cards for candidates to declare their race or ethnicity, the idea was immediately rejected on the grounds that it would be perceived as discriminatory (Conversation with Eugenía María Zamora, Vice President of Electoral Court, San José, Costa Rica, July 26, 2011).

[5] A mere 1.5 percent of the population claimed to identify as a member of a "black community," fewer than those who claimed an indigenous identity (Barbary & Urrea, 2004).

in a group, *pueblo*, or nationality; language use (and parents' language use); ancestry; culture; or traditions. Most censuses asked people to identify with specific indigenous ethnic groups and not the generic "indigenous" category (Del Popolo et al., 2009; Loveman, 2014, pp. 252–265).

Beginning in the 2000s, public opinion surveys offered another way of estimating the size of the Afrodescendant and indigenous populations. The Latin American Public Opinion Project (LAPOP), based at Vanderbilt University, includes questions on ethno-racial self-identification. In addition, PERLA administered nationally representative surveys in 2010 in Brazil, Colombia, Mexico and Peru that measured ethno-racial identity in distinct and innovative ways, including through the use of a skin color ranking scored by the interviewer (Telles, 2014b).[6]

Variation in counting criteria has produced different estimates of the size of indigenous and Afrodescendant groups. For example, the size of the Afrodescendant population in Colombia changed from 1.5 to some 11 percent between the 1993 and 2005 censuses owing to changes in the categories used to assess Afrodescendancy. The same happened in Costa Rica, where the group's size changed from 2 to 8 percent of the population between the 2000 and 2011 censuses (Telles, 2014a, p. 8). In Brazil, different methods of determining who is black produce dramatically different estimates of population size. In the PERLA survey, for example, the size of Afrodescendant group varied from 6 to 60 percent of the sample depending on classification criteria. Whereas only 6 percent of those surveyed self-identified as "negro" in response to an open-ended interviewer question, 55 percent self-identified as "preto" or "pardo," and some 60 percent were so categorized by the interviewer (Silva & Paixão, 2014, p. 191). A different Brazilian survey from 2002 employed six different methods of racial classification: depending on the method, the non-white group ranged from 11 to 59 percent of the sample (Bailey, Loveman, & Muniz, 2013).

Indigenous group size also fluctuates according to counting method. Consider the results of the PERLA survey administered in Peru. When asked to identify with the generic category of "indigenous," fewer than 5 percent of the sample responded affirmatively, but 35 percent of the sample reported having an indigenous parent and just under 40 percent reported having another indigenous ancestor (Sulmont & Callirgos, 2014, pp. 149–153). A similar pattern held for Mexico, according to the PERLA survey: 12 percent of the sample identified with the generic term "indigenous," 20 percent identified with a specific

---

[6] The skin color ranking was meant to capture the external dimensions of racial classification, since racism and discrimination often occur via the external, social classification of individuals, not their own self-identification. In addition, the color palette facilitated analysis of phenotypical variations within each racial and ethnic category (e.g., lighter versus darker mestizos). Telles and his collaborators found that skin color mapped more closely onto educational and income inequality than did ethnic and racial categories (Telles, 2014b).

TABLE 2.1. *Afrodescendant and Indigenous Populations in Latin America (numbers are rounded to the 1,000s)*

Countries	Total Population	Year	Afrodescendant Population	Percentage	Indigenous Population	Percentage
Argentina	40,117,000	2010	150,000	0.4	955,000	2.4
Bolivia	10,027,000	2012	24,000	0.2	2,790,000	40.6
Brazil	190,733,000	2010	97,083,000	50.9	897,000	0.5
Chile	16,636,000	2012	97,000	0.6	1,700,000	10.3
Colombia	42,954,000	2005	4,274,000	10.5	1,393,000	3.4
Costa Rica	4,302,000	2011	334,000	7.8	104,000	2.4
Cuba	11,163,000	2012	3,885,000	34.8	—	—
Dominican Republic	9,445,000	2010	8,980,000 (*indio*)	89.0	—	—
Ecuador	14,484,000	2010	1,043,000	7.2	1,014,000	7.0
El Salvador	5,744,000	2007	7,000	0.13	13,000	0.23
Guatemala	14,713,000	2011	5,000	0.0	4,428,000	30.0
Honduras	8,448,000	2011	59,000	1.0	428,000	7.0
Mexico	112,337,000	2010	2,366,000	2.2	11,133,000	9.9
Nicaragua	5,142,000	2005	23,000	0.4	444,000	8.6
Panama	3,454,000	2010	313,000	9.2	418,000	12.3
Paraguay	6,673,000	2012	234,000	3.5	116,000	1.7
Peru	27,412,000	2007	411,000	1.5	7,600,000	27.0
Uruguay	3,286,000	2011	255,000	7.8	159,000	4.8
Venezuela	27,228,000	2011	14,534,000 (*moreno*)	53.4	725,000	2.7
Totals	554,298,000		133,027,000	24.0	34,317,000	6.2

Source: Telles (2014a, pp. 26–27). His data are mostly from the latest round of national censuses, with the following exceptions: data on Chile (Afrodescendants), the Dominican Republic, and Mexico (Afrodescendants) come from LAPOP, and on Paraguay (Afrodescendants) from the Inter-American Development Bank.

ethnic category (Mayan, Mixtec, Zapotec, etc.) based on ancestors or customs, and 44 percent acknowledged having an indigenous ancestor (Martínez Casas et al., 2014, pp. 52–53). In the Mexican census, the indigenous group grew from 6 to 15 percent of the population between 2000 and 2010, which the PERLA scholars attribute to the inclusion of a reference to "culture" (Ibid.).

Table 2.1 contains the most recent available data (as of 2014), mostly from national censuses, on the percentage of the population that is Afrodescendant and indigenous in 19 countries.

Based on the census and other data, Telles and other PERLA scholars estimate that Afrodescendants make up some 20 to 25 percent of Latin America's total population. They offer a range, rather than a precise figure, owing to the difficulty enumerating the racial composition of the Dominican Republic and Venezuela. Table 2.1 categorizes people who self-identified as "*indio*" and "*moreno*" as Afrodescendant in the Dominican Republic, though the category likely includes people who are not. The same holds for the *pardo* category in Brazil. (Telles, 2014a). At the same time, however, the practice of self-definition used by national censuses has tended to underestimate the size of the Afrodescendant population. As a result of negative social stigmas attached to both categories, many people who can pass prefer to identify as white (Ibid.).

As we see in this book, the difficulty of pinning consistent boundaries around Latin America's racial and ethnic groups poses a challenge not just for census counting but also for electoral engineers designing institutions to promote inclusion and representation. Most states cannot count and classify voters in consistent ways. And even those that can – such as Brazil and Cuba, where historically there has been more regularity in practices of self-definition and classification by others, may not want to. Many citizens object in principle to their segregation into distinct racial and ethnic categories by the state. And if the state cannot construct constituencies of minority voters, how can these voters select and hold accountable their designated representatives? Before addressing these questions, let us first examine trends in women's, Afrodescendants', and indigenous peoples' presence in power.

Women

Women's presence in power has grown significantly over time, with variations across countries and branches and levels of government.[7] As many existing works analyze women's representation in elected office (see, e.g., Hinojosa, 2012; Jones, 2009; Piscopo, 2010; Schwindt-Bayer, 2010), this treatment will highlight only major trends. Unlike Afrodescendants and indigenous peoples, women are easy to count. Data were available for all countries, though not for all levels of government.

Women's presence in national legislatures has increased significantly over time. Their share of seats in single or lower houses of parliament climbed steadily between 1990 and 2014: it averaged 9 percent in 1990, 13 percent in 2000, 21 percent in 2010, and 25 percent in 2014. Cross-national differences are important, as revealed in Table 2.2: in 2014, women's presence ranged from a high of around 40 percent in the Argentine and Nicaraguan lower houses and Costa Rica's unicameral parliament to a low of 9 percent in the Brazilian lower house and the Panamanian parliament. As we see later in this chapter, a great deal of this variation can be attributed to the presence or absence of a gender quota law.

Women's presence in cabinets has grown. In 2000, they made up 10 percent of ministers in South America and 16 percent of ministers in Mexico and Central America; in 2014, these figures had increased to 26 percent and 27 percent, respectively. These averages obscure large amounts of variation: women's share of cabinet seats ranged from highs of 44 percent in Nicaragua, 42 percent in Peru, 39 percent in Chile (under the second Bachelet administration), to

---

[7] This section draws from Htun and Piscopo (2010, 2014).

TABLE 2.2. *Women in Congress in Latin American Countries, 2014*

	Election Year	Lower House	Upper House
Argentina	2013	36.2	39.4
Bolivia	2009	25.4	47.2
Brazil	2010	8.6	16
Chile	2009	14.2	13.2
Colombia	2010	12.1	16
Costa Rica	2010	38.6	
Cuba	2013	48.9	
Dom. Republic	2010	20.8	9.4
Ecuador	2013	38.7	
El Salvador	2012	26.2	
Guatemala	2011	13.3	
Honduras	2009	19.5	
Mexico	2012	36.8	32.8
Nicaragua	2011	40.2	
Panama	2009	8.5	
Paraguay	2013	17.5	20
Peru	2011	21.5	
Uruguay	2009	12.1	12.9
Venezuela	2010	17	
Average		24.5	

Source: Htun and Piscopo (2014, p. 8).

lows of 8 percent in El Salvador, 13 percent in Uruguay, and 14 percent in the Dominican Republic (Figure 2.1).

Women are less present in executive office at the subnational level. Few women have been elected as governor in federal countries. Argentina elected its first women governors in 2007; Mexico and Brazil have elected only a handful of women governors since the mid-1980s. Women held an average of 9 percent of mayoral posts in Latin America and the Caribbean in 2010, an improvement over 1990 and 2000, when women made up some 5 percent of mayors (Htun, 2001; Htun & Piscopo, 2014).[8]

In general, women's numbers are lower in executive than in legislative offices. It is harder for women and other relative newcomers to win the majoritarian or plurality elections characterizing most executive contests. When only one seat is in dispute, parties tend to field the strongest candidates. Owing to their greater financial power, these are usually men. In addition, governor and mayor positions involve control of local tax resources and federal disbursements ("pork"), and can therefore be used to construct and maintain patronage

---

[8] Data on women's political participation at the local level are drawn from the 2010 Gender Equality Observatory, organized and published by the United Nations' Economic Commission on Latin America and the Caribbean (ECLAC).

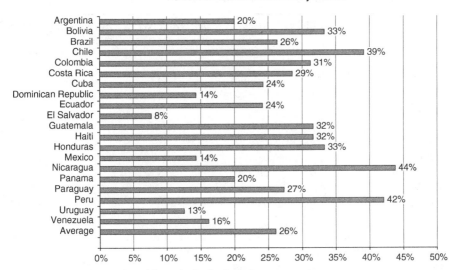

FIGURE 2.1. Women in cabinets in Latin American countries, 2014.
Source: Htun and Piscopo (2014), p. 4.

networks (Htun & Piscopo, 2010, p. 4). These networks confer power across multiple areas of government. Franceschet and Piscopo (2013), for example, link women legislators' exclusion from power networks in Argentina to the fact that they are significantly less likely than men to have occupied "high pork" positions such as governor and mayor.

Afrodescendant Representation in National Legislatures

Composing a picture of Afrodescendant presence in national elected office required collecting original data. As mentioned earlier, only in 2014 did one country – Brazil – begin to collect data on the race/ethnicity/color of candidates (and by extension, elected officials) as a result of a directive from the Supreme Electoral Court.[9] For this book, I focused on seven Latin American countries: Brazil, Colombia, Costa Rica, Ecuador, Peru, Uruguay, and Venezuela. Almost all of these countries have significant Afrodescendant population presence, Afrodescendants in the national legislature, and civic organization around black rights. I estimated numbers of Afrodescendants in national legislatures by classifying legislator photos available on congressional websites for every country except Brazil.[10] This method has precedent: Brazilian scholars

---

[9] Resolution 23.405/2014, Tribunal Superior Eleitoral – TSE. Retrieved from www.seppir .gov.br/noticias/ultimas_noticias/2014/04/tse-inclui-quesito-2018cor-ou-raca2019- em-registros-de-candidaturas-ja-nas-eleicoes-de-2014 (accessed August 30, 2014).

[10] A small team of researchers from the University of New Mexico and Vanderbilt University coded the photos separately. There was significant agreement on visible Afrodescendancy for

TABLE 2.3. *Afrodescendants in National Legislatures, 2014*

Country	Total Blacks	Black Women	Total No. of Legislators	Blacks as a% of Total
Brazil				
Chamber	103	n/d	513	20
Senate (2010)	1	0	81	1.2
Colombia				
House	9	0	166	5.4
Senate	1	0	102	1
Costa Rica				
Unicameral	0	0	57	0
Ecuador				
Unicameral	9	5	137	6.6
Peru				
Unicameral	3	3	130	2.3
Uruguay				
House	1	0	99	1
Senate	0	0	31	0
Venezuela				
Unicameral	4	1	165	2.4

Sources: Author's calculations; afrocolombianosvisibles (2014); Locatelli (2014).

at the Laboratory for Economic, Historical, Social, and Statistical Analysis of Race Relations (LAESER), in Rio de Janeiro, had also estimated the racial composition of the legislature by classifying photos on file with the TSE (Paixão & Carvano, 2008). Ideally, this strategy would be supplemented by two additional levels of measurement: (1) validation by the legislator in question that she or he identifies as Afrodescendant; and (2) intersubjective confirmation by legislative staff, political journalists, and others in the milieu that the legislator is "known as black." For the 2014 Colombian elections (but not previous legislatures), I relied on data from the "Afrocolombianos visibles" blog. Data are presented in Table 2.3.

These numbers are low in light of the Afrodescendant presence in society. The degree of Afrodescendant underrepresentation is pronounced in Brazil (51 percent of society, compared to some 20 percent of the lower house of Congress), Colombia (11 percent of society; 5 percent of the lower house), and

every country except Venezuela. This methodology was used by Paixão and Carvano's team at the Federal University of Rio de Janeiro for the 2008–2009 report on Brazil's racial inequalities. The Brazil data in this chapter (for a more recent legislature than that studied by Paixão and Carvano) come from Universo Online's "Congresso em foco" and for the 2014 elections, from the Electoral Court's official data. I am grateful to Elvira Pichado Delacour, Margarita Corral, and Jason Morin for their assistance.

Costa Rica (8 percent of the population, no deputy). In Ecuador and Peru, by contrast, Afrodescendants were close to proportionally represented in 2014, and in Peru all three Afrodescendant legislators were women.

In Brazil, the parliamentary presence of Afrodescendants appeared to grow significantly after the Supreme Electoral Court began requiring candidates (and by extension elected officials) to declare their race/color. Official data suggest that *pretos* and *pardos* made up 20 percent of deputies elected to lower house of Congress in 2014 overall (see Table 2.3). Of the twenty-eight parties with some presence in the Chamber of Deputies, only five did not have any legislators assuming a black identity.[11]

In 2010, only 9 percent of the federal deputies were black (forty-four total) including seven women.[12] As this number was supplied by a different source with a different method, it is not strictly comparable to the 2014 data. In 2006, roughly the same number of black deputies were elected (forty-five), again using different counting methods, but with only three women (Paixão & Carvano, 2008, p. 148). In the 1990s, there were only about fifteen black deputies in the lower house of Congress (Johnson, 1998).

Black legislators were elected from parties across the political spectrum. As Table 2.4 shows, a variety of parties had elected deputies self-identifying as *pardo* and *preto*, including parties classified as Left (Partido dos Trabalhadores [PT], Partido Socialista Brasileiro [PSB], Partido Democrático Trabalhista [PDT]), those as the Center (Partido da Social Democracia Brasileira [PSDB], Partido do Movimento Democrático Brasileiro [PMDB]), and those as the Right (Democratas [DEM], Partido Progressista [PP], Partido Trabalhista Brasileiro [PTB]) (Power & Zucco, 2012). (Not everyone agrees that Brazilian parties can be classified ideologically on the left–right spectrum, though skeptics agree that the Workers' Party (PT) can be considered left of the spectrum, with other major parties (PSDB, PMDB, DEM) farther to its right (Lucas & Samuels, 2010).) Blacks made up some one-quarter of deputies from the Workers' Party (PT), the largest and governing party. Several smaller parties had proportionally large numbers of Afrodescendant deputies: six of ten deputies from the Brazilian Communist Party (Partido Comunista do Brasil [PC do B]), for example, self-identified as *preto* or *pardo*.

In the United States, all forty-three black members of the House of Representatives were Democrats in 2014 (Manning, 2014). In Brazil, by contrast, deputies identifying as *pretos* and *pardos* did not cluster by party, ideology, or party type. In this respect, the 2014 elections conformed to past trends. After

---

[11] According to TSE data, none of the elected deputies declared themselves as *amarelo* or *indígena*. At least one deputy was of Japanese descent, however: Walter Ihoshi, of the PSD and from São Paulo, who declared himself *branca* to the TSE.

[12] For a count, see "Os deputados que se autodeclaram negros." Retrieved from http://congressoemfoco.uol.com.br/noticia.asp?cod_canal=21&cod_publicacao=36175 (accessed July 11, 2011). I added one person (Eliane Rolim – PT/RJ) to the list. As a *suplente*, she was not part of the original count.

TABLE 2.4. Pretos _and_ Pardos _elected to Brazil's Chamber of Deputies,_ 2014

Party	_Pardos/Pretos_	Total Deputies	% _Pardo/Preto_
PT	18	70	26
PMDB	7	66	11
PSDB	3	54	6
PSD	4	37	11
PP	5	36	14
PSB	10	34	30
PR	7	34	21
PTB	3	25	12
DEM	4	22	18
PRB	7	21	29
PDT	7	19	37
SD	6	15	40
PSC	4	12	33
PROS	3	11	27
PC do B	6	10	60
PPS	0	10	0
PV	3	8	38
PSOL	2	5	40
PHS	1	5	20
PTN	1	4	25
PMN	1	3	33
PRP	0	3	0
PTC	1	2	50
PEN	0	2	0
PSDC	0	2	0
PRTB	0	1	0
PSL	0	1	0
PT do B	0	1	0
Total	103	513	20

Please see list of acronyms following the Preface and Acknowledgments in this book.
Source: Supreme Electoral Tribunal (Brazil). Note these figures reflect candidates who were elected by party, and may differ from those who actually assumed seats due to leaves of absence, the assumption of power by _suplentes_ (alternates), and the formation of multiparty blocks and coalitions.

the 2006 elections, some 45 percent of black deputies were elected from Leftist parties and some 55 percent from parties of the Center and Right (Paixão & Carvano, 2008, pp. 149–151).[13]

---

[13] Women may cluster by party or ideology more than men. After the 2010 elections, six of seven black women in the Chamber of Deputies were from parties of the Left: four were elected by the ruling Workers' Party (PT) and two by the Communist Party of Brazil (PC do B). Only one deputy – Andreia Zito of the Brazilian Social Democratic Party (PSDB) – came from a Center party. No black female deputies were elected from parties of the Right.

In Colombia, Afrodescendants made up a mere 5 percent of the Chamber of Deputies in 2014 (some 9 of 166, not counting the two deputies elected for the seats reserved for "black communities") and 1 percent of the Senate (1 of 102). There was only one woman among them.[14] As in Brazil, Afrodescendants in the Colombian Congress were affiliated with a broad range of political parties (including four from the Liberal Party, two from the "Partido de la U," and one each from the Movimiento Político 100% por Colombia, Movimiento de Integración Regional, Centro Democrático, and Movimiento Independiente de Renovación Absoluta). (For more details, see Chapter 5 on Colombia.)

Costa Rica did not have a single Afrodescendant man or woman in parliament in 2014, a significant break from past practice. From 1953 until his death in 1990, former president and chief political boss José Figueres used his power to guarantee the presence of at least one Afrodescendant member of the fifty-seven-person Congress. He made sure the National Liberation Party (PLN, the dominant party) put a black candidate in an electable position on a party list, usually in Limón province. In total, there have been seventeen black legislators elected via this route.[15]

In 2014, Ecuador was the only Latin American country where Afrodescendants were proportionally represented in parliament relative to their population size. That year, the country had approximately nine black legislators, almost 7 percent of parliament. According to the census, Afrodescendants made up 7 percent of the total population. Five of the nine legislators were women, and eight legislators came from President Rafael Correa's party (PAIS). In a pattern similar to Colombia's (more on this in Chapter 5), two of the male Ecuadorian representatives were famous soccer players. In the previous legislature (2009–2013), there were three Afrodescendant legislators, including one woman.

In Peru, three Afrodescendant women held seats in Congress in 2014; all were former volleyball players elected from different parties (Fuerza 2011, Perú Posible, and Gana Perú). Uruguay had one Afrodescendant male legislator elected from the Frente Amplio. Of Venezuela's four Afrodescendant legislators, three came from the United Socialist Party of Venezuela (PSUV) and one from the Progressive Outpost (*Avanzada Progresista*).[16]

Across all seven countries, two trends are evident. First, Afrodescendants are underrepresented relative to their presence in the overall population, though over time data from Brazil and Ecuador, while not strictly comparable, suggest that their numbers in power are growing. Two, Afrodescendants do not cluster

---

[14] These data are based on a list from the Afrocolombianosvisibles blog (afrocolombianosvisibles, 2014).

[15] Interview with Walter Robinson, San José, Costa Rica, July 26, 2011. Robinson was the fourteenth deputy elected this way and Epsy Campbell the fifteenth.

[16] There was high variation among coders in estimates of the number of Afrodescendant legislators in Venezuela, from a low of three to a high of eleven.

by party. They tend to get elected from parties across the spectrum, including parties from the Right.

Indigenous Presence in National Legislatures

In some ways, measuring indigenous presence in national legislatures is even trickier than measuring Afrodescendant presence. In the past, scholars have estimated indigenous inclusion simply by counting the number of representatives elected by ethnic parties (see, e.g., Van Cott, 2005). Yet many so-called indigenous parties, such as the Movimiento al Socialismo (MAS) in Bolivia, the Alianza Social Indígena (ASI) in Colombia (now called the Alianza Social Independiente), and Pachakutik in Ecuador, have nonindigenous members and elected officials (and their numbers have grown over time). What is more, not all indigenous peoples are elected via these parties. In the Guatemalan election of 2011, only two of nineteen indigenous legislators were elected by an indigenous party. The other seventeen were from other parties, including nine elected from the right-wing party of President Otto Pérez Molina (Soberanis, 2011).

Classification of legislator photos is not a feasible option. Unlike Afrodescendancy, which tends to be visible, indigenous identity is difficult to ascertain from photos. Whether a person considers herself to be indigenous may change over time or from context to context depending on education, language acquisition, employment, residence, and political socialization. Historically, the distinction between indigenous and mestizo has been primarily cultural and flexible (Harris, 1964; Knight, 1990). What is more, as data from Bolivia show, many people identify *both* with one of the country's many indigenous communities (Quechua, Aymara, Guaraní, Chiquitano, etc.) *and* as mestizo (Zavaleta, 2008).

Table 2.5 presents data on indigenous presence in national legislatures for those countries for which data were available. The data come from nationally-specific secondary sources, personal correspondence with staff in field offices of the United Nations Development Program (UNDP), and from my own coding. Each source is identified in the table. In the event of contradictions between sources, I relied on the one with the most specific information (such as lists of names).[17]

Bolivia has the highest indigenous presence of the countries included in the table, reflecting recent growth, not an historic pattern. Figure 2.2 charts data compiled by Cárdenas (2011). In spite of the fact that recent census data indicate that people identifying with indigenous groups make up more than 60 percent of the population, indigenous peoples made up less than 10 percent of Congress until the 2000s. Numbers spiked in that decade, due largely to the emergence of the *Movimiento al Socialismo* (Movement toward Socialism, or MAS), led by Evo Morales (more on this in Chapter 4), and also the dramatic

---

[17] For example, three different sources gave different numbers for indigenous legislators in Peru. I relied on the report published by the National Electoral Court.

TABLE 2.5. *Indigenous Presence in Latin American Legislatures, circa 2013*

Country	No. of indigenous	Total Number	Indigenous as% of Total	No. of Indigenous Women
Bolivia				
Chamber	32	130	24.6	5
Senate	6	36	16.7	3
Brazil				
Chamber	0	514	0	0
Senate	0	80	0	0
Chile				
Chamber	0	120	0	0
Senate	0	38	0	0
Colombia (2014)				
Chamber	1	166	0.6	0
Senate	2	102	2	0
Ecuador				
Unicameral	7	137	5.1	5
Guatemala				
Unicameral	20	158	12.7	3
Mexico				
Chamber	14	500	2.8	3
Senate				
Peru				
Unicameral	1	130	0.8	0
Venezuela				
Unicameral	3	165	1.8	0

Sources: For Bolivia, Cárdenas (2011); for Brazil, Fernando (2011); for Chile, Jouannet (2011); for Colombia, Laurent (2012a); for Guatemala, Soberanis (2011); for Mexico, Cabrero, Pop, Morales, Chuji, and Mamani (2013); for Peru, Pinedo Bravo (2012); for Ecuador and Venezuela, author's coding.

growth in the number of voters (from around 3 million in 2005 to almost 5 million in 2009) (Cárdenas, 2011). Numbers of indigenous women were historically low, not exceeding one or two, until the 2005 elections (when they came to occupy four lower house seats) and especially the 2009 elections (when indigenous women came to hold five lower house seats and three Senate seats) (Cárdenas, 2011). As Chapter 4 discusses, the application of a gender parity law had a dramatic effect on women's numbers in the Senate. It was less effective in lower house races because of the tendency of political parties to place women in *alternate*, rather than *titular*, positions.

Indigenous presence in the Colombian Congress (1 of 166 in the lower house and 2 of 102 in the Senate) is largely the product of statutory legislative reservations, as Chapter 5 discusses. In the 1990s, however, several indigenous

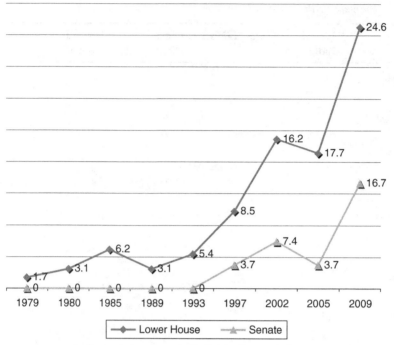

FIGURE 2.2. Indigenous presence in Bolivia's Congress (1979–2009).
Source: Author's presentation, based on data from Cárdenas (2011).

candidates successfully contested elections outside of the reserved seats, bringing their numbers to a high of four senators after 2002. After political reforms adopted in 2003, which privileged larger parties, indigenous strategies changed to focus on the reserved seats, though nonindigenous parties began contesting these as well. In the 2010 elections, indigenous parties captured both reserved Senate seats but a nonindigenous party won the reserved seat in the lower house.

Five of Ecuador's seven indigenous representatives are women. Four of the indigenous deputies were elected by Pachakutik, the principal indigenous party, and three were from the PAIS party of President Rafael Correa. Interestingly, Pachakutik also elected two nonindigenous deputies (Cabrero, personal correspondence, 2013).

In Guatemala, five different political parties elected indigenous deputies in the 2011 elections. The most (nine) came from the right-wing party of President Otto Pérez Molina; four deputies came from two other center-right parties; five from the UNE (center-left, Christian Democratic party), and two from the left-wing URNG-WINAQ alliance (Soberanis, 2011, p. 226). Of the six regions with majority indigenous populations, only a third (thirteen of thirty-six) of the deputies elected were indigenous (45 percent of candidates were indigenous)

(Ibid., pp. 224–225). Representation was greater at the local level: 110 of 333 mayors were Mayan (Ibid., p. 224).

Mexico's indigenous representatives came from nine different *pueblos* (and one identifies as *mestizo*) (Cabrero et al., 2013). Seven were elected from the PRI, five from the PRD, one from the PAN, and one from Citizens' Movement (*Movimiento Ciudadano*) (Ibid.). The low numbers (14 of 500, or 2.8 percent) are surprising in light of the fact that, for the 2006 and 2009 elections, twenty-eight electoral districts had been deliberately engineered to contain a minimum of 40 percent indigenous residents (more on this later).

Indigenous presence is low in Peru. Though indigenous people make up some 30 percent of the population, there was only one indigenous legislator elected to Congress for the 2011–2016 term (according to a publication of the National Electoral Court).[18] The previous congress (2006–2011) had two indigenous legislators, both highland women. An indigenous woman, Paulina Arpasi, was elected from Perú Posible in 2001. All four indigenous representatives won seats by receiving high numbers of preference votes that elevated them from lower positions on party lists (Pinedo Bravo, 2012). The fact that three of four indigenous representatives in the 2000s were women may be attributable to the country's gender quota law and thus reflect growth in women's inclusion, not the greater inclusion of indigenous peoples (Salmón, 2011, p. 287, citing Torres, 2008).

The congressional presence of people with indigenous ancestry is likely higher in Peru, but legislators may not identify publicly in that way. In the PERLA study, some 60 percent of people who reported having indigenous ancestry did not identify as indigenous (Sulmont & Callirgos, 2014). Identification in Peru is complicated by the fact that historically, state policy reclassified highland indigenous peoples as "peasant communities" (*comunidades campesinas*), a category that differentiated them legally from the numerically smaller "native communities" (*comunidades nativas*) occupying the Amazonian region. Only these latter groups were considered – by law, public policy, and society – to be indigenous (Smith, 1982). In spite of recent efforts to bring local categories into conformity with international norms, many communities in the coastal and highland regions believed to be indigenous do not regard themselves as such (Aragón, 2012; Pinedo Bravo, 2012; Salmón, 2011).[19]

Venezuela's indigenous representatives were elected in seats engineered for that purpose: three single-member districts encompassing different states (more on these below). After the 2010 elections, each of the three representatives came from a different indigenous organization, though most indigenous

---

[18] Other sources give different numbers: Villanueva Montalvo (2012) lists three indigenous representatives, while UNDP (2013) gives nine!

[19] Legislation adopted in the 2000s attempted to incorporate, though not without contradictions, international language on "indigenous or originary peoples" (Pinedo Bravo, 2012; Salmón, 2011).

organizations in Venezuela are allied with mainstream political parties, without whose support it would be impossible to win. Conflict between government and opposition shapes the competition for the reserved seats (Angosto Ferrández, 2011).

Mechanisms to Promote Inclusion in Latin America

Latin America has led the world in the adoption of gender quota laws, but lagged with respect to mechanisms to promote racial and ethnic inclusion. Beginning with Argentina's early adoption of a national gender quota in 1991, by 2014, fifteen countries had quota laws applied at the national and subnational levels (see Tables 2.6 and 2.7). Unlike policies to promote racial and ethnic inclusion, the *form* of gender quota laws varies little from country to country. All require that women comprise a certain percentage of the total number of candidates postulated by a party for legislative elections. As Piscopo puts it, "quotas ... restructure electoral lists and intervene in the 'inner life' of political parties, using state authority to make candidate recruitment and nomination more permeable to women" (Piscopo, 2013, p. 10).

There is more variation in the details of the quota laws, such as the percentage level of the quota. Most countries have reformed their gender quota laws over time to strengthen their requirements. Changes have included the raising of threshold percentages, the addition of oversight mechanisms, the extension of quotas to additional legislative chambers, and the introduction of placement mandates in closed-list systems (Jones, 2009; Piscopo, 2015).

Legislative quotas have spilled over into other areas of governance. As Piscopo reports, quotas are now applied in a variety of institutions, including both appointed and elected positions in the executive branch, the judiciary, and the boards of civil society organizations (see Table 2.8).

Fewer countries have introduced mechanisms to promote the inclusion of groups defined by race or ethnicity. In 2014, five countries applied them: Bolivia, Colombia, Mexico, Peru, and Venezuela (see Table 1.1 in the Introduction).

Bolivia's reserved seats, analyzed in greater detail in Chapter 4, were introduced in the 2009 Constitution. Indigenous groups had initially demanded more (thirty-six) but the final text conceded only seven. The seats are elected from single member districts in which only certain groups recognized by the constitution can run but for which all residents of the district are eligible to vote. In the district created in Beni province, the single seat is designated to represent eighteen different indigenous groups; in the other six districts, the seat represents between one and six groups.[20] The La Paz district is intended to represent Afro-Bolivians as well as five other groups (in the 2009 elections, an Afro-Bolivian candidate won the seat).

---

[20] Gaceta Oficial de Bolivia. 2009. *Regimen Electoral Transitorio. Ley no.* 4021. Gaceta No. 0018, April 14, 2009. La Paz.

TABLE 2.6. *Gender Quota Laws in Latin America (National Level)*

Country	Quota Law	First Adopted	Major Reforms
Argentina	Both chambers, 30%	1991	1993, 2000 (placement mandates) 2000 (quota extended to Senate)
Bolivia	Both chambers, 50%	1997	2009/2010 (threshold raised from 30%)
Brazil	Lower chamber, 30%	1997	2000 (threshold raised from 25%) 2009 (closed loophole)
Colombia	Both chambers, 30%	1998	2000 (declared unconstitutional) 2011 (quota reinstated)
Costa Rica	Unicameral, 50%	1996	1999 (placement mandate) 2009 (threshold raised from 40%)
Dominican Republic	Lower chamber, 33%	1997	2000 (threshold raised from 25%) 2002 (Senate exempted from quota)
Ecuador	Unicameral, 50%	1997	2000 (threshold raised from 20% to 30%, placement mandate) 2008 (threshold raised to 50%) 2008/2009 (extended to senate)
El Salvador	Unicameral, 30%	2013	
Honduras	Unicameral, 40%	2000	2009 (threshold lowered to 30%) 2012 (threshold raised to 40%, increasing to 50% in 2016)
Mexico	Both chambers, 50%	1996	2008 (threshold raised from 30%) 2014 (threshold raised to 50%)
Nicaragua	Unicameral, 50%	2012	Applies beginning in 2016
Panama	Unicameral, 50%	1997	2012 (threshold raised from 30%)
Paraguay	Both chambers, 20%	1996	
Peru	Both chambers, 30%	1997	2000 (threshold raised from 25%)
Uruguay	Both chambers, 33%	2009	Applies to 2014 elections only

Source: Piscopo (2015).

TABLE 2.7. *Gender Quota Laws in Latin America (Subnational Level)*

Country	Quota Law	First Adopted	Reformed
Argentina	Varies by province		
Bolivia	Departmental, municipal, 50%	2009	2010
Brazil	Municipal, state, 30%	1995	1997, 2000
Colombia	Departmental, 30%	2011	
Costa Rica	Municipal, 50%	2009	
Dominican Republic	Municipal, 33%	1997	2000
Ecuador	Municipal, 50%	2000	2008, 2009
El Salvador	Municipal, 30%	2013	
Honduras	Regional, municipal, 30%	2009	
Nicaragua	Municipal, 50%	2012	
Mexico	State, 50%	2014	
Paraguay	Departmental, 20%	1996	
Peru	Regional, municipal, 30%	1998	
Uruguay	Departmental, 33%	2009	
Venezuela	Regional, municipal, 50%	2008	

Source: Piscopo (2015).

Colombia's seats (analyzed in Chapter 5) were introduced by the 1991 Constitution and different pieces of implementing legislation. Unlike Bolivia's seats, which are elected by geographically defined constituencies, Colombia's seats are elected nationwide. Indigenous and "black community" candidates appear on every ballot in the country. This practice conforms to the Senate's national district, but is at odds with the regular methods used to elect representatives to the lower house (where legislators are elected by province). Only indigenous candidates can run in the indigenous seats, but they may be postulated by both indigenous and nonindigenous parties meeting requirements established by the National Electoral Court. To field candidates for the "black community" seats, a group needs to be registered with the Interior Ministry.

In Mexico, the San Andrés accords stipulated that the indigenous population be taken into account in routine redistricting. For Mexico's 2006 and 2009 elections, twenty-eight electoral districts had been deliberately engineered to contain a minimum of 40 percent indigenous residents. Few indigenous politicians were elected, as political parties failed to run indigenous candidates in those districts and few organizations mobilized to demand effective implementation of the measure. For its part, the state offered no mechanism to gather data on whether the districts had succeeded in electing indigenous candidates (Villanueva Montalvo, 2012, pp. 55–56).

Since a 2002 reform established regional elections, Peruvian electoral law has required that 15 percent of candidates on party lists contesting subnational legislative elections (regional and municipal councils) in eleven of twenty-five regions be members of "native communities." As mentioned earlier, the term "native communities" refers only to members of indigenous groups in the

TABLE 2.8. *Quotas for Executive and Judicial Branches, and Civil Society*

Country	Quota Rule	Year Adopted	Juridical Status
Argentina	30% for trade union directorates	2003	Statutory
Bolivia	50% for all posts in the judiciary at all levels, including the Constitutional Court and the independent Electoral Tribunal	2009, 2010	Constitutional[a]
	50% for all elected *and designated* government authorities and representatives at all levels (including the indigenous territories)		
Colombia	30% for highest executive branch positions at all levels of government	2000	Statutory
Costa Rica	50% quota for one of the two vice presidency positions	1996	Statutory[a]
Costa Rica	50% for the boards of trade unions, charity organizations, and voluntary organizations	2011	Statutory
Dominican Republic	50% for mayors and deputy mayors	2000	Statutory[a]
Ecuador	50% in elected or appointed decision-making positions in all public offices, including the National Equality Councils	2008	Constitutional[a]
	50% in the Electoral Tribunal, all branches of the judiciary, and the judicial civil service		
Haiti	30% in all elected and appointed positions at the national level, including the civil service	2011	Constitutional[a]
Honduras	30% for mayors and deputy mayors	2000, 2004	Statutory[a]
Nicaragua	50% for mayors and deputy mayors	2012	Statutory[a]

[a] Included in the legislative quota law.
Source: Piscopo (2013).

Amazonian lowland regions, not to groups from the highlands. Peruvian quotas thus apply only to a small subset of the indigenous population. The quotas have been much criticized, first for undermining indigenous organizations and parties (as mainstream parties poach indigenous leaders to comply with the quota), and second, for not being part of a larger package of reforms to promote indigenous autonomy and self-governance (Aragón, 2012 citing Espinosa and Lastra 2011; Htun, 2004b).

Venezuela's seats date from the 1999 constitution establishing the Bolivarian Republic. The constitution guaranteed the three seats in the national assembly as well as indigenous participation in local and federal deliberative bodies in areas with indigenous presence (article 125, cited in Angosto Ferrández, 2011). Implementing legislation mandated that indigenous peoples occupy one seat in the legislatures of eight states (2005 Organic Law on Indigenous Peoples and Communities) and one seat in municipalities and "parroquias" with more than 300 or 180 indigenous residents, respectively (2009 Organic Law on Electoral Processes, cited in Angosto Ferrández, 2011). To contest any of these seats, a candidate must have exercised a position of traditional authority in her or his community; have a recognized history in the social struggle for the recognition of cultural identity; have engaged in behavior to benefit indigenous peoples; and be member of a legally recognized indigenous organization that is at least three years old (Ibid., p. 21). Between 2004 and 2010, a total of 171 organizations had contested seats (though 121 of these had contested a seat in one municipal election only), 23 different organizations had won at least one seat, 11 at either the national or regional level, and only one group (CONIVE) had won seats at all three levels.

Conclusion

Though gender quota laws have increased the political inclusion of women, reserved seats for Afrodescendants and indigenous peoples have had a more mixed effect. In some cases, such as Venezuela and Colombia (for indigenous peoples but not Afrodescendants), the application of reserved seats has improved minority presence in politics. In others, such as Bolivia, Mexico, and Peru, statutory inclusion mechanisms appear to be more epiphenomenal to other factors affecting political presence. In the case of Bolivia, the main factor increasing indigenous presence has been general electoral reform, the expansion of the electorate, and the rise of the MAS (Madrid, 2012). In Mexico, efforts to engineer a higher indigenous presence have failed because of party behavior, while in Peru the indigenous quotas apply to only a small minority of the indigenous population.

Numbers of Afrodescendants show little correlation with inclusionary mechanisms. Those countries with the highest levels of Afrodescendant presence (in terms of a percentage of all legislators) – Brazil and Ecuador – have not applied any mechanism to promote political inclusion. Yet countries with low levels – Costa Rica, Uruguay, and Venezuela – do not have inclusionary mechanisms either. As we see later on, Afrodescendant presence in Colombia (the only country in the region with any affirmative action in politics for Afrodescendants) seems more related to black presence in mainstream parties and the high numerical presence of blacks in provinces such as Chocó and San Andrés and in cities such as Cali than to the "black community" reservations introduced by the 1991 Constitution.

What explains the adoption of gender quotas and their success in getting women elected? Have they produced any broader consequences on legislative behavior? Why were ethnic and racial quotas and reservations not more widely introduced? How have the policies worked? Have they improved the representation of interests of disadvantaged groups? The chapters to follow will explore these questions, beginning first with the story of why and how women from different political parties mobilized successfully around gender quotas.

3

Gender Quotas: Why and How?

In 1991, Argentina became the first country in the world to introduce a gender candidate quota to national electoral legislation.[1] Since then, fifteen other Latin American countries followed suit (though Venezuela subsequently revoked the law). In 2014, the median country in the region – fifteen of nineteen, or 79 percent – applied gender quotas in every election. Not all the laws are perfect: in the years after adoption, many underwent reforms to facilitate implementation, add sanctions for noncompliance, and raise target percentages (see Table 2.6). Overall, the policies have led to major gains in women's presence in power in some countries; in others, the results have been less impressive.

Latin America's embrace of gender quotas led world trends. Overall, some fifty-six countries (and two polities – Kosovo and the Palestinian Authority) have national laws guaranteeing women's inclusion in politics through candidate quotas or reserved seats. Some forty-five countries apply such guarantees at the local level (Paxton & Hughes, 2013).

Why are so many countries adopting quotas? What is the problem that the policies are responding to? Why did some countries, but not others, introduce these measures? Did they succeed in getting more women elected? In a fascinating book, Ann Towns argues that the status of women has become a measure of civilization and a way to "evaluate and rank states in a hierarchical manner" (Towns, 2010, p. 6). Countries interested in improving their status in international society must attempt visibly to demonstrate their efforts to improve the condition of women. Policies like gender quotas offer a means for states to ascend in the global hierarchy. They adopt quotas to seem modern and to prove their credentials on democracy and human rights. In an earlier era, by contrast, it was the opposite phenomenon–women's political exclusion– that

---

[1] Other countries had previously introduced mechanisms to guarantee women's presence, but these took the form of reserved legislative seats, not candidate quotas in political parties.

constituted an international status symbol. "Civilized" states kept women out of politics (Ibid., chapter 4).

The emergence of gender quotas as a "standard of modernity" may be a necessary condition for policy adoption. But it is not sufficient. Many more states are affected by, and participate in, international society than have quota policies.[2] International norms and hierarchies are thus an important part of the explanation for quotas but do not adequately distinguish between adopters and nonadopters. To explain variation in policy patterns, we need to look at the political agency of women politicians. Women in some countries crossed party lines to forge a common political identity; in others, they did not.

Women do not naturally share interests. They must mobilize a perception of shared interests as the basis of a political identity. In this chapter, I analyze women's collective action and the formation of multipartisan coalitions of politicians. Quotas were achieved when women from Right, Center, and Left parties united against their shared exclusion from political power. They formed single-issue coalitions to advocate quotas as a mechanism to rupture institutionalized patterns of sex discrimination in political parties. Women from the Peronist and Radical parties in Argentina; the Party of the Democratic Revolution and National Action Party in Mexico; and the Workers' Party and Party of the Brazilian Democratic Movement in Brazil (among others) joined together to defeat the arguments of male colleagues that quotas were undemocratic and unconstitutional. These tactics helped maximize support for quotas across the party system. When women did not unite in multipartisan alliances, as in Chile, quotas were not adopted.

The chapter also begins to reflect on the potential – and limitations – of quotas as a mechanism to induce political representation, reflections that continue in a later chapter on the aftermath of quotas. Women did not gain access to power via a women's party, or authorization by a women's electorate. Rather, quotas put women into power through parties, most of which are still dominated by men. After the adoption of the laws, women's coalitions tended to disband as their members returned to their prior commitments and became reabsorbed into their parties. Party loyalty and discipline often thwarted gender-based collective policy advocacy.

This chapter provides an account of where gender quotas came from and how they were achieved. It differs methodologically from subsequent chapters focusing on ethnic and racial struggles for inclusion. Unlike the following chapters on Colombia, Bolivia, and Brazil, this chapter does not focus on a single country but is broadly comparative. I draw on evidence from various countries, including Argentina, Bolivia, Brazil, Chile, Costa Rica, Mexico, and Peru, and offer an explicit comparison of the achievement of quotas in Argentina and Mexico and nonachievement in Chile. This difference in research design reflects my belief that the logic of women's struggles for quotas is more similar

---

[2] I am grateful to Lisa Baldez who has made this point repeatedly for more than ten years.

cross nationally than the politics of ethnic and racial inclusion. As a result, telling the story of national struggles for quotas in separate chapters would be repetitive theoretically (though it would supply rich details). When there is cross-national variation, for example, in the role of multipartisan coalitions or the effects of institutions, it is noted within this chapter.

Early History of Quotas

The first example of political guarantees for women at the national level may have been India, where British colonial rulers allocated seats to women within the reservations system for Dalits, or untouchables, under the terms of the Poona Pact between Ambedkar and Gandhi.[3] After independence, India abandoned the reservations systems for women and religious minorities in favor of principles of individual rights. However, the 1950 constitution kept reserved seats for Dalits (Scheduled Castes) and aboriginal groups (Scheduled Tribes) (Galanter, 1984). Pakistan, by contrast, kept women's reserved seats until the 1980s (they were later reintroduced in 1999). Applied in elections between the 1950s and the 1980s, these seats were responsible for the election of most female members of parliament (Krook, 2010a).

Taiwan's constitution, drafted on mainland China in the late 1940s, upheld affirmative action for women, Tibetans, overseas Chinese citizens, and certain occupational groups. The most numerically significant of these were the women's reservations. In line with Sun Yat-Sen's beliefs in gender equality, and resulting from struggles of women's organizations and their male supporters during the twists and turns of the constitutional drafting process, the 1946 constitution contained a chapter on the special rights of women, and declared that women and population groups with "special modes of living" should have guaranteed presence in the national legislature. The reservations system was intended to compensate for women's disadvantaged position in Confucian society and to open up more opportunities for women in politics and society. The Kuomintang (KMT) may have been influenced by the first-wave feminist movement and the granting of woman suffrage in dozens of countries after World War II, but there was almost no precedent for guarantees of political

---

[3] The problem of "untouchability," not women's rights, occupied center stage in Indian politics in the 1920s and 1930s. The British had already granted separate electorates and reservations first for Muslims, and then for Christians and Sikhs, in 1909 and 1919. Proposals to introduce similar provisions based on distinctions within the Hindu community, however, triggered Mohandas Gandhi's famous hunger strike. The Indian National Congress and the biggest national women's associations objected to all legal distinctions among Indians (whether by gender, religion, or caste), which they suspected to form part of a British efforts divide-and-rule strategy against the nationalist movement (Pedersen, 2004). Under pressure to avert Gandhi's death, Dr. Bhimrao Ramji Ambedkar, spokesman for untouchables, relinquished the idea of separate electorates in exchange for a system of reserved seats to be elected by all voters (Galanter, 1984). This agreement, known as the Poona Pact, also granted seats to women.

presence. Taiwan gave representatives elected by registered women's organizations presence in the National Assembly. For elections to the Legislative Yuan, a certain proportion of seats (from 5 to 20 percent, depending on the size of the constituency) elected by the general public are reserved for women. Women's reservations also apply to provincial and municipal elections.[4]

A few North African countries also had an early experience with women's reservations. In 1978, Sudan introduced a reservations system. Though specific provisions have varied over time, today the country continues to guarantee 36 of its 350 national assembly seats for women (Abou-Zeid, 2006, p. 180). In 1979, Egypt reserved 30 of 360 parliamentary seats for women, though it revoked this policy in 1984. The government had introduced the quota without much consultation with civil society, including the women's movement, leading to strong opposition. What is more, the women MPs who held the reserved seats were relatively inactive and ineffective politicians (Abou-Zeid, 2006, pp. 189–190).

The idea of mechanisms to guarantee women's presence in power had been around for much of the 20th century. Until the 1980s, however, it was not an idea that many women were mobilized around and advocating. Why did women begin to organize around quotas? Even as they advanced in economy and society, few women were gaining access to elected office. Persisting discrepancies between women's presence at the middle and bottom of organizations and their numbers motivated greater numbers of women to activism. Until institutionalized patterns of exclusion were broken, few women would reach the top. International norms and activist networks foregrounded quotas as the way to break entrenched practices of sex discrimination in candidate selection.

Political Mobilization for Quotas

Women were excluded from politics for most of history. In the West, women's scarcity in decision making was not incongruent with their political disenfranchisement, legal subordination, and low participation in the formal labor market. In the last third of the twentieth century, women's roles were revolutionized in Latin America and most of the world (Esping-Andersen, 2009; Goldin, 2006). Women gained ground in society and economy and most – though not all – countries ended legal sex discrimination and took action to promote equality (Glendon, 1989; Htun & Weldon, n.d.).

As the end of the twentieth century approached, the gap between women's participation in society, economy, and lower levels of the polity on the one

---

[4] For Legislative Yuan elections, one seat is guaranteed for women (and given to the woman receiving the most votes) in a constituency electing up to ten representatives; an additional seat is reserved each time the district increases by ten more seats. In practice, this means that the size of the women's reservation varies from 5 to 20 percent (Bih-Er, Clark, & Clark, 1990; Chien, 1950).

hand and their presence at the top only grew wider. Though women's presence at the middle and bottom of organizations was approaching parity with men's in many countries, their numbers in power remained small. In 1990, women's literacy and educational attainment rates equaled men's in much of Latin America. They made up 30 percent of the labor force region-wide, and as much as 40 percent in some large economies. They were half of students enrolled in universities – more in some countries including Brazil and Colombia – and prestigious academic majors such as law. Yet women accounted for an average of only 9 percent of legislators in lower houses of Congress across the region (Htun, 1998a; Valdés & Gomariz, 1995).

Within political parties, women comprised close to half of affiliates but had almost no presence among the leadership or on candidate lists. In Argentina's Radical Party (UCR) in the early 1990s, for example, women made up 49 percent of members nationwide (53 percent in the city of Buenos Aires) but not one woman served on the party's national board (Htun, 1997, p. 12). Similarly, women accounted for 39 percent of the Brazilian Workers' Party (PT) affiliates in São Paulo and 43 percent in Rio de Janeiro in 1991, but a mere 6 percent of the national board members (Htun, 1997).

In the past, many observers attributed women's exclusion from political office to their lower overall social and economic status. Countries with higher levels of economic development and more egalitarian cultural values tended to have more women in positions of power (Inglehart & Norris, 2003). Yet although women in Latin America had advanced overall, they had not achieved equivalent gains in political presence. Their scarcity in elected office could not be explained by a low supply of qualified or aspiring women (Hinojosa, 2012). This seemed to invalidate the prediction that women would enter power incrementally as their social standing improved (Dahlerup & Friedenvall, 2005).

Nor could women's low numbers be attributed to voter biases. In surveys, Latin Americans reported overwhelming support for female candidates. In 2000, 93 percent of respondents in five countries said they would vote for a woman for president; 94 percent for mayor. Subsequent polls by LAPOP and Latinobarometro reported similar results (Hinojosa, 2012). World Values Survey results also showed that the vast majority of Latin Americans thought that women were as good at being leaders as men (Htun & Piscopo, 2010, p. 18, Table 3). Studies from the United States indicated that when women became candidates, they received the same amount of money, media time, and votes as men. Women's low numbers owed to their scarcity among candidates, not funder, media, and voter discrimination (Darcy, Welch, & Clark, 1994).

As this suggests, women were qualified to be leaders, wanted to hold power, and voters wanted to support them. But they were being excluded. Why? Women's absence could not be explained merely by observing the interaction between the supply of, and demand for, women candidates (Krook, 2010b). Rather, processes of candidate selection in political parties were biased toward men and against women. Institutionalized sex discrimination in candidate selection – not women's own positions or ambitions – had kept them out of power.[5]

In light of the diversity of women, we cannot assume they will mobilize collectively. Though gender institutions position women in similar ways, forging shared disadvantages, women continue to be deeply divided by differences of class, race, culture, geography, education, and ideology, not to mention their connection to an organized women's movement or their degree of "gender consciousness." Women are raced, classed, rendered ethnic, and affected by normative heterosexuality (Crenshaw, 1991; Garcia Bedolla, 2007; Hancock, 2007; Weldon, 2008). Though a woman's body is what makes a woman, each woman exercises unique choices in doing what she wishes with this body (Moi, 2001).

Many episodes of collective action among women have been prompted by a gender-based exclusion. The denial of rights or opportunities on the basis of sex – either explicitly, as in the case of the vote, or implicitly, through sexism in political parties – motivated women to organize along these same lines (Baldez, 2002). Gender-based exclusion from power compelled women to acknowledge their shared disadvantages, and the desire to challenge it facilitated their collective action (Ibid., p. 13). Political mobilization around quotas began as women from different backgrounds, sectors, and political parties united to combat their common exclusion, suffered because they were women, not because of their other characteristics.

Common interests in securing greater access to politics cut across party lines. As Friedman notes, "Although all women may not agree on the substance of specific policy outcomes, they do have a common interest in being present when policy is being made" (Friedman, 2000, p. 291). Shared experience of disadvantage inspired many – but not all – women to unite in pro-quota coalitions. As we see below and in Chapter 4 on Bolivia, the achievement of quotas depended on the formation of alliances between women from different parties and backgrounds.

Why did women endorse quotas? Before turning to quota laws, women politicians had tried other strategies to combat discrimination such as leadership training, greater access to campaign finance, mentoring, networking, and gender preferences. Organizations such as the United Nations Development Fund for Women (UNIFEM, now called UN Women) and the Ford Foundation

---

[5] Many scholars and others continue to focus on women's ambition as a factor behind their scarcity at the top (see, e.g., Lawless & Fox, 2005; Sandberg, 2013). Though likely a factor in some cases, it could also be the case that weaker ambition is a response to historical patterns of exclusion and the scarcity of women role models. Women are less likely to run if they believe they will not be competitive (Hinojosa, 2012, p. 45). In any event, supply factors such as lack of ambition cannot explain the significant variation in women's numbers across parties, even within the same country. As Hinojosa points out, processes of candidate selection differ between parties. The more centralized and exclusive the process, the more women are chosen. By contrast, when candidate selection is decentralized and inclusive (such as in local primaries), fewer women emerge as candidates (Hinojosa, 2012).

sponsored national efforts to convince women to run for office and prepare them to conduct successful campaigns. Since the 1980s, many parties had included rhetorical commitments to equality in their statutes. For example, in response to a national gender equality law, Costa Rica's Partido de Liberación Nacional (PLN) reserved 10 percent of its budget for leadership training for women and required parity in nominations for internal executive posts. Yet the measure was inconsequential: the number of women in party leadership was virtually unchanged between 1985 and 1993 (Htun, 1997, p. 25). In Mexico, parties began to introduce gender preferences in the early 1990s, and in 1996 the electoral law exhorted parties to nominate women to 30 percent of candidate slots. Yet following the 1997 elections, the number of women in Congress actually went down. Chilean parties from the governing Concertación coalition introduced internal quotas in the mid-1990s (the Partido Por la Democracia [PPD] quota, for example, was 40 percent) but women's presence in the legislature barely changed (Htun, 1998b).

Gradualist and rhetorical measures made little headway against sex discrimination in the short term. Why? Male preference in candidate selection is not merely a behavior. It is an institution: a norm, pattern, and social practice that conditions individual choices and motivations. Men began to control politics long ago (Bjarnegård, 2013). Social expectations and practices congealed around this fact and set in motion processes of increasing returns in which "preceding steps in a particular direction induce further movement in the same direction" (Pierson, 2000, p. 252). People became accustomed to seeing men in power, masculine characteristics and roles became virtues of leadership, and places men socialized with one another (poker dens, private clubs, and locker rooms) turned into the sites of political negotiation and pact making. Norms of work evolved to accommodate individuals who could delegate child rearing and other domestic tasks to caregiving partners, and formal arenas of power (such as Congress) adapted to male needs by installing urinals, weight rooms, spittoons, and pool tables.

As Hinojosa explains, historic male dominance makes it less likely that women will self-nominate as candidates. In addition, women tend to be absent from "power monopolies" – "small, informal groups of people connected by kinship, social, or business associations, which concentrate power" (Hinojosa, 2012, p. 48). Such monopolies or networks are crucial for candidate recruitment and fundraising. As Sanbonmatsu notes in the case of the United States, "leaders who recruit candidates tend to look to whom they know – people they do business with, people they play golf with, and so on" (Hinojosa, 2012, p. 49, citing Sanbonmatsu, 2006, pp. 201–202).

Conceptualizing male dominance as an institution suggests that women can be excluded without men *actively and consciously* discriminating against them (though such discrimination undoubtedly also occurs). Conducting business as usual ends up excluding women, as business as usual consists of rules and practices that are gendered, that is, constructed and functioning according to men's lives, men's needs, and prevailing social images of manliness. Argentine deputy Inés Botella noted that, "when, at 4 or 5 in the morning, the men get around to formulating party lists, they don't have time to think about the female party activists who are equally capable of doing the job" (quoted in Marx, Borner, & Caminotti, 2007, p. 68). An Argentine deputy interviewed by Jennifer Piscopo complained that "meetings happen late at night at hotels, but I cannot go without putting my reputation at risk" (quoted in Piscopo & Thomas, 2012, p. 17). When Marcela Durrieu assumed a seat in the Argentine Congress, she was registered as absent even when present in the plenary. The reason? A petite woman weighing fewer kilograms than the average male deputy, her presence on her seat was not heavy enough to tip the Chamber's automatic means of registering attendance.[6] Women are excluded and marginalized de facto, not necessarily because men are trying to keep them out.

Conceptualizing male dominance in candidate selection as an institution makes it possible to understand its ubiquity while remaining cognizant of its inefficiency and irrationality. Simple institutional inertia helps explain a great deal of the persisting male power of political life.[7]

Conceived in this way, the quota was a bet that an exogenous shock would have a better chance at changing institutions of candidate selection than incremental measures or the gradual growth in women's participation. Though some institutions change incrementally and surreptitiously (Mahoney & Thelen, 2010; Streeck & Thelen, 2005b), others are difficult to modify in light of vested interests in existing arrangements and other obstacles (Pierson, 1996b, 2000). In some cases, institutional change must be forced through war, revolution, natural disaster, radical imposition from a higher power, and other shocks or crises (Krasner, 1984).

The institution of sexism in politics would probably have changed eventually, but not at a rate that satisfied women politicians. More female politicians – including women from the Right – turned to quotas when it became increasingly clear that radical, not gradual, measures were needed to break with ingrained institutional patterns.[8] They were convinced that without drastic imposition from

---

[6] Interview with Marcela Durrieu, Buenos Aires, July 1998.

[7] Both women's and men's behaviors enforced the institution: the former opted out and the latter opted into politics as rational responses to the incentive structures in political parties. In Germany, for example, the Social Democratic Party had long required prospective candidates to spend years working as apprentices inside the party. This practice, though apparently gender-neutral, favored men and excluded women who tended to have less time for party work. When the party adopted a quota in 1988, leaders discovered that there were actually multiple other ways to recruit candidates (Krook, 2008, p. 48).

[8] The quota movement involved a paradigm shift from an "incremental" to a "fast track" approach among feminist activists, women politicians, and international organizations (Dahlerup & Friedenvall, 2005). The "incremental" approach, which informed the adoption of quotas by Scandinavian political parties in the 1970s and 1980s, maintains that women's representation will gradually increase as they advance in society and acquire similar political resources to men. The "fast track," by contrast, rejects the incrementalist confidence in change and reflects a feminist desire for immediate results.

a higher power – in the form of a national quota law enforced by the state –
parties would be slow to change their locked-in institutional rules and procedures to accommodate women. As former president of Mexico's Party of the
Democratic Revolution and senator Amalia Garcia put it, "Politics is a rude fight
where what matters is beating the other. Women should not have to descend to
this level. That's why we need a quota."[9] As we see in the text that follows, even
women from right-wing parties opposed to the idea of affirmative action began to
endorse quotas once the intractability of male dominance became clear. As Senator
Cecilia Romero, from Mexico's right-wing PAN (Partido Acción Nacional) party,
said: "It's a necessary measure. Without a quota, things would take too long."[10]

The quota was a tool to rupture ingrained patterns of sex discrimination in
candidate selection. It forced parties to nominate women, thereby increasing
their presence in power. Quotas, however, did not change the other institutions
that shape political inclusion. As we see later on in the book, quotas were
compatible with practices that continued to marginalize women from centers of power and decision making (Franceschet & Piscopo, 2008; Piscopo &
Thomas, 2012; Schwindt-Bayer, 2010).

The Spread of Coalitions for Quotas

In the 1980s and 1990s, pro-quota coalitions emerged across Latin America,
Europe, Asia, and Africa and by the 2000s, they had become more numerous
in the Middle East as well. Organized women pushed for international agreements that endorsed measures to promote women's presence in politics. The
Convention on the Elimination of All Forms of Discrimination against Women
(CEDAW), endorsed by the United Nations in 1979, had already endorsed
affirmative action as a justifiable means to end sex discrimination. In working for consensus around the positions endorsed by international and regional
agreements and other statements of principle, women activists and politicians
promoted the growth of international norms. These norms, in turn, inspired
women's activism in additional countries and offered leverage and legitimacy
to groups lobbying for quotas.[11]

Parties in European countries had earlier begun to experiment with voluntary candidate quotas. Unlike the reserved seats in British India, Taiwan, and
North Africa, these were not national laws but voluntary policies introduced
by mostly left-wing political parties to govern the candidate selection process.
Beginning in the 1970s, feminist movements and women's groups inside political parties had pressured party leaders to adopt these quotas. The Norwegian
Labor Party and Danish Social Democratic Party set a level of 40 percent for
women's presence; the Swedish Social Democratic Party declared that every

---

[9] Interview, Mexico City, January 1998.
[10] Interview, Mexico City, May 9, 2001.
[11] See Htun and Weldon (2012) on how women's organizing promoted international agreements
on violence against women, which in turn triggered further organizing.

second candidate on the political party list had to be a woman (Dahlerup, 2002).[12] The Spanish Socialist Party adopted a quota in the late 1980s, as did the German Social Democrats and several left-wing parties in Italy. Overall, fifteen European parties adopted quota policies between 1985 and 1992: most tended to have women present among the party leadership, a leftist ideology, or pressure from other parties with quota policies (Kittilson, 2001).

In Europe, regional debates on quota laws began at a Council of Europe seminar in 1989 and continued through the establishment of an EU-wide network of experts on women in decision making in 1991 (Mazur, 2001). In 1992, the EU summit on "Women in Power," held in Athens, involved feminist researchers and activists, government officials, and EU bureaucrats. The conference declaration, signed by ministers and parliamentarians from throughout the region, noted that women's representation had not improved since the 1970s in many countries and called on governments to take measures to ensure the balanced participation of men and women in decision making.[13]

Some Latin American parties adopted quotas as well. At its 1991 party congress, the Brazilian Workers' Party (Partido dos Trabalhadores [PT]) resolved that 30 percent of party leadership positions be occupied by women; Mexico's Party of the Democratic Revolution (Partido de la Revolución Democrática [PRD]) did the same in 1993 (Htun, 1997). Then, in July of 1995 in São Paulo, women legislators from fifteen countries gathered at the Latin American Parliament (Parlatino) headquarters to discuss women's rights and gender quotas (Suplicy, 1996).

International activism around gender quotas coalesced around the Fourth World Conference on Women, held in Beijing in 1995. Endorsement by dozens of governments of the "Platform for Action" helped propel a shift in global discussions of sex equality in politics (Dahlerup, 2006a, p. 4). The document attributed low levels of women in decision making not to their lack of interest, will, or qualification (as had been the case in the past), but to institutionalized sex discrimination. This shifted the "responsibility for promoting change" from "the individual woman to [government] institutions." In addition, the Platform redefined the goal of policy as "equitable distribution of power and decision-making" between women and men, not women's minimal or token presence. Finally, the document recommended that states take "positive action" and adopt "specific targets and implementing measures" to encourage political parties to integrate women into elective and nonelective leadership positions (Dahlerup, 2006a, p. 5). Overall, Beijing marked a fresh way of thinking about political equality, especially among state officials and international development practitioners.

---

[12] The Danish quotas applied only to elections to local and county councils, not to the national parliament (Dahlerup, 2002).

[13] "Athens Declaration." Retrieved from www.eurit.it/Eurplace/diana/ateneen.html (accessed July 25, 2006).

The Platform was merely a statement of principles: it was not binding on signatory states. Yet such statements are powerful, for they represent a broad consensus among diverse countries and cultures about values and the objectives of government policy (see quote by Brazilian activist Sonia Corrêa in Htun, 2003a, p. 150). The platform gave gender quotas an international seal of legitimacy and global reach.

Endorsement at Beijing lent power and visibility to objectives the feminist movement had been advocating for years. Many women politicians attended the Beijing Conference. Not all had been concerned with gender issues in the past, and not all had much contact with one another. At Beijing, however, they bonded, they learned, and they got motivated to lobby for quotas and women's rights in their home legislatures. As then-deputy in the Brazilian Congress Marty Suplicy explained to me in an interview, "We returned from Beijing with quota bills in hand."[14]

Beijing also influenced men. Then-president of Peru Alberto Fujimori was the only head of state to attend the conference. There, he proclaimed his government's commitment to advancing women's rights and on returning home became a staunch supporter of a gender quota law. Presidential influence helps explain why, in June of 1997, a quota law was passed unanimously by Peru's Congress. Though women politicians had already introduced various versions of a quota bill, the proposal encountered resistance and did not make it to the floor. Members of the president's coalition were reportedly opposed to quotas but changed their mind after their electronic pagers beeped with news of the president's wishes.[15]

Though the Platform diffused ideas about affirmative action in politics, not all countries bought in. To understand this variation in behavior, we need to investigate the domestic agents of quotas: multipartisan coalitions of women politicians and activists. As I argue later, multipartisan coalitions were crucial to the achievement of quota laws. Across countries, women from Left and from center parties tended to endorse quotas. More variable was the position of women from the Right. When women from the Right endorsed quotas – as in Argentina and Mexico – laws were passed. When women from the Right rejected quotas – such as in Chile – they were not adopted.

Argentina's Quota Law

Prior to Argentina's audacious adoption of gender quota law in 1991, there were scattered governmental experiments promoting women's presence and a growing trend among European parties voluntarily to adopt quotas, as described earlier in this chapter. These experiences helped inform the Argentine

[14] Interview, Brasília, August 7, 1997.
[15] Interviews, Lima, November 1997.

reform, but cannot fully account for it. As we see in the text that follows, local actors got the idea of quotas on party lists from Europe but, in pushing for a national law, they went far beyond it. Argentina's adoption of a gender quota law in 1991 was *sui generis*. It did not respond to but rather inaugurated regional and global trends. The main global impetus for quotas – the Fourth World Conference on Women, held in Beijing in 1995 – took place four years *after* Argentina approved its law.

Argentina's pioneering adoption of a candidate quota law and struggle to implement it changed the course of women's inclusion in the rest of the region. Politicians such as Marcela Durrieu traveled around Latin America in the early 1990s holding seminars to share their experience with quotas. They told women in other countries how they lobbied for quotas and how they monitored enforcement of the law.[16]

As the Argentine story has been told extensively elsewhere (Durrieu, 1999; Krook, 2008; Lubertino Beltrán, 1992; Marx et al., 2007) I sketch it only briefly here, highlighting the formation of cross-partisan alliances among women and emphasizing one factor insufficiently addressed by other scholars: the role of the president. As we see later, the influence of Argentine president Carlos Menem and Peruvian president Alberto Fujimori was decisive in the success of their respective countries' quota laws.

Argentine advocates were influenced by Eva Perón's application of gender targets in the Peronist Party in the 1950s, international agreements and conferences, and the quota policies used by several parties of the European Left. After reaching an historic high under the Peróns in 1955, when women made up 22 percent of the Argentine Chamber of Deputies and the Senate, numbers of women in elected office had only declined. In the 1970s they made up about 9 percent of Congress but occupied only 6 percent of seats through the 1980s. To women active in political parties, social movements, and the human rights organizations that had helped usher in the transition to democracy, this scarcity was fundamentally unjust. Feminists had worked throughout the decade to achieve equality in family law, the legalization of divorce, and the creation of a national agency to advance women's rights. Several had traveled to Nairobi to attend the nongovernmental organization (NGO) forum parallel to the United Nations World Conference on Women in 1985. This international discussion about women's rights motivated them to begin annual meetings of women's groups throughout the country to discuss political participation, among other issues (*Encuentros Nacionales de Mujeres*) (Htun, 2003b; Marx et al., 2007, pp. 51–59).

---

[16] Interview, Marcela Durrieu, Buenos Aires, June 1998. University of San Francisco Professor Elisabeth Friedman recalls meeting a slender, chain-smoking Argentine woman (whom she later acknowledged was Marcela Durrieu) in Venezuela in the early 1990s as she spoke with feminists and politicians about her experience lobbying for quotas.

Frustrated by the almost complete absence of women from party lists, activists meeting at the Radical Civic Union's Women's Congress (Unión Cívica Radical [UCR]) proposed that the party apply a 35 percent candidate quota on its lists for popular election. The country's other main political party – the Peronist Party (Partido Justicialista [PJ]) – had an equally poor record: women's presence among deputies oscillated between 3 and 6 percent in the 1980s even though party statutes required that the women's, labor, and political wings of the party be equally represented in leadership and on electoral lists (Marx et al., 2007, pp. 59–60). As deputy Inés Botella noted in her speech during congressional debates, "We make up 59 percent of the electorate but only three percent of political representatives. This situation is absolutely unjust" (quoted in Marx et al., 2007, pp. 67–68).

The UCR's male leadership was lukewarm to the quota proposal. Their refusal to apply voluntary quotas prompted women to go over the heads of individual party leaders and seek a national law. (As we see below, similar events occurred in Mexico's PRD party). In late 1989, a female UCR senator and a multipartisan group of women deputies submitted two separate bills to Congress requiring *all* political parties to apply gender candidate quotas. Women from the major parties and different social sectors organized collectively to push the quota bills. They formed a multipartisan network (the Feminist Political Network or *Red de Feministas Políticas*), held meetings with municipal, state, and national legislators, and organized demonstrations throughout the country. Meanwhile, women leaders from the Peronist Party raised the issue with President Carlos Menem (in power from 1989 to 1999), who declared his support for quotas and advised them to continue to mobilize public opinion (Ibid.; Durrieu, 1999).

The bill passed the Senate relatively easily but stalled in the lower house. On the day when it was eventually discussed there, November 6, 1991, women filled the galleries of the chamber and the neighboring streets. Durrieu recalls that, "the Congress was practically taken over by women activists from all the political parties" (Durrieu, 1999, p. 144).

In spite of this pressure, by the early morning it appeared that the bill was headed for defeat. At that moment, President Menem sent Interior Minister José Luis Manzano to speak to the party caucus on his behalf. Manzano told the recalcitrant deputies that the president supported the bill and made a speech appealing to Peronist traditions and the gender quota applied by Eva Perón in the 1950s. This intervention united the Peronists behind the law and influenced politicians from other parties who did not want to stand out as its only opponents (Durrieu, 1999, pp. 144–145).

Given the controversy over quotas in Argentina, the president's endorsement of the bill was decisive. Why did Menem, not known as a feminist (later in his presidency he sought to include a ban on abortion in the constitution), support quotas? Some observers argue that he wanted to attract women's votes and close a gender gap suffered by the Peronists in relation to the opposition

UCR party as well as "modernize the country and reposition it to the world" (Marx et al., 2007, p. 62). Interior Minister Manzano told me in an interview that the president was embarrassed by the historically low numbers of women in power and that he harbored hopes of going down in history as the person responsible for a revolutionary improvement in women's rights in line with the Peronist tradition.[17]

Menem's role did not end with approval of the law in Congress. He also promulgated a decree that proved crucial for its successful application. The decree (issued on March 8 – International Women's Day – 1993) clarified that 30 percent was intended to be a minimal presence: one woman should be included for every two men on party lists and, in the event that only two candidates appeared on the list, one should be a woman. In elections in 1993 and 1995, multipartisan networks of women throughout the country used this decree to challenge in court those party lists that failed to place women in the appropriate positions. With the help of the National Women's Council (a government agency), they overcame legal hurdles (such as the requirement that only the wronged party – in this case, the female candidate – could impugn a noncompliant list), and saw that several lists were thrown out by electoral tribunals.

By 1995, the National Electoral Court ruled that the Women's Council could initiate suits on behalf of female candidates throughout the country. In 2000, President Fernando de la Rúa emitted another decree to clarify the law's placement mandates. The decree gave electoral judges the power to reorder party lists and gave any voter in a district the right to impugn party lists in court (Durrieu, 1999; Marx et al., 2007). After the electoral law was changed in 2001 to institute direct, popular elections of Senators (previously, federal senators had been elected by provincial legislators), another decree clarified that if parties were contesting two or fewer seats, one of each party's top two candidates had to be a woman (effectively, a gender parity mandate) (Piscopo & Thomas 2012).[18] These institutional reforms gave advocates the tools they needed to make quotas effective. In 2014, women made up a whopping 36 percent of the lower house and 39 percent of the Senate.

Mexico: Women from the Right Endorse Quotas

As in Argentina, the struggle for quotas in Mexico began within the parties. The battle commenced within the left-wing PRD in the early 1990s as women leaders pressured for inclusion in internal decision making positions and among candidates. The party narrowly adopted a candidate quota of 20 percent at its congress in 1993 (the quota was later raised to 30 percent), but failed to

---

[17] Interview with Manzano, Buenos Aires, August 1998.
[18] Since each province elects a total of three senators (two from the victorious party and one from the runner-up), a 30 percent quota law (even with women in the third place on party lists) would likely result in few women getting elected.

TABLE 3.1. *Arguments for and against Gender Quotas in Mexico's PRD*

Arguments against Quotas	Women's Responses
There aren't enough women to fill the slots	Women are 52 percent of the electorate; the major force at party rallies; they run political campaigns; and, because the PRD includes leaders from social movements, there are plenty of women to pick from
Women aren't prepared	This may be true in some cases but neither are the men! Women responded with the slogan: "Nobody is born a PRDista! She makes herself one. No one is born a deputy! She makes herself one"
Women don't want to be candidates	But we are asking for the quota!
Women must earn positions on their own	This presumes that men become candidates through their own merits, which isn't the case. They are recruited through their networks
Quotas lead to the filling of party lists with aunts and mothers-in-law	The same happens with men
The issue is unimportant	On the contrary: you cannot make decisions on major national issues with a partial (exclusively male) perspective

Source: Interview with PRD women's secretary Malu Mícher, Mexico City, May 9, 2001.

meet this percentage in elections in 1994 (Baldez, 2004, p. 240; Bruhn, 2003). Through the late 1990s, PRD women lobbied to increase the party's quota to 50 percent, but the proposal narrowly lost at the 2001 party congress. After the count was announced, some male delegates yelled to their female counterparts, "Don't cry!" This response, especially in a party explicitly committed to inclusion and social justice, infuriated women and hardened their resolve to seek a tough national law.[19]

The arguments for and against quotas within the PRD are instructive, for they mirror negotiations in parties and legislatures throughout the region (see Table 3.1). Male opponents claimed that there weren't enough women to fill the slots; they weren't prepared; women didn't want to be candidates; women must gain candidacies through their own efforts; the issue lacked importance; and so forth. To this, women responded that, in reality, women made up 52 percent of the electorate; they were the major force in party rallies and they ran

[19] Interview with Malu Mícher, Mexico City, May 9, 2001.

political campaigns; there were plenty of women because the party included leaders from social movements; women may not all be qualified, but then neither were the men; and that the quota was necessary because national decision making could not rely on only one perspective.[20]

Similar deliberations about women's leadership were occurring in the center-left Partido Revolucionario Institucional (PRI) and the right-wing PAN. Women activists from all parties had met regularly throughout the 1990s to exchange strategies and opinions about promoting women's candidacies, among other topics (Bruhn, 2003, p. 112). This network helped spread the example set by the PRD's earlier introduction of quotas. Also influential, however, was the experience of Argentina and the 1995 Fourth World Conference on Women, discussed earlier. Like in Brazil, the Beijing Conference stimulated a great deal of activism in Mexico. As PRI Deputy María Elena Chapa recalled: "We traveled around the entire country organizing meetings about women's participation in diverse areas and women's common concerns: health, education, employment, politics, poverty, self-image, environment, violence, children, among others, in line with the issues granted global attention in the Beijing Platform for Action" (quoted in Htun & Jones, 2002, p. 35).

In 1996, the ruling PRI adopted a quota of 30 percent on proportional representation (PR) lists and on territorial committees, but stipulated only a weak placement mandate that would work for every ten list slots (Bruhn, 2003, p. 112). Later that year, under the ruling party's influence, the national congress approved a weak and largely rhetorical quota law. Though the law stipulated that women make up 30 percent of candidates, it permitted parties to comply by including them as alternate candidates (*suplentes*) on party lists. (By Mexican law, the ballot specifies an alternate for each titular candidate [*propietario*] in single-member districts and on PR lists who will take office in the event the *propietario* dies or resigns.) What's more, there were no specified penalties for noncompliance. Parties obeyed the law by naming women primarily as *suplentes*, and they made up 60 percent of *suplentes* contesting the 2000 elections. After the elections, women's presence in Congress actually declined (Htun, 2001). Why was the law so weak in content and enforcement? According to one observer, it was a last-minute addition to the legislative agenda and approved only to placate women activists within the ruling party. It was not the product of sustained discussion or the consequence of a campaign by a multipartisan coalition.[21]

Female party leaders and activists worked hard so their parties would adopt quotas. Yet in comparative perspective, the embrace of quotas by the Left PRD and the center-left PRI is not too surprising. Leftist parties around the world favor interventions promoting social justice, tend to elect more women, and are more likely voluntarily to adopt quota rules than their counterparts on the

---

[20] Interview with PRD women's secretary Malu Mícher, Mexico City, May 9, 2001.
[21] Interview with Cecilia Romero, Mexico City, May 9, 2001.

Right (Caul, 1999; Inglehart & Norris, 2003; Norris, 2004). More intriguing is the behavior of the right-wing PAN. PANista women's eventual (and grudging) acceptance of quotas in the early 2000s was the decisive factor in the formation of the multipartisan coalition of women that achieved Mexico's tough law.

Throughout the 1990s, PANista activists, led by the National Secretariat for the Political Promotion of Women, pressured the party to promote more women. The PRD's early embrace of quotas produced contagion effects: it increased the perception that other parties would be electorally vulnerable if they failed to respond to women's demands (Matland & Studlar, 1996). Between the 1994 and 1997 elections, women's presence on the PAN's PR lists increased from 10 to 24 percent (Bruhn, 2003, p. 114). Before the 2000 elections, women pressed for more explicit affirmative action measures. They convinced the party to require that a woman occupy one of the first two positions on each PR list, that a woman be named as the alternate if the titular candidate were a man (and vice versa), and that, among the candidates presented by each state's central committee for primary elections, men and women be equally represented (Htun, 2002a, pp. 27–28). These are striking moves for a party whose leadership explicitly rejected the quota and they exceeded the requirements of the weak national law in effect at that time.

Yet these internal measures proved inadequate. Women still occupied fewer seats among the PAN's caucus (12 percent of lower house deputies and 13 percent of senators) than among its rival parties on the left; their presence also lagged the national average. This poor performance, in spite of strong internal pressure from women activists and party leaders, compelled politicians previously opposed to quotas to join their left-wing counterparts in endorsing a strong national law. As PAN Senator Cecilia Romero told me in an interview:

> The demand for quotas came about because party leaders failed to respond to our demands for participation. It doesn't matter if we like the quota. It's a necessary measure: without a quota, things would take too long. Some women are enthusiastic about the quota; others simply recognize that there isn't any other way. It should be a temporary thing.[22]

> For women of the PAN, support for quotas did not reflect an ideological commitment. In fact, they disliked the idea. But they recognized that to promote women's leadership, quotas were a tactical necessity.

Once women from Mexico's three main parties joined together, they still had to convince recalcitrant male politicians to support the law. Some PRD and PRI politicians opposed quotas, but most of the resistance came from the PAN. Its president opposed quotas; other leaders joked that quotas for women would lead to quotas for homosexuals (Baldez, 2004, p. 246). To confront this skepticism, women relied on a novel lobbying strategy. Believing that male politicians would be less dismissive of arguments made by women from other

---

[22] Interview, Mexico City, May 9, 2001.

parties, they assigned PRD and PRI women the task of lobbying PAN men, and vice versa. It worked. As one PAN politician reported in an interview with Lisa Baldez: "It's one thing to confront the women from your own party. But when you are up against women from the other parties, it's difficult to say no," (Baldez, 2004, p. 247).

Ultimately, the PAN supported the law for pragmatic reasons. They were motivated by the desire to avoid blame for failing to advance women's rights and were afraid of being portrayed in the media as sexist and anti-women. As leader (and first lady between 2006 and 2012) Margarita Zavala told Lisa Baldez: "We do not have the money to counteract the impact that voting against the quota would have in the media; this is what finally convinced the last holdouts, that we would have to explain why we voted as we did" (quoted in Baldez, 2004, p. 249 and passim). The Chamber of Deputies approved the bill by a 403–7 vote (12 abstentions); the Senate passed it unanimously. The law was tough: in addition to proscribing compliance with the 30 percent quota by including women as *suplentes*, any party not applying the law would be issued a public reprimand by the Federal Electoral Institute. Failure to enforce the law after another twenty-four hours would disqualify a party from competing in the district in question (Baldez, 2004, pp. 248–249).

Chile: No Quota

Unlike in Argentina and Mexico, women from parties of the Chilean Right failed to support a quota. By the second decade of the twenty-first century, the number of people advocating a quota law had grown steadily – to include some right-wing politicians, including the male president of the lower house of Congress – but a multipartisan pact remained elusive. Chile's experience vividly demonstrates that collective action among women, even in the face of a shared disadvantage, cannot be assumed. It must be constructed, and the success of such efforts at gender-specific mobilization varies across countries and over time.

Since the return to democracy in 1990, women politicians of the left and center-left parties of the governing *Concertación* coalition on several occasions tried to get a quota law passed by Congress. These efforts failed, even during the presidency of Michele Bachelet (2006–2010), a socialist and quota supporter. The country's resistance to the quota trend is surprising. It possessed a strong and legislatively active women's agency (Servicio Nacional de la Mujer [SERNAM]), underwent nineteen years of left and left-of-center governments (1990–2009), and promoted other reforms such as parental leave, day care centers, family courts, and women's police stations (Blofield & Haas, 2005; Haas, 2000).

At the beginning of the 2000s, there was little discussion in Chile of gender quotas, low public awareness, and lack of consensus among the ruling coalition on the issue (Franceschet, 2005; Hola, Veloso, & Ruiz, 2002). Though all three parties of the governing Concertación coalition (consisting of the Socialist Party [PS], Democratic Party [PPD], and Christian Democratic [DC] Party) had applied quotas for internal leadership positions and for candidate positions since the 1990s (Htun, 1997), these were poorly enforced, leaving a significant gap between the level of the quota and women's actual participation. The internal quotas were controversial and not widely supported, even by women (Franceschet, 2005, pp. 98–101). The socialist government of Ricardo Lagos (2000–2005) named five women (of sixteen ministers) to the cabinet, but neglected to support a quota bill presented to Congress in 2003. This bill, which would require that women make up 40 percent of candidates fielded by political parties in national and municipal elections, was ranked as the lowest priority by the Family Committee (Franceschet, 2005, p. 101).

Advocacy for quotas gathered steam in the second half of the decade under the first Bachelet presidency. By this time, quota experiences in other Latin American countries – not to mention their use in Europe, Asia, and Africa – had dispelled some earlier skepticism among Chileans about the advantages of such a policy. On assuming power, Bachelet set a regional record by appointing a cabinet of ten men and ten women. Concern for gender balance spilled over into other areas: state-owned enterprises appointed women to their governing boards and women were appointed to high-level commissions.[23] The government's parity policies were widely supported. One study of public opinion found that 73 percent of respondents agreed with the policies, including 60 and 70 percent of those identifying their political affiliation as center-right and right, respectively (SERNAM, 2008).

Bachelet announced her support for the 40 percent quota bill, still languishing in Congress.[24] As with the official parity measures, public opinion studies evinced support for quotas. Some 63 percent of respondents in 2006 confirmed their agreement with the establishment of a candidate quota for popular elections (SERNAM, 2008, p. 30). Yet opinion was divided across the political spectrum. Whereas 85 percent of the non-Concertación Left and 68 percent of the Concertación-affiliated respondents favored quotas, merely 40 percent of the Alianza por Chile (the coalition of right-wing opposition parties consisting of the Renovación Nacional [RN] and Unión Democrática Independiente [UDI]) supporters did. In fact, 55 percent of Alianza partisans opposed them (SERNAM, 2008, p. 32). On the Right there was a significant gender gap: only 30 percent of Alianza men declared support for quotas, compared to 49 percent of women (63 percent of men and 47 percent of women opposed quotas) (SERNAM, 2008, p. 33).

Unlike in Mexico, multipartisan coalitions of women politicians backing quotas failed to form. Though women from the governing Concertación

---

[23] Jane Jaquette, personal communication, April 26, 2006.
[24] Jen Ross, "Chile Kick Starts Debate on Gender Quotas," Women's e-news, February 16, 2007. Retrieved from www.womensenews.org/article.cfm/dyn/aid/3069 (accessed August 28, 2009).

have tended to favor quotas, women from the opposition Alizana have been resolutely opposed. When I visited Chile in April, 2012, UDI deputy Claudia Nogueira spoke to me about the relationship between women politicians on the Right and the Left. She said that, whereas they could find common ground on women's access to work and the problem of violence, they would continue to disagree on abortion and on quotas.[25] UDI Deputy María Angélica Cristi summed up their views: "We have always been against bills that purport to establish any type of discrimination, that tend to reward or encourage the inclusion of women in politics only because of their gender. We don't believe that merely being a woman qualifies one for political office, such as a candidate for congress, mayor, city council or even president of the Republic."[26]

Politicians and intellectuals on the Right tend to interpret women's scarce presence in politics in different ways than quota advocates. The latter focus on sexism in political parties and discrimination in candidate selection procedures. Politicians and intellectuals on the Right, by contrast, point to women's gender roles, lack of interest, and lack of preparation as more salient explanations (Hola et al., 2002, p. 32). As two advisors from the right-wing think tank Liberty and Development put it, "It's a self-evident fact that availability for a political career is lower in the feminine universe than in the masculine universe" (Cámara de Diputados de Chile, 2007, p. 36). Deputy Cristi believes that, if exceptional women are committed to succeeding in politics, they will become candidates. In her view, demonstrating oneself to be a woman capable of confronting masculinist biases in politics is an asset.[27]

Women politicians from the Right and the Left disagreed not only about the desirability of quotas. They also disagreed about how women's underrepresentation should be explained, whether it violated principles of fairness and social justice, and what kind of response was needed from the state, if any. Women on the Right attributed women's low presence in power to their own choices, though most acknowledged that these choices were shaped by gender roles and responsibilities. What's more, they believed that propping women up with a quota was not just unnecessary (since committed women could become candidates through their own efforts) but counterproductive and unfair.[28] They did

[25] Personal conversation, Santiago, April 25, 2012.

[26] "Ley de cuotas: Más mujeres en la política." Biblioteca del Congreso Nacional de Chile, November 28, 2007. Retrieved from www.bcn.cl/carpeta_temas_profundidad/temas_profundidad.2007-11-27.0456839556 (accessed September 2, 2009).

[27] "Ley de cuotas: Más mujeres en la política." Biblioteca del Congreso Nacional de Chile, November 28, 2007. Retrieved from www.bcn.cl/carpeta_temas_profundidad/temas_profundidad.2007-11-27.0456839556 (accessed September 2, 2009).

[28] "Ley de cuotas: Más mujeres en la política." Biblioteca del Congreso Nacional de Chile, November 28, 2007. Retrieved from www.bcn.cl/carpeta_temas_profundidad/temas_profundidad.2007-11-27.0456839556 (accessed September 2, 2009); Hola, Velasco, & Ruz (2002); interview with Evelyn Matthei by Camila Vergara.

not buy into the "fast track" approach endorsed by international organizations and women from the Right in other countries, such as Mexico and Argentina.

In January of 2007, the 40 percent quota bill was defeated in the lower house's Family Committee. The vote divided largely along partisan lines: the five deputies from the Concertación and one independent voted in favor; the five deputies from the Alianza por Chile voted against; and there was one abstention (Cámara de Diputados de Chile, 2007).[29] This abstention, by a Concertación deputy, denied the bill the majority endorsement it needed to be transferred to the floor.

Bachelet responded to this defeat by submitting her own quota bill to Congress in October of 2007. It was the first time the executive had authored such a bill (Franceschet, 2010, p. 251). In addition to calling for a 30 percent (minimum) quota in party candidate nominations and internal leadership posts, the bill establishes financial incentives for parties to nominate women candidates. It promises them extra public funding for increasing the number of women candidates above 30 percent and even more funding above 40 percent (Presidencia de la República de Chile, 2007). The bill sat for two years until, on September 1, 2009, Bachelet denoted it "urgent," implying that the bill would be considered in the following extraordinary legislative session. At a meeting of a multipartisan group of women legislators, she declared that the scarcity of women in elected office and among candidates had to change, adding that, "No one could imagine that the national football team could win a match with only half its players. We are about to see a match [the 2009 elections] and hope that the team will be complete and play very well" (Bachelet, 2009).

Partisan conflict has precluded change in other areas related to women's rights. Opposition from the Right (and the government's fear of confronting it) delayed the legalization of divorce until 2004. Abortion is forbidden under all circumstances, even to save the mother's life, and there has been little public discussion of reform because of conservative pressure (Htun, 2003a). To the extent that women's rights reforms have passed, advocates have portrayed the changes in socially conservative terms. A law requiring employers to provide day care, for example, was framed as a way to protect motherhood and not to facilitate women's economic independence (Blofield & Haas, 2005).

Opposition from right-wing parties is the most salient obstacle to Chile's adoption of a quota law, but the electoral system context must also be taken into account. Comparative research has shown that quotas work best in closed-list PR systems with large districts and placement mandates (Htun & Jones, 2002; Jones, 1998, 2009).[30] Chile, by contrast, has a district size of only

---

[29] Voting record from the Family Commission. Retrieved from www.camara.cl/trabajamos/comision_sesiondetalle.aspx?prmTAB=votacion&prmID=415&prmIDSES=8111 (accessed August 31, 2009).

[30] Closed-list systems allow parties to determine the order of candidate on the list and to apply placement mandates guaranteeing that women are ranked in electable positions. The larger the size of the district, the more candidates each party is likely to elect from deeper positions on

two, uses open lists, and requires that, to win both seats, a party or coalition capture two-thirds of the total vote. These rules create strong incentives for the parties to group themselves into two coalitions; generate competition among each coalition's candidates for preference votes; and mean that, in most districts, only one candidate per coalition actually wins a seat.[31]

How would a quota be applied in such a system? Unless it required parity in candidacies (leading each coalition to field one man and one woman per district), it is difficult to see how parties would determine the allocation of their female candidates across districts and how this would relate to intracoalition bargaining over candidacies. Even if women were nominated, many would fail to gain seats because of intracoalitional competition and the tendency of each district to elect only one candidate per coalition. Several politicians interviewed by SERNAM in 2002 said they did not see how the quota could be applied and, even if it was attempted, it would not change anything (Hola et al., 2002, p. 54). As this suggests, quota legislation, although symbolically important, could be practically ineffective in Chile without broader electoral reforms. It might allow men to claim credit (for very little), distract attention from other problems of gender inequality, and have the potential to weaken the women politicians who advocated it (Jones, 2005).

The outlook for quotas is thus tied to a broader package of electoral reforms. Since the return to democracy in 1990, there has been considerable discussion about increasing district size and moving to a more proportional system, but every attempt has failed. A high-level commission appointed by President Bachelet in 2006, which included two feminist academics, included a gender quota among its recommendations for reform. Yet opposition from the parties of the right compelled Bachelet to withdraw the proposal in 2007 (Franceschet, 2010, p. 250). There was also resistance from the governing coalition: when confronted with the prospect of real change, many Concertación politicians realized that the system had served them reasonably well.[32]

In addition, the Chilean feminist movement initially failed to mobilize for quotas in the same ways that assisted the cause in other countries. In the Mexican and Argentine cases discussed previously, civil society groups worked in concert with women politicians to lobby and raise public awareness. Chile's movement, by contrast, grew weaker with the return to democracy in 1990 and

---

their lists. By contrast, if a party elects only one or two candidates in a district, a woman ranked third on the list will never gain a seat.

[31] The system is biased against women in various ways. The small district size encourages parties to field their strongest candidates, not to balance the ticket with a diverse field. Even when a woman is the preferred candidate of her party, she is still susceptible to being bumped in the interparty bargaining that determines the coalition's choice of candidates in the district (Franceschet, 2010, p. 249). What's more, the system favors incumbents: more than 70 percent of incumbents seek reelection and, of these, more than 80 percent win (Franceschet, 2010, p. 249 citing; Navia, 2008).

[32] Personal communication with John Carey, August 29, 2009.

considerably more distanced from the political class. By the mid-2000s, there were few links between women politicians and women active in civil society and little sense that the former represented the interests of the latter. The idea that electing more women would make a difference, a key motivator in other countries, thus seemed unrealistic in Chile. As Franceschet puts it: "The popular perception in Chile that politics is an elite affair and that agreements are negotiated behind closed doors undercuts any arguments that electing more women will make a substantial difference to women's lives" (Franceschet, 2010, pp. 253–354).

After 2010, civic activism around quotas increased. Comunidad Mujer (Women's Community), a women's rights NGO, launched its "Political Participation and Leadership Project" in 2008. By 2012, the group had sponsored campaigns to gain support among politicians, intellectuals, and other elites for gender quotas as well as to change public opinion more broadly. It made several videos featuring celebrities voicing their support for quotas, sponsored a petition drive, and lobbied politicians. Other activities included leadership training for women candidates in popular elections, civic engagement programs for young women, a prize to recognize organizations promoting gender equality, and diversity consulting for private sector organizations. The staff of Comunidad Mujer regularly contributes op-ed articles to major newspapers; the group also sponsors public conferences, workshops, and lectures. It was at a Comunidad Mujer forum in April of 2012 when the (male) President of the Chamber of Deputies publicly announced his support for a gender quota law.[33]

Some officials in the government of President Sebastian Piñera (2010–2014), including the director of the state women's agency, SERNAM, supported the adoption of a quota law.[34] Piñera himself was reportedly open to the idea, but his government ended up endorsing only financial incentives to political parties as a mechanism to promote women's inclusion. In March of 2013, SERNAM presented a bill to Congress that would reward parties that increased the number of women candidates by 20 percent over previous elections, with the funds allocated in proportion to the number of votes received by each woman.[35] As reported earlier, similarly gradualist, pool-enlarging methods to promote inclusion failed to produce results in other countries, constituting a main motivation for women from different backgrounds to endorse quotas.[36]

---

[33] I gave the keynote speech at this forum in Santiago and was in the audience when Nicolas Monkenberg made these remarks.

[34] Interview with Minister Carolina Schmidt, Santiago, April 26, 2012.

[35] "President Piñera y Ministra Schmidt firmaron proyecto para incentivar participación política de las mujeres." Retrieved from http://portal.sernam.cl/?m=sp&i=3445 (accessed March 8, 2013).

[36] By the time this book was going to press, Chile had approved a massive electoral reform that included a 40 percent gender quota law, to be phased out in 2029. The new law, promulgated by Bachelet in April of 2015, introduced proportional representation, created larger multimember

Conclusion: Quotas as a Self-limiting Device

Quotas are not a mechanism to represent women's interests. Though many quota advocates hoped for more – that is, they expected that women in power would advocate gender interests – the minimum common denominator uniting women from the left and right, from parties and social movements, was the goal of increasing women's inclusion. They demanded quotas for the sake of fairness, not because they believed that women in power would advance group-specific policy interests.[37] As Mexican feminist Cecilia Loria argued, the quota is "not for the representation of women, as this is impossible. Rather, it is because having a woman's body should not be an impediment to being a candidate. It's a question of fairness, not of representation."[38]

Multipartisan coalitions were dominated by elites. In Bolivia, for example, demands for quotas did not originate from a grass-roots movement and were only remotely connected to the demands of average women. According to political scientist Ximena Costa: "Quotas were achieved by a group of middle class female intellectuals who had access to power and wanted to extend this right to others. It wasn't a massive demand surging from society but rather from a small group of women."[39] In Brazil, the movement for quotas was spearheaded by Deputy Marta Suplicy, a Paulista from a wealthy family (and a member of the Workers' Party). Though Suplicy mobilized other women in Congress and forged ties to feminist intellectuals and members of the women's movement, in many ways, the effort behind quotas was a one-woman show (Marx et al., 2007).

Quotas were conceived, advocated, and won by elite women as a way to break sexism in candidate selection, a temporary fix that, over time, would become obsolete. As the quota is implemented, procedures for candidate selection change, gradually rendering obsolete the reasons for quota adoption in the first place. During debates about quotas in the Argentine Congress, deputy Gabriela Gonzáles Gass argued that quotas are temporary measures that, "with the passage of time – as they produce real equality – will disappear on their own" (quoted in Marx et al., 2007, p. 68). Or, as León and Holguín argue, "As an affirmative action, quotas have a temporary character whose limit is given by the inclusion of the marginalized group ... in the process of political decision making" (León & Holguín, 2005, pp. 47–48).[40] As more women

---

districts to replace the old binomial system, and increased the number of senators. Quota will be applied for the first time in the 2017 elections.

[37] To be sure, some quota advocates claimed that women would bring distinctive perspectives and interests to the political process and that their presence would promote gender equality policy. These views were not shared by all members of the multipartisan coalitions behind quota adoption. Only the argument from fairness was supported across the political spectrum.

[38] Interview, Mexico City, May 8, 2001.

[39] Interview with Jimena Costa, La Paz, May 13, 2005.

[40] In a public opinion study carried out by the Chilean women's agency, SERNAM, in 2008, respondents indicated that they supported gender parity in politics because "equality implies that everyone has the chance to exercise public office" (51 percent selected this answer to a multiple

gain power, they break down the obstacles holding others back. Over time, the quota will become less necessary as institutionalized sex discrimination is gradually reversed.

The articulated logic behind quotas contrasts vividly with the language of group rights in proposals for ethnic and racial reservations. The point of quotas is not to *recognize* women's difference from men but to render it *irrelevant* for holding national office. By accomplishing their objectives, quotas render themselves unnecessary.

Activists and academics often inflated the meaning and implications of quotas in hopes that they would translate into better representation and more extensive policy changes. Yet there is nothing inherent in the quota that justifies these expectations. In fact, quotas offer grounds for some pessimism about any longer term effects on representation or policy change. Quotas enable women to gain access to power as individual members of political parties. Beneficiaries are nominated by their parties and elected by the general pool of voters. They are not nominated by group-specific parties or organizations and not elected by a subset of voters, as is usually the case with reserved seat arrangements. Put another way, candidate quotas are not based on the assumption that women form a political constituency nor do they engineer one. As Mexican Senator Cecilia Romero put it: "As women, we are not a group. Women are not a collective."[41]

To maintain unity, quota coalitions tended to limit their objectives to enactment of the quota. They did not promote an additional agenda on women's rights such as sexual harassment penalties, maternity leave, equal pay, or greater reproductive rights. In France, for example, advocates of the gender parity constitutional amendment and law (2000) avoided broader considerations such as socio-economic equality and anticipation of what, if any, policy changes women's presence in power would bring about. This separation of the goal of parity from the substantive representation of women's interests enabled politicians of diverse political and ideological stripes to smooth over their differences and unite in the parity movement. This self-limitation strategy helped defray fears that right-wing and conservative women would be attacked or disqualified (Bird, 2002; Giraud & Jenson, 2001; Jenson & Valiente, 2003; Mazur, 2001).[42] In other areas as well, disaggregating issues has enabled people

---

choice question). Fewer (35 percent) favored gender parity on the grounds that "Women have different views than men and it's important that such views be present in politics" (SERNAM, 2008, p. 22).

[41] Interview, Mexico City, May 9, 2001.

[42] Crucial in the French case was the distinction between inclusion rights for women and for other excluded groups. Advocates were able to gain wide partisan support by denying that parity would legitimize demands for inclusion by these other groups. And indeed, the installation of parity has done little to bring the concerns of ethnic minorities and women ethnic minorities into political life (Bird, 2001, pp. 279–280).

of diverse beliefs to find common ground. Aggregating issues into omnibus proposals, by contrast, has stalled change (Htun, 2003a, p. 181).

Pro-quota coalitions tended to disband after the laws were adopted (though they occasionally reunited for defined policy objectives) as women became reabsorbed into their parties and occupied with partisan agendas. And, though many women acted on behalf of gender interests – by introducing legislation, making speeches, and developing connections to female constituents – a significant number did not. As we see in Chapter 7, some women who tried to change politics confronted institutionalized gender biases in legislatures. Quotas gave women presence in power, but not the power to make effective use of their presence.

4

Indigenous Reservations and Gender Parity in Bolivia
(written with Juan Pablo Ossa)

This chapter explores how intersectional differences and institutions helped structure the terms of inclusion by focusing on Bolivia, which applies both a gender parity law and reserved seats by ethnicity. The country's experience is puzzling. As is well known, the first (self-identified) indigenous president was elected in 2005 and reelected in 2009. Evo Morales and his party, the *Movimiento al Socialismo* (MAS, Movement toward Socialism), have defended indigenous interests. After assuming office, Morales appointed people of indigenous descent to cabinet positions and required state officials to speak one of three indigenous languages (Aymara, Quechua, or Guaraní) (Albró, 2006, p. 210). He presided over a constitutional convention and adoption of a new constitution that upholds numerous indigenous rights, including collective land rights, political and legal autonomy, and control over natural resources (República de Bolívia, 2009, Article 30). The national development plan promotes universal health care and income supports while showcasing indigenous cosmovision – including the Andean principle of "living well" – as the paradigm for state policy (Johnson, 2010, p. 143).

Yet the MAS rejected a central demand of indigenous movements. They had requested thirty-six reserved seats in parliament: one for each *pueblo* (or people) recognized by the constitution. In the end, the electoral law approved by the MAS-dominated legislature guaranteed a mere seven seats to indigenous groups, one-fifth of the number originally proposed and a mere 5 percent of the total seats in the lower house of Congress.

When it came to women, the opposite occurred. In spite of its *machista* tendencies, the MAS adopted and applied a parity rule leading to the political inclusion of record numbers of women. Then, the Congress approved laws to establish parity between men and women in the national electoral court, the state electoral courts, the Constitutional Court, and in the selection of leaders in autonomous indigenous regions.[1] Though not all of the party caucus agreed,

---

[1] "Balance de 5 Leyes Aprobadas" Observatorio de Genero Coordinadora Mujer, Julio de 2010.

and women deputies had to struggle against recalcitrant male legislators to get the rules adopted, the remarkable parity provisions were adopted without roadblocks, strikes, or intimidation.

Bolivia's indigenous-led government guaranteed indigenous peoples a mere 5 percent of parliamentary seats while women got a gender parity law granting them 50 percent of positions on candidate lists. Why was Evo Morales's government stingy in its response to the demands of indigenous movements for greater political inclusion? How were women able to convince the government to approve a gender parity law? Wasn't it supposed to be the other way around? Does Bolivia's experience imply more general conclusions about marginalized groups' empowerment and struggle for inclusion?

Following theories of intersectionality, this chapter highlights differences and disagreements *within* marginalized groups and the potential for *intra*group conflicts of interest. Arguing that shared membership in a group is not sufficient to guarantee mobilization, it demonstrates that group success depends in part on the ability to overcome differences and forge a common political strategy. In addition, its approach links intragroup dynamics to institutional factors and party interests. Excluded groups tend to demand logically appropriate, but differing, institutional changes to promote their inclusion (Htun, 2004b). Parties are not agnostic vis-à-vis these policies. Inclusion mechanisms that further – or at least fail to jeopardize – party interests in gaining power will be more acceptable than those that pose a threat to the party's position.

Armed with this approach, the chapter identifies three factors behind Bolivia's endorsement of gender parity and rejection of (a significant number of) ethnic reservations:

1. *The relative unity of the women's movement and disunity of the indigenous movement.* The women's movement overcame the historic division between urban feminists and women from indigenous, popular sectors to unite around the goal of parity in Congress and other arenas of public decision making. The indigenous movement was divided in its support for reserved seats.

2. *Gender parity is a majority issue affecting all women; indigenous reservations pertain to a disadvantaged subgroup of indigenous peoples.* Though parity in electoral lists and public institutions affects (or has the potential to affect) *all* women, indigenous reservations were designed for numerically small and rural groups.

3. *Inclusion through quotas or parity on party lists is more acceptable to a party than the reservation of seats in parliament.* Candidate quotas or parity allows parties to bring in women as individuals, to dilute their group strength by partisan divisions, and to control them through the sanctions and incentives inherent in the nomination process. Legislative reservations give indigenous groups access to power independent of mainstream parties.

Intersectionality, Institutions, and Inclusion

As an approach to the study of social experience, intersectionality emphasizes the plurality of differences within and across groups (Garcia Bedolla, 2007; Hancock, 2007; Jordan-Zachery, 2007; Nash, 2008; Weldon, 2008, 2011). Bisected by multiple axes of power and difference, any single marginalized group is not a homogeneous entity but a collection of categories or coalitions. Excluded groups may disagree over the terms of their own inclusion, the nature of their disadvantage, and whether and how any disadvantage should be addressed. The convergence of group interests, preferences, and perspectives is an *outcome* of politics, not the *premise* of politics. As we see in the text that follows, collective action across subgroup categories helps explain why some groups successfully pushed the state to grant them political inclusion. When members of a more encompassing category are able to join into a larger and more effective coalition, their demands for inclusion (and perhaps other issues) are more likely to be granted.

Intersectionality implies that different sectors of marginalized groups may have different interests. Though some issues may affect all members of a marginalized group, others are more relevant to their disadvantaged and/ or advantaged subgroups (Crenshaw, 1991; Strolovitch, 2007). The number of constituents affected by an issue is directly related to the attention that advocacy organizations devote to it. Organizations promoting the interests of marginalized groups therefore have a tendency to promote issues affecting the majority of members more than those issues affecting only disadvantaged subgroups. Feminist groups in the United States, for example, are more likely to work on violence against women (a majority issue) than on welfare reform (an issue affecting primarily poor women) (Strolovitch, 2007, pp. 93–95).

Intragroup divisions help account for differences in their interests and the priorities of advocacy organizations. Explaining the adoption of policies to address marginalization and inequality, however, requires an additional analytical step. Groups do not advance their demands in a vacuum but in the context of already existing political institutions. They achieve their policy goals when they can take advantage of points of access and leverage. We must therefore examine the relative opportunities that political institutions offer to differently constituted groups and different types of claims (and deny to their competitors and opponents) (cf. Amenta et al., 2010; Skocpol, 1992, pp. 54–57; Skocpol, Ganz, & Munson, 2000, pp. 298–300).

Political parties have inherent interests that shape their positions vis-à-vis policies to promote the inclusion of historically marginalized groups. This argument rests on two widely accepted propositions about parties. First, they are the primary agents of representation and hold a monopoly on access to elected office (with some exceptions) (see, e.g., Mainwaring & Scully, 1995, p. 2). Second, parties are oriented toward the goal of electoral victory (Schlesinger, 1984, pp. 383–384). As Downs puts it, they are "teams" seeking to win elections, a goal that subordinates other objectives (Downs, 1957, pp. 25–28). This implies that parties are unlikely willingly to engage in behavior that jeopardizes their ability to hang onto power.

Party interest in electoral victory implies a preference for candidate quotas over reserved parliamentary seats. Why? Candidate quotas, a policy that is logically appropriate for groups that cross-cut partisan divisions, are a mechanism to promote individuals from the bottom of party ranks to electable positions on candidate lists (Htun, 2004b). As long as parties control the nomination process,[2] candidate quotas involve the mere addition of individuals of a different sex, race, or ethnicity to party lists. While threatening to some of those individuals occupying top positions, candidate quotas pose little threat to the party as a whole. The included group is weakened as it is divided across party lines. And through nominations, party leaders have the power to impose sanctions and offer incentives to shape the behavior of members of the recently included group.

Reserved seats – provided they are filled by election from special districts or separate voter rolls – enable groups to gain access to power independently of existing parties (Htun, 2004b). Logically appropriate for groups whose boundaries coincide with partisan divisions or who form their own party, legislative reservations may involve changing the size of parliament, the number of seats elected per district, the relative weight of proportional and majoritarian contests (in mixed systems), and other structural features of an electoral system. As a result, reserved seats may threaten existing parties' share of seats, alter the proportionality between votes and seats, give small parties coalition (or blackmail) potential, and otherwise alter the partisan balance of power.[3] Rather than impose adjustments within individual parties, they produce changes that alter relations across parties, potentially to the detriment of the party in power. As a result, rational parties will be less receptive to claims for reserved seats than to candidate quotas. Ceteris paribus, groups demanding quotas are more likely to succeed than groups demanding reserved seats.

This approach forms part of a growing body of work that highlights the varying ways that different groups gain access to politics, a challenge to earlier literature that assumed that the mechanisms behind the inclusion of women and minorities were similar (see, e.g., Lijphart, 1999). In an earlier work I showed that, across electoral democracies, women tend to demand and receive candidate quotas in parties while ethnic groups prefer and are granted reserved parliamentary seats (Htun, 2004b), a pattern that holds in the Bolivian case

---

[2] Not all systems give parties control over the nominating process. Examples include Colombia before the single nontransferable vote (SNTV) system was reformed in 2003 and in Brazil before the "*candidato nato*" (birthright candidate) rule was abrogated in 1998.

[3] If the reserved seats are filled through nomination by parties or by a particular category of party candidates receiving the most votes in general elections (e.g., women in Afghanistan), they will not be as threatening to a dominant party's position.

examined in this chapter (and in Latin American countries more generally).[4] Moser and Holmsten argue that, whereas women benefit from party systems emphasizing *depth*, politically mobilized ethnic groups tend to do better in party systems that prioritize *breadth* (2008). In *deeper* systems, political parties attempt to balance their tickets by nominating more women as candidates and more candidates tend to get elected from each party. *Broader* party systems, by contrast, incorporate a greater diversity of small parties, including those formed by ethnic minorities, but tend to elect fewer candidates – and therefore fewer women–per party. Hughes's study of some eighty countries found that guarantees of group representation benefit some subgroups while hurting others. Though a combination of national gender quotas and provisions for minority representation (which she calls "tandem quotas") helped more ethnic minority women gain access to power, they created a disadvantage for women and men from majority ethnic groups (2011).[5]

This chapter differs from other contributions in one key respect: its arguments apply to claims and strategies for inclusion, not to specific groups (such as women or indigenous peoples). Though group features imply a better fit with some representational policies than others (Htun, 2004b), this relationship is not fixed in stone. Conforming to regional and historical repertoires of group representation, women have demanded and received reserved seats in parliament, and some parties and governments have applied ethnic candidate quotas (Krook & O'Brien, 2010b). It is not the *type* of group that drives the different outcomes analyzed in this chapter but its cooperation amidst diversity, the mobilization of a political strategy, and the "fit"[6] (or lack thereof) with prevailing political institutions, particularly parties.

The Struggle for Gender Parity

Historically divided along class, ethnic, regional, and other lines, Bolivian women united to demand parity in access to decision making. How did this coalition come about? As this section shows, the MAS's electoral successes in 2005 and 2009 helped forge greater connections between the urban feminist movement and women from indigenous and popular sectors. Sex discrimination by the government and gender-based political assault caused women to recognize their shared position of disadvantage. Urban feminists began to forge links with indigenous women and indigenous women began to assume

---

[4] I argued that this variation derives from the fact that gender tends to cross cut partisan divisions whereas mobilized ethnicity frequently coincides with them (2004b). Other scholars have argued that the variation in inclusion policies owes to transnational and regionally specific "repertoires" of group representation (Krook & O'Brien, 2010b). Once a policy has been accepted as legitimate, for example, it is likely that it will be sought by and extended to another group seeking rights (Krook & O'Brien, 2010b; see also Skrentny, 2002).

[5] Tandem quotas compel party elites to add minority women to the legislature because by doing so they comply with both types of quotas simultaneously (Hughes, 2011).

[6] The notion of "fit" comes from Skocpol (1992, p. 54).

an increasingly assertive stance on women's rights vis-à-vis the men in the MAS and other organizations.

Divisions among "Women"
In the 1990s and early 2000s, middle-class, urban feminists were largely unconnected to the social base of the MAS and few indigenous women participated in their movement. For their part, few indigenous women advanced feminist claims. In 1997, the feminist movement convinced the Bolivian Congress to adopt a gender quota law requiring that women make up 30 percent of candidates in proportional elections (but not all elections). Pushed by feminist nongovernmental organizations (NGOs), women in Congress, and the Subsecretariat for Gender Issues (part of the Ministry of Human Development), the pro-quota advocacy movement consisted of urban elites with connections to international development agencies and to elected officials: "It was not a demand emerging from mass society but rather from a small group of women ... intellectuals from the middle classes."[7] The "Women's Political Forum" (*Foro Político de Mujeres*) spent one year practically living in congress to lobby politicians; they held seminars and workshops around the country; they campaigned the press and other media; and they even distributed propaganda with popcorn at a soccer match.[8] They convinced traditional elites and parties to endorse quotas, including then-president Gonzalo Sánchez de Lozada (who was completing his first term). Baldez and Brañez report that Sánchez de Lozada's daughter helped change the president's mind about quotas. She told a local newspaper that, though her father had never limited her aspirations at home, she regretted that in four years in power he had never appointed a single woman to his cabinet. The day after the interview was published, his party (Movimiento Nacionalista Revolucionario [MNR]) announced that 40 percent of candidates in the 1997 elections would be women (2005b, pp. 150, fn. 116). Indigenous and popular sector women did not participate in this coalition, though several were elected to Congress in the 2002 elections thanks to the quota.

The initial results of the quota law were disappointing. Women's presence in the lower house of Congress rose by only three percentage points in the 1997 elections (from 8 to 11 percent). Women made up 18 percent of those elected from proportional representation (PR) lists but only 3 percent (two seats) from the single-member districts (SMDs). Most of the parties complied with the quota law by nominating women as alternates (*suplentes*). In the 2002 elections, the results improved and women made up 19 percent of those elected to Congress, including 26 percent from the PR lists and 13 percent from the SMDs (Baldez & Brañez, 2005).[9]

---

[7] Interview with Jimena Costa, La Paz, May 13, 2005.

[8] Interview with Diana Urioste, La Paz, May 12, 2005.

[9] In between the two elections, the *Foro Político de Mujeres* lobbied parties and the Supreme Electoral Court to apply the quota law in a way more favorable to women. Instead of counting from the top of the titular list to the bottom, and putting women in every third titular slot (from

This tradition of elite women's organizing was largely unconnected to the rise of radical movements and the growth of the MAS. Most of the relationships between urban feminists and popular sector (or lower-class), indigenous women stemmed from NGO service provision or gathering data for studies (Monasteiros 2007, cited in Rousseau, 2011, p. 13). According to a former deputy and former minister, movements of indigenous women did not advocate an end to gender discrimination. Instead, their main concerns were the eradication of poverty and the protection of *usos y costumbres*.[10] Another analyst predicted that if indigenous peoples gained more national power the movement for gender equality would suffer a setback.[11]

According to urban feminists interviewed, indigenous women did not share the demand for gender quotas and their communities lacked a concept of discrimination and affirmative action.[12] During our meeting, one NGO leader waved her hand around the office and said, "There aren't any indigenous women here. We live in parallel worlds. But we should make hiring them a priority."[13] These urban activists expected, however, that their work on behalf of women's rights would benefit their indigenous counterparts. As another activist put it: "When we are demanding women's rights, we are demanding the rights of indigenous women."[14]

Indigenous women interviewed around the same period readily acknowledged the gender hierarchies in their communities. A vice presidential candidate from the 2002 elections affirmed that the male leadership of peasant unions was sexist (*machista*). They relied on women's work but refused to cede them any power. As a result, the vast majority of indigenous women rarely spoke in public or engaged in autonomous political action, whether on national issues or in civic organizations.[15] A former Vice Minister for Indigenous Affairs added that: "Women are the majority in the marches but when it comes to decision time, men make all the decisions."[16]

which they stood little chance of gaining a seat), the *Foro* proposed that the lists be counted horizontally, from first titular position to first *suplente* position and so on, so that the third (women's) position would correspond to the second titular position on this list (Baldez & Brañez, 2005). The court denied the petition but the public opinion campaign succeeded in compelling parties to improve women's list placement.

[10] Interview with Gloria Ardaya, La Paz, May, 2005.

[11] Interview with Jimena Costa, La Paz, May 13, 2005.

[12] This chapter reports these statements, even if we do not necessarily agree with them, since they reveal the lack of cooperation and mutual understanding among women.

[13] Interview with Diana Urioste, La Paz, May 2005.

[14] Interview with Rosario Paz, La Paz, May 12, 2005.

[15] Interview with Esther Balboa, La Paz, May 12, 2005. Balboa, who did graduate work in Canada and Mexico, was selected by Felipe Quispe to be his vice presidential candidate in the 2002 elections for the Movimiento Indígena Pachakuti (MIP) party. The objective was to achieve both male/female and Aymara/Quechua parity.

[16] Interview, La Paz, May 16, 2005.

Interviewees also noted that indigenous women had largely neglected to organize around gender discrimination. According to a former Vice Minister for Women, who was the first indigenous person to lead a state women's agency, women had always played a part in indigenous struggles and organizations but they had not developed their own movements *as women*. One important exception was the Bartolina Sisa Federation, a peasant women's union formed in 1980. Yet until the late 2000s, the Bartolinas and other base organizations had little contact with the "Western" feminist movement and did not assume feminist goals such as political inclusion and reproductive rights. Their connection to the male-dominated peasant and workers' unions had precluded alliances with "whites." Our interviewee believed at the time that: "Cultural divisions are more pronounced than gender solidarity."[17]

"Women" as a Coalition of Urban and Indigenous Feminists

The assumption of power by the MAS created several incentives for these different groups of women to cooperate. As scholars have pointed out, a common experience of discrimination and exclusion often helps to forge a political identity among diverse groups of people (Baldez, 2002; Friedman, 2000; Jung, 2008). The government demonstrated strong *machista* tendencies and took measures that denied the importance of women's rights. At the same time, rising reports of gender-related political assault fortified women's solidarity.

After assuming office in 2006, Morales's government demoted the Gender Subsecretariat created in the 1990s to a "Directorate on Gender and Generational Violence" under the Vice Ministry for Equal Opportunities. Vice President Garcia Liñera had said that the MAS intended to "transversalize" gender throughout the government, arguing that, like the indigenous peoples, women are not a minority and so their issues could be not relegated to one ministry.[18] Yet feminists pointed out that gender had not been mainstreamed. Though virtually every government policy and agency focused on indigenous issues, only three of twenty ministries had created gender-related focal points or programs.[19]

---

[17] Interview, La Paz, May 13, 2005.

[18] In an interview with *The Nation*, he observed: "Very early on we discussed gender inequality at the highest levels of government. We agreed that you can either opt for an understanding from a minority perspective or a majority one. It turns out that gender inequity is quite similar to the discrimination faced by indigenous people. During previous governments, a special ministry was established for indigenous groups. But why should the majority of the population be relegated to just one ministry? The same is true of women. Why should they be treated like a minority when they are, in fact, the majority? We believe women should be present in every level of government according to ability. Our first minister of government was a woman, and this is a position that is always perceived as requiring a strong and authoritative man. So we feel that by having women stuck off in a ministry or vice-ministry, we are marginalizing them. Just like indigenous people, women should participate fully" (Farthing 2009). Ironically, the same "gender" perspective informed creation of the Subsecretariat under the government of Gonzalo Sánchez de Lozada (Paulson & Callá, 2000).

[19] Interview with Pilar Uriona and Dunia Mokriani Coordinadora Mujer, La Paz, June 22, 2009.

Under the MAS government, gender equality did not receive the same emphasis as indigenous rights. Rather than an important cause on its own, gender equality was subsumed to the decolonization of the state. Official discourse held that once ethnic oppression was eliminated, patriarchy would erode. The national development plan, for example, assumed that gender inequality – and other inequitable relations of power – would be resolved automatically once colonialism has been eradicated.[20]

Much of the MAS's male leadership – especially the president – displayed little awareness of gender discrimination. President Morales was notorious for making insensitive and even sexist comments in public. There were other complaints that, if not explicitly sexist, other leaders of the governing coalition were insensitive to issues of gender discrimination. One female deputy recalled that:

The Movement toward Socialism is not exactly linked to a feminist movement or a recognition of gender. It is an indigenous project that hasn't really looked at gender issues. As a result, it's difficult for a parliamentary group dominated by men to understand our issues and even more to see them as real problems. I'll give you an example from a congressional debate on the [proposed] law on gender-based political assault. It had already been largely discussed and approved. When we were in the process of approving it one of my male colleagues [compañeros] turned to me and asked why we hate men so much.[21]

In this context, the convening of a constituent assembly in 2006 – fulfillment of a campaign promise – offered a chance for women to mobilize to press for greater recognition of their rights. In spite of a history of distance and even mistrust, urban feminists groups believed it critical to link their demands to those of the indigenous movement (Novillo Gonzáles, 2011, pp. 36–37). In the name of a coalition, Women Present in History (*Mujeres Presentes en la Historia*), more than 25,000 women, from rural indigenous groups to urban intellectuals, organized a network of workshops to formulate a joint proposal for the assembly (Novillo Gonzáles, 2011, p. 39). Parity on party lists was a central demand. Meanwhile, proposals from the Bartolina Sisa peasant women's union included the demand for parity in presence in Congress, parties, and all decision-making bodies, as did the platform developed by the united front of all indigenous groups, the *Pacto de Unidad* (Unity Pact).[22] Women delegates,

---

[20] Interview with Pilar Uriona and Dunia Mokriani, Coordinadora Mujer, La Paz, June 22, 2009.
[21] Interview with MAS Deputy Ximena Florez, La Paz, June 17, 2009.
[22] "De la protesta al mandato: una propuesta en construcción. Presentes en la historia: Mujeres en la Asamblea Constituyente" Proyecto Mujer y Asamblea Constituyente, Junio de 2006; "Las Bartolinas en la Asamblea Constituyente: Propuesta para el nuevo Estado Pluri- Nacional Unitario," Federación Nacional de Mujeres Campesinas de Bolivia "Bartolina Sisa" FNMCB, "BS," Enero de 2007; "Constitución Política del Estado Boliviano: Por un Estado Pluri- Nacional Comunitario, Libre, Independiente, Soberano, Democrático y Social," Propuesta Consensuada del Pacto de Unidad, Sucre, Mayo 23 de 2007; "Propuesta de las Organizaciones Indígenas, Originarias, Campesinas y de Colonizadores de Bolivia hacia la Asamblea Constituyente" Julio de 2006. See also discussion in Rousseau (2011, pp. 18–20).

who comprised one-third of the constituent assembly, organized under the leadership of the assembly's president, an indigenous woman, to present a joint platform on women's rights and coordinated their lobbying work (Rousseau, 2011, pp. 12–13).[23]

Urban feminists and indigenous women had different philosophical reasons to support gender parity. For indigenous women, it flowed from a concept of complementarity between the sexes. In many Andean cultures, the union of a man and a woman – the *chachawarmi* in Aymara, *qhari-warmi* in Quechua – constitutes the basic social, moral, and economic unit of society. Men and women are not considered full members of their community until they enter into such a union. Far from endorsing women's isolation in the home, complementarity implies that sexual dualism should be present in all spheres, including public decision making (Rousseau, 2011, pp. 17–18). For urban feminists, by contrast, parity in decision-making is implied by principles of democracy and equal rights and was the logical step given their history of advocacy for gender quotas (Mokrani & Uriona, 2009).

Women disagreed about other issues such as abortion. Indigenous women's organizations including the Bartolina Sisa peasant federation were opposed to elective abortion (Rousseau, 2011, p. 18). As a result, the Women Present in History coalition's platform called only vaguely on the state to "guarantee sexual and reproductive rights," and the September 28th Campaign (for the legalization of abortion) strategically dropped the abortion issue (Mujeres Presentes en la Historia, 2007, p. 7; Rousseau, 2011, p. 23).[24]

The Constitution – approved after a process fraught with conflict[25] – codified numerous women's rights, including guarantees of equality in elections to Congress; freedom from violence; protection during pregnancy; equal pay for work of equal worth; protection from employment discrimination for reasons of pregnancy, civil status, age, or physical traits; reproductive and sexual rights (without defining what these are); and equal access to land in indigenous communities (República de Bolívia, 2009). Yet the text did not specify exactly how equality in political participation would be implemented. Article 147 merely stated: "Equal participation of men and women will be guaranteed in the election of legislators" (República de Bolívia, 2009). Congress had a

[23] The government bowed to pressure from women's movements and agreed to alternate men and women's names on party lists for election to the assembly. (Alternation had also been included in plans of the previous government.) As a result, women made up one-third of delegates to the constituent assembly overall and almost half of those from the MAS. Approximately half – and likely more – of the female delegates were indigenous (Rousseau, 2011, pp. 12–14).

[24] The decision to avoid issues provoking conflict resembles patterns in other countries. Women in Mexico's Congress, for example, explicitly decided to leave abortion off the agenda to preserve their multiparty political alliance (author interview with Patricia Mercado, Mexico City, July, 2000).

[25] For more information on the constituent assembly conflicts, see Laserna (2010).

60-day window to approve a temporary electoral law implementing various constitutional provisions, including gender parity and indigenous seats.

The process of electoral reform in 2009 and 2010 furnished another incentive and opportunity for women to cooperate, revealing the common obstacles women faced such as hostility by male partisan colleagues and harassment of elected female officials. Feminist groups from civil society and an alliance of women in Congress campaigned for a parity law with public demonstrations, media interventions, and lobbying in Congress. They encountered sexist remarks and hostility from male legislators who removed the proposal from the electoral law at one point (Novillo Gonzáles, 2011, pp. 47–58).

In addition to alternation on party lists, women politicians wanted the electoral law to address the phenomenon of gender-based political assault, on the rise in Bolivia as women's opportunities for participation expanded. Women elected officials had been the target of harassment, public humiliation, and even death and kidnapping threats to pressure them to resign their positions so that their posts could be assumed by a male alternate (*suplente*). In some cases, the *suplente* himself organized the campaign of intimidation; in others, women were forced to sign an undated resignation letter before assuming office.[26] Between 2000 and April of 2011, the Bolivian Association of Women City Councilors recorded 572 episodes of gender-based political assault.[27] Women politicians believed that tightening the procedures surrounding political resignation – essentially by requiring that officials resign in person at an electoral court and not in writing or in their communities – would reduce the opportunities for intimidation.

When it looked like the tide was turning in Congress against gender parity, indigenous women took action. Senator Leonida Zurita, a leader of the Bartolina Sisa women's peasant union and internationally known advocate of indigenous rights, gathered the women legislators together. According to our interviewee who was present at the meeting, she scolded women who had failed to support the cause of parity and called on an indigenous woman in traditional dress (*de pollera*) to speak on behalf of the proposal. When the plenary session resumed, the intervention of Cristina Rojas proved a turning point. Our interviewee reports that: "It was decisive because the men were indigenous originary peasants too [*indígenas originarios campesinos*] ... so they listened to her and agreed. If one of us had spoken, as the urban women we are, they would not have listened and we would have ended up with nothing."[28]

The temporary electoral law approved by Congress in 2009 neglected to use the term "parity," referring instead to "equality of opportunities" between

---

[26] Interview with Deputy Elizabeth Salguero, La Paz, June 14, 2009.
[27] "Desde 1999 hubo 572 casos de violencia política contra las mujeres: despatriarcalización, las mujeres se empoderan y ahora impulsan una ley en el legislativo." Retrieved from www .cambio.bo/noticia.php?fecha=2011-02-28&idn=39887 (accessed August 3, 2011).
[28] Interview with Ximena Florez, La Paz, June 17, 2009.

TABLE 4.1. *Results of Gender Quotas in Bolivia 1997–2009*

Year	Quota (% of candidates who must be women)	Women as a Percentage of Elected Senators	Women as a Percentage of Elected Deputies
1997	30	4	11
2002	30	15	18
2005	30	4	17
2009	50	47	25

Source: Electoral Results, Corte Nacional Electoral Bolivia; Inter-Parliamentary Union Database.

women and men and requiring that they alternate on party lists and in the titular-alternate formula in SMDs. To promote implementation, the feminist movement organized a massive campaign – Women Ready for the Lists (*Mujeres Listas para las Listas*) – directed at parties and citizen awareness, in which important sectors of the indigenous movement also participated.[29]

Notwithstanding these efforts, parties complied with the parity law in a minimalist manner, conforming to a common tendency in Latin American elections (Jones, 2009). Of the 1,046 candidates who were registered to compete, 494 were women, but only 179 women were placed as titular candidates. The rest were alternates.[30] Though the law led to the election of record numbers of women (see Table 4.1), the vast majority came from PR lists. Forty seven percent of the PR list deputies were women, compared to only 11 percent of deputies elected from SMDs, and none of the candidates elected from the seven indigenous districts was a woman.

In 2010, the newly elected Congress discussed and adopted a permanent electoral law whose provisions reflected the strength and influence of the coalition of women. To preclude parties from exploiting loopholes and nominating women as *suplentes*, the new law required that 50 percent of the titular candidates in all the SMDs nominated by each party be women. In addition, the law recognized gender-based political assault as an electoral crime, with penalties of up to five years of prison. Finally, the law established that the principle of parity also covered reserved indigenous districts.[31] In addition to elections, Congress approved laws to establish parity between men and women at the Electoral Tribunal, the Judicial Branch, the Constitutional Court, and the selection of leaders in autonomous indigenous territories.[32]

[29] "Mujeres exigen respeto del 50% en lista de candidatos." *Los Tiempos*, September 9, 2010.
[30] "Candidatos presidenciales no lograron incorporar el 50% de mujeres en sus listas", Jornada. net, September 9, 2009; "La cuota femenina en listas electorales llega al 17.1%," *La Prensa*, November 12, 2009; "Solo el 30 por ciento de los candidatos a la asamblea nacional son mujeres," *La Patria*, November 13, 2009.
[31] "Mujeres vigilan avances de paridad en la Ley del Regimen Electoral," *La Patria*, Junio 22, 2010.
[32] "Balance de 5 Leyes Aprobadas." Observatorio de Genero, Coordinadora Mujer, Julio de 2010.

Meanwhile, at the beginning of his second term, Morales attempted a new start on the issue of gender. Under pressure from the Bartolina Sisa women's union, in a move he described as a homage to his mother, sister, and daughter, the president appointed women to ten (half) of cabinet positions. Though the president of the indigenous federation Consejo Nacional de Ayllus y Markas del Qullasuyu (CONAMAQ) complained that the cabinet lacked any indigenous participation, the photos of the new ministers clearly showed that at least two of the female ministers were indigenous.[33] The title of a newspaper article similarly referred to women's inclusion while denouncing indigenous exclusion. These critical comments reveal that, while women bridged the cultural divide and forged a coalition to combat shared disadvantages, indigenous peoples remained divided, including about who counts as indigenous. As explained later, these divisions precluded the formation of a common project of political inclusion.

The Politics of Indigenous Reservations

On the face of it, Bolivia's adoption of reserved seats for indigenous people is curious. Most countries use legislative reservations to guarantee the political presence of minority ethnic or cultural groups who, owing to their small numbers, would not otherwise be able to compete in general elections (Htun, 2004b; Lijphart, 1986b; Reynolds, 2005). In Bolivia, however, people of indigenous ancestry, far from a numerically small minority, are the majority. Many studies report that, according to the 2001 census, 62 percent of the population identifies as indigenous (see, e.g., Assies & Salman, 2005; Lucero, 2008; Madrid, 2008; Van Cott, 2005).

Yet in fact, the generic category "indigenous" has little salience in Bolivia. The widely used 62 percent census figure refers to the total number of Bolivians identifying with a specific group such as Aymara, Quechua, Guaraní, Chiquitano, or Mojeño. (Thirty-six different groups are recognized in the 2009 Constitution.) When surveys ask about generic "indigenous" or "originary" identity, the number of people responding is quite small, between some 16 and 19 percent of the sample. More people identify as "mestizo" (see Table 4.2).

Table 4.2 compares results of the census with LAPOP and UNDP sample surveys. It reveals that, though well over a majority of Bolivians identify with specific indigenous ethnic groups, well over a majority of these also opt to identify as "mestizo."[34] Indigenous and mestizo are not mutually exclusive

---

[33] "El Nuevo gabinete tiene rostro de mujer, tecnócrata y obrero, pero sin indígenas," *ERBOL Periódico Digital*. Enero 23, 2010. Retrieved from www.erbol.com.bo/noticia.php?identificador= 2147483923118 (accessed July 27, 2010).

[34] According to a public opinion survey conducted in 2006, 76 percent of people identifying as Quechua also identified as mestizo. The same was true of 56 percent of Aymaras and 79 percent of Chiquitanos (Toranzo, 2008, p. 39).

TABLE 4.2. *Ethnic Identification in Bolivia*

	1900 Census (%)	1950 Census (%)	2001 Census (%)	Latin American Public Opinion Project (LAPOP) Survey (2006, %)	United Nations Development Programme (UNDP, 1996, %)
Indigenous or *originario* (generic term)	51	63		19	16
Total number of people who identify with specific group (including Quechua, Aymara, Guaraní, Chiquitano, Mojeño, or other)			62		
Mestizo	27	37			67
Mestizo or *cholo*				65	
White	13			11	17
None or other				4	

Source: Adapted from Zavaleta (2008, p. 52). Blank cells indicate that the survey did not include this category. Note that because the census, LAPOP, and UNDP studies ask different questions they are not directly comparable.

categories. In addition, there is a considerable degree of heterogeneity and distinct levels of identification within each ethnic category, reflecting patterns of migration, geography, economic activity, and interaction with the state (Albó, 2008; Zavaleta, 2008). "Indigenous peoples" include rural communities with traditional cultural and social practices as well as groups that speak only Spanish, live in urban areas, and work in the formal economy. There are multiple ways of being "indigenous" and a plurality of forms of indigenous agency (Albró, 2006, pp. 420–422; see also Jung, 2008).

Divisions among the "Indigenous"
Intra-indigenous differences have given way to a variety of political organizations and projects. Though a complete analysis of the evolution of indigenous politics is beyond the scope of this chapter,[35] it presents a brief trajectory to illustrate the way that the discussion over reserved ethnic seats reflected diverse

---

[35] For more comprehensive analysis of the evolution of indigenous politics in Bolivia, see Albó (2002, 2008), Assies & Salman (2005), Gustafson (2009a, 2009b), Hylton & Sinclair (2007), Lucero (2008), Madrid (2012), Postero (2006, 2010), Regalsky (2010), Van Cott (2005), Webber (2010), and Yashar (2005).

interests among indigenous peoples. The geographical cleavage between the eastern, tropical lowlands and the western, Andean highland regions divides the indigenous movement and virtually every other feature of the Bolivian polity.[36] Lowland and highland peoples have "different modes of economic and social organization and distinct histories of relations with political parties and the state" (Van Cott, 2005, p. 52). Fewer in number than their highland counterparts, lowland groups have organized primarily in defense of their autonomy, access to land, and control of natural resources. The lowland federation Confederación de Pueblos Indígenas de Bolivia (CIDOB), representing dozens of groups in several departments, was never able to forge a national organization of highland and lowland movements (Yashar, 2005, pp. 198–204).

Different highland indigenous movements had different political projects. Beginning in the 1960s, *Indianista* (Indianist) movements were focused primarily on racism and the defense of Indian rights while *Kataristas* organized along both ethnic and class lines, both as indigenous peoples and as peasants. *Kataristas* formed the Confederación Sindical Única de Trabajadores Campesinos de Bolivia (CSUTCB, Single Peasant Union Federation of Peasant Workers of Bolivia) in 1979. By the beginning of the twenty-first century, it remained Bolivia's largest indigenous organization (Van Cott, 2005, pp. 52–59; Yashar, 2005, pp. 167–181).

The "second generation" of movements that emerged in the wake of free-market reforms of the 1980s had at least two distinct orientations. Coca growers unions – formed by miners dismissed by the closure of state-owned enterprises and other peasants – sought the legalization of coca production and consumption, a goal they defended, in part, with reference to indigenous traditions. The *cocaleros* formed parties and began competing in elections, eventually forming the *Movimiento al Socialismo* (MAS) in 1999 (Albó, 2002, 2008; Postero, 2010; Van Cott, 2005; Yashar, 2005). Meanwhile, other indigenous groups organized to reconstitute the *ayllu*, the basic unit of pre-Colombian social and political organization that had been displaced by the peasant revolution of the 1950s. Their umbrella organization – Consejo Nacional de Ayllus y Markas del Qullasuyu (CONAMAQ) – became a principal defender of the classical Indianist project of political and cultural autonomy.

Though the governing party (the MAS) emerged from one sector of the indigenous movement, it grew by recruiting politicians from the traditional left to fill slots on candidate lists and by forging alliances with a broad range of social movements (Anria, 2013; Madrid, 2012; Van Cott, 2005). The MAS's inclusiveness was largely responsible for its electoral success: it has been able to win votes from people that identify with particular indigenous groups *and* as mestizo (Madrid, 2012, pp. 99–100). The party has three primary tendencies: an indigenist one responsible for deploying and managing cultural

---

[36] For more information on the politics of regionalism in Bolivia, see Barragan (2008), Eaton (2007), and Roca (2008).

symbols; a state-interventionist, socialist sector that controls public policy; and a populist sector rooted in the radical movements that brought down the previous government (Laserna, 2010, pp. 39–42). The populist tendency – rooted in the personal fame and charisma of Evo Morales – is oriented toward the poor and deploys a fierce antiestablishment discourse (Laserna, 2010; Madrid, 2012, pp. 100–107).

In the clash between these multiple projects, the indigenist one has tended to lose out. Development of the hydrocarbon sector offers one example. The state's commitment to explore new and untapped reserves to fund social programs put it at odds with indigenous groups seeking control over ancestral territories (Farthing, 2009; Gustafson, 2011; Kaup, 2010). In addition, the MAS actively opposed the creation of self-governing indigenous units (*autonomías indígenas*), fearing they would exclude the party from participation in local politics.[37] In elections held in eleven municipalities to choose authorities to steer the communities toward the new autonomy regime, the MAS fielded slates of candidates to compete against leaders that had been preselected by communal assemblies, against the explicit wishes of indigenous organizations (Cameron, 2010, pp. 10–12). Further disagreements over the autonomy process provoked a march by the lowland indigenous federation CIDOB and mutual accusations of foreign financing and traitorous behavior, a pattern that repeated itself in 2011 during conflicts over the government's proposal to build a highway through the Territorio Indígena Parque Nacional Isiboro (TIPNIS).[38] The proposal for indigenous reserved seats must be seen in this context. Disadvantaged sectors of the indigenous movement, engaged in mounting conflicts with the government over indigenous rights, have sought reserved seats to preserve their independence. Reserved seats, however, conflicted with the majority interests of the indigenous movement, which centered on maximizing the power of the MAS party organization.

Majority Interests and Interests of a Disadvantaged Subgroup: Party Power and Reserved Seats

Shortly after assuming power in January of 2006, the MAS government made moves to fulfill its campaign promise to convoke a constituent assembly. Already underway during the previous government, plans for the assembly raised the question of who would be represented and how. Would indigenous people gain presence directly as peoples (*pueblos*), chosen through their own *usos y costumbres*, or would they gain access only as individual candidates postulated by political parties? Whereas the former strategy would benefit

---

[37] In various local referenda held in late 2009, many indigenous voters also opposed the creation of indigenous autonomies.

[38] "Consulta previa TIPNIS no tendrá carácter vinculante," *La Razón*, October 12, 2011; "El conflicto del Tipnis podría derivar en guerra de tierras," Jornada.net, August, 2011.; "Indigenas dan ultimatum a Evo para dialogar hasta el Lunes," Paginasiete.bo, August 19, 2011; "Evo revela detalles del llamado entre indígenas y EEUU," *La Razón*, August 22, 2011.

disadvantaged subgroups within the indigenous movement, the latter would help larger groups expand their hold on power.

Several indigenous movements demanded reserved seats exempt from the general partisan contest. This was not a new demand: it had been expressed in every constitution-related workshop organized by the various federations since 2001.[39] A declaration signed by the indigenous federations CONAMAQ, CIDOB, CSTUCB, and Bartolina Sisa in 2007, for example, demanded the right of indigenous nations to appoint half of the government's cabinet and inclusion of a representative for each indigenous nation in the legislature, elected based on *usos y costumbres*.[40] Yet almost immediately, the government distanced itself from the proposal for reserved seats, declaring its principled opposition to all guarantees of representation and rebuffing demands by unions, peasants, and the police.[41] All constituents were to be elected from party lists.

In spite of the MAS's rejection of ethnic reservations, many indigenous delegates were elected to the constituent assembly. Representatives from different organizations formed the Unity Pact (Pacto de Unidad) to advocate indigenous rights. Though popular participation in the assembly was thwarted by the violence and conflict surrounding it,[42] indigenous groups succeeded in the sense that the document was packed with rights.[43] Provisions on political inclusion

---

[39] See, e.g., "Propuesta sobre Reforma a la Constitución Política del Estado," Confederación de Pueblos Indígenas de Bolivia (CIDOB), Santa Cruz, December 2001; "Propuesta para la Asamblea Nacional Constituyente," Unibamba, Cochabamba, July 2005; "Sistematización de Propuestas para la Asamblea Constituyente", CSCB, CONAMAQ, CRSUCIR, May 13, 2006; "Propuesta de las Organizaciones Indígenas, Campesinas y Originarias hacia la Asamblea Constituyente," CSUTCB, CIDOB, CSCB, FNMCB-BS, CONAMAQ, July 2006.

[40] "Constitución Política del Estado Boliviano, Acta Consensuda", CIDOB, CONAMAQ, CSUTCB, Bartolina Sisa, May 2007.

[41] "El MAS desecha la cuota para los indígenas y los sindicatos," *La Razón*, February 23, 2006. Ironically, the government of Carlos Mesa – which indigenous movements had helped depose – had accepted indigenous demands for direct representation. Its proposal for a constituent assembly included twenty-six reserved seats elected through *usos y costumbres* (interview with José Luis Exeni, Director of the National Electoral Court, La Paz, May 17, 2005). See also Ley de 6 de Marzo de 2006, Ley Especial de Convocatoria a la Asamblea Constituyente. The seats would have made up 14 or 22 percent of the total, as the government's bill contemplated an assembly of either 180 or 116 delegates. Exeni was certain that far more indigenous people would be elected than those representing the reserved seats.

[42] For discussion of the political conflicts, violence, and maneuvering during the constituent assembly process, see Laserna (2010).

[43] Rights protected include, among others, the right to cultural identity, religious belief, traditions, and customs; self-determination and territory; collective land titling; the protection of sacred places; collective intellectual property over knowledge and science; the practice of political, legal, and economic systems that conform to indigenous cosmovision; prior consultation with regard to the exploration of subsoil resources in Indian lands; autonomous management of indigenous territory and exclusive use of renewable resources (without prejudice to "rights legitimately acquired by third parties"); and participation in state institutions (República de Bolívia, 2009, Article 30). Article 32 guarantees the "Afrobolivian people" all the rights granted to the "indigenous originary peasant peoples."

for indigenous groups – which the constitution approved in principle – were contradictory, likely owing to the fact that the vast majority of constitutional provisions were approved hastily and with little discussion by constituents meeting in a temporary location in the city of Oruro, far from the city of Sucre where the assembly was supposed to be held (Laserna, 2010, p. 31).[44]

The MAS's heavy-handed behavior during the constituent assembly created conflict with many of its supporters. Indigenous movements that had initially supported the party became disenchanted. When we interviewed leaders of the indigenous federations CIDOB and CONAMAQ in 2009, they expressed distrust of the MAS. CIDOB vice president Pedro Nuni, for example, argued that the MAS is a unionist party, not an indigenous one, and therefore does not represent his group: "We believe that the MAS has Marxist tendencies that most of us indigenous peoples of the lowlands do not understand."[45] When it chooses to represent indigenous interests, it prioritizes those of the Andean groups and has failed genuinely to reach out to the lowland groups.[46] Survey results on the 2005 elections provide support for the party's Andean orientation. Whereas speaking the highland languages Aymara or Quechua made a respondent more likely to vote for the MAS, speaking a lowland indigenous language did not (Madrid, 2012, p. 115).

The perceived regional bias of the MAS made the achievement of reserved seats – as a guarantee of direct representation – even more important to disadvantaged subgroups of the indigenous movement. Distinguishing between "political" and "indigenous" inclusion, several leaders claimed that the genuine participation of originary peoples could not occur through mainstream political parties. As one put it, "There's no representative for the *sullos*, for the *markas*, let alone for the *ayllus*." Another indigenous leader confirmed that, "We, the indigenous people, have always determined ourselves to be independent and non-political."[47] A leader of the highland indigenous federation CONAMAQ argued that the federation, "remains as our ancestor left us. We are not of the left or the right. We uphold the position of the originary indigenous people of the Collasuyo."[48]

When Congress began to debate the temporary electoral law, the lowland federation CIDOB presented a proposal for thirty-four seats and CONAMAQ,

---

[44] For example, Article 146 states that the districts for indigenous, originary, peasant groups should be proportional to population density, established in rural areas in those departments where indigenous are a minority, and should not cross departmental boundaries. Article 147 states the opposite: it instructs legislators to establish the seats without regard to population density or departmental boundaries (República de Bolívia, 2009).

[45] Interview with Pedro Nuni, vice president CIDOB, June 16, 2009.

[46] Interview with Pedro Nuni, vice-president of CIDOB, June 16, 2009.

[47] Interviews with Tata Elias Quelca, director of CONAMAQ, June 11, 2009; Nilda Copa, executive of the *Confederación Nacional de Mujeres Campesinas Originarias de Bolivia*, Bartolina Sisa, June 13, 2009; Pedro Nuni, vice president of CIDOB, June 16, 2009, respectively.

[48] Interview with Tata Elias Quelca, June 11, 2009.

the highland federation, for twenty-four. They insisted that officials be chosen through *usos y costumbres* instead of open competitive elections.[49] At the same time, the National Electoral Court introduced a proposal that largely mirrored indigenous demands for direct representation, though it refrained from proposing a fixed number of seats, arguing that these could be determined later based on "scientific" criteria.[50]

The bill proposed by the MAS-led government, by contrast, proposed to create only fifteen reserved indigenous districts. This number was intended as a compromise between the indigenous demand that each nation have its own congressional seat and their actual demographic weight.[51] Indigenous leaders claimed that the government had elaborated the bill without consulting them and maintained that fifteen seats would not be enough to guarantee their representation. Attempting to modify the government's initial decision, representatives from the major indigenous federations went on a hunger strike to highlight the importance of their cause (Mokrani & Uriona, 2009).[52]

After tough negotiations between the MAS and the opposition party, Poder Democrático y Social (PODEMOS, the largest opposition party in Congress that opposed high numbers of reserved seats),[53] the final law reserved merely seven seats for indigenous peoples in the 2009 elections, a significantly smaller number than the thirty-four demanded by CIDOB and fewer than half of the government's original proposal for fifteen.[54] Any party or group could nominate candidates for election in the indigenous districts and *usos y costumbres* were not protected.

---

[49] "CONAMAQ pide 24 escaños, La propuesta será presentada hoy," *Erbol*, La Paz, February 13, 2009; "Organizaciones indígenas presentan al Congreso sus proyectos de Ley Transitoria Electoral," cidob-bo.org, February 13, 2009; Proyecto de ley no. 176 de 2009 referido a la Ley Transitoria de Regimen Electoral, Cámara de Diputados, Bolivia, February, 2009.

[50] The Electoral Court believed that it could determine the number of indigenous seats and their geographical distribution in a scientific manner based on population data, information about communal land holdings, and records of indigenous political participation. Interview with José Luis Exeni, former president of the *Corte Nacional Electoral,* June 14, 2009.

[51] The fifteen seats proposed by the government included thirteen seats for indigenous minority groups and an additional seat each for Quechuas and Aymaras. If the thirty-six constitutionally recognized indigenous groups divided themselves between *titulares and suplentes* (alternates), the proposal could offer representation to a total of thirty groups, so argued the government (interview with Oscar Cámara, Ministro de Control Social de Empresas, Junio 6, 2009). In addition, only the main indigenous federations CIDOB, CONAMAQ, and the CSTUCB were entitled to nominate candidates for the seats, giving them a monopoly on indigenous representation in the special districts and preventing opposition parties from competing. What's more, the number of reserved seats in each province was to be subtracted from their number of proportional (PR) seats, not the single member districts (*uninominales*).

[52] "Organizaciones indígenas presentan al Congreso sus proyectos de ley transitoria electoral." February 13, 2009. Retrieved from www.cidob-bo.org (accessed November 1, 2009).

[53] Interview with Sergio Medinacelli, PODEMOS adviser and former delegate to the constituent assembly, La Paz, June 8, 2009.

[54] "El Congreso negocia la ley y revisa los escaños indígenas," *La Razón*, April 9, 2009.

Indigenous federations were disappointed with the final outcome of the electoral law, which they felt had failed to recognize indigenous peoples as subjects constituting the nation (Mokrani & Uriona, 2009). The lowland federation CIDOB's reaction was more radical: the group felt that the government had betrayed the indigenous movement, the constitution, and the constitutional process. Pedro Nuni believed they were fooled. "They let us down, they didn't tell us the truth. We were tricked by the politicians in Congress."[55] CIDOB issued a resolution asking indigenous communities to mobilize publicly to reject the law, denouncing it as a renewed assault on indigenous rights.[56]

Though the outcome of the 2009 electoral law could be partially explained as the result of opposition from PODEMOS, the same cannot be said for the permanent electoral law approved in 2010. The government – unconstrained because it had won a two-thirds congressional majority in December, 2009 – had a chance to raise the number of seats from seven. Yet indigenous proposals for more seats were not even considered. In fact, Evo Morales borrowed the arguments made earlier by the opposition party PODEMOS to disqualify indigenous demands: "Some congresspeople are elected with 120,000 votes and others with 500 ... it is okay for minorities to have representation, but this difference amounts to discrimination against the majority."[57]

This MAS's opposition to giving each indigenous group a seat in Congress conformed to its ambivalence about the project of indigenous autonomy more generally. Over the course of 2009 and 2010, the MAS grew increasingly hostile to indigenous demands that challenged the authority of the party or the state (Cameron, 2010, p. 10). Some observers have claimed the MAS is not truly an indigenous party and fails to represent indigenous interests.[58] Yet this view, which seems to presume that there is an "authentic" indigeneity, flies in the face of most contemporary social theory. Cultures, social groups, and the normative traditions they uphold do not possess an essential core but are continually engaged in contestation and resignification (see, e.g., Benhabib, 2002, pp. 82–104). People of indigenous descent who defend a classical project of autonomy and those who militate in the MAS are staking out diverse ways of being indigenous. The intersectional approach adopted in this book

[55] "Indígenas acusan al Mas de traición y acuden a la ONU," *La Razón*, April 9, 2009.
[56] Coordinadora de Pueblos Étnicos de Santa Cruz, Resolution signed on April 8, 2009.
[57] "Presidente dice que demandas de CIDOB son imposibles de atender," *La Prensa*, June 28, 2010.
[58] Since its rise, many Bolivians have denied that the party possesses a legitimate indigenous project. Felipe Quispe, former presidential candidate and leader of the MIP, has declared that, "Evo is not an Indian. He's a socialist," and that the MAS "is not the expression of the indigenous nation. They are from the middle class and the sour destitute Left," (quoted in Albró, 2006, p. 416). The vice president of the lowland federation CIDOB opined that, "The MAS is a leftist political party ... that did not emerge from the real indigenous movement" (interview, La Paz, June 16, 2009). Other analysts suggest that the MAS's ethnic project is more opportunistic: "[Quispe's] MIP is the real ethnic party. In MAS it's a secondary issue. Evo doesn't use ethnic card that much but he knows that the ethnic theme sells very well abroad" (Salvador Romero, interview, May 17, 2005).

incorporates these contradictions: it admits that different sectors of a (for-merly) marginalized group may have different views on the group's interests and purpose. We should be less concerned about who represents the "authen-tic" core of the group than whether deliberative processes that express inter-ests and collective identities are fair and inclusive (Benhabib, 1992, 2002; Habermas, 1996). What is most worrisome about the MAS is not its diver-gence from indigenous authenticity but its willingness to resort to intimidation against its opponents.[59]

The MAS's unwillingness to cede to indigenous demands for autonomy must be seen in light of the challenge to its rule posed by elites in the Eastern provinces. Regional oligarchies fed by soy, sugar, and cotton exports as well as hydrocarbon extraction defend free market policies, privatization, and the rights of multinationals against the MAS's redistributive and nationalist pro-ject (Eaton, 2007; Gustafson, 2008; Kohl, 2010). Alienated by the party's pro-motion of indigenous cultural identity and fearing its plans for land reform, these elites sought an exit from central government domination and com-pelled Morales to hold a national referendum on autonomy in 2006. It won in the eastern provinces but lost in the western ones. In 2008, the four eastern provinces held their own autonomy referenda to secure regional control over natural resources and tax revenues. (Unsanctioned by the National Electoral Court, the election was widely seen as illegal.) Eastern elites have resorted to violence and the massacre of popular protestors; there is also evidence that quasi-paramilitary rural defense committees have formed to fight migrants and squatter encroachment. Like indigenous movements defending the *ayllu* and *usos y costumbres*, the Eastern oligarchy deploys a discourse of autonomy. But the extent of autonomy they demand far exceeds anything else in the recent wave of decentralization in Latin America and would significantly constrain the redistributive capacity of Bolivia's central government (Eaton, 2007, p. 74; 2011; Gustafson, 2008).

[59] It could also be argued that Bolivia is a poor example of the way that inherent party interests drive preferences for policies to include marginalized groups. As Kurt Weyland asked us, "Is the MAS 'enough of a party' to possess and pursue interests concerning political inclusion?" Though structured like a party (at least on paper), the MAS's statutes are not implemented in practice, the party lacks administrative structure in the most important regions of the country, and can-didate selection depends largely on the approval of Evo Morales, though in some cases candi-dates are elected by social movements and popular assemblies (Anria, 2009, pp. 76–78). What's more, the MAS rose to power on an anti-party platform, calling for an end to party-dominated representation and referring to itself as a "political instrument" of grassroots movements and unions, not a party (Abou-Zeid, 2006; Anria, 2009; Do Alto & Stefanoni, 2009; Madrid, 2008, 2012). The weakly institutionalized nature of the MAS enhances the role of Evo Morales as ultimate decision maker and arbiter of conflict, rendering the MAS as unpredictable as the man who leads it. Yet we still believe that the MAS meets the minimalist criteria of a party as a team seeking to win elections: it has selected candidates to run for office (albeit through procedures that are not predictable or transparent), contested elections by following the rules (though it has tried to rig these in its favor, such as during the constitutional convention of 2007–2008), and formulated policy while adhering to legislative procedures.

Conclusion

These stories about Bolivia show that not all good things go together. Though women mobilized across class and ethnic lines and succeeded in gaining parity in participation, indigenous movements continued to have their demands for inclusion rejected by a government that had otherwise pledged itself to their cause. To explain these diverse outcomes, this chapter demonstrated that the Bolivian movement for gender parity and the movement for indigenous reservations differed in significant ways. Whereas women strategically put aside their differences over other issues to unite behind gender parity, different sectors of the indigenous movement entertained different proposals for inclusion and reserved seats. What's more, the parity issue affected women across the board while reservations were targeted at numerically small, rural groups. This disadvantaged sector of the indigenous movement sought to protect its independence from a governing party that was evolving to embrace a wider set of actors and issues. Over time, the MAS grew increasingly hostile toward the project of indigenous autonomy.

Bolivia's experiences do not reflect universal features of gender or indigeneity but the particular ways these social groups and their demands evolved in that country. What may be generalized is the theoretical lens this chapter brought to bear on the puzzle of political inclusion. The intersectional approach reveals that marginalized groups are not a single group but a collection of groups. The unity of the group is a political achievement, not a premise of politics. Explaining group success in achieving policy goals requires a prior analysis of a group's ability to construct a common political strategy amidst diversity (Lee, 2008).

In addition, the chapter argued that parties prefer candidate quotas and parity to reserved seats. By requiring parties simply to add individual women to party lists, quotas pose less of a threat to party interests than reserved seats, which hold the potential to reduce the party's share of seats and alter the partisan balance of power. The aftermath of quotas confirms these expectations about relative threat. As other chapters of this book show, almost nowhere has the growing presence of women on party lists led to a revolution or significant changes within parties.[60] In Argentina – the country that pioneered a candidate quota law in 1991 – women's presence in Congress has not challenged the control of male party leaders over the legislative agenda, committee assignments, or the incentives of legislators to avoid specializing in public good policy issues (though it has led to the introduction of more bills and greater awareness of gender issues) (Piscopo & Thomas, 2012). Even though women have come to occupy thirty to 40 percent of legislative seats, they are included as members of different parties, not as their own party. Coalitions forged by women to

[60] In fact, many male party leaders endorsed quotas for women in an effort to shore up their own position (e.g., Carlos Menem in Argentina and Alberto Fujimori in Perú) (see also Baldez, 2004; Dahlerup, 2008).

achieve quotas are often weakened inside of a legislature once they become subject to agenda control, and discipline imposed by party leaders.

The rise of the MAS and its rejection of more than a token number of indigenous reservations confirm a central tenet of intersectional analysis: individuals and groups can be simultaneously privileged and marginalized (see, e.g., Crenshaw, 1991; Garcia Bedolla, 2007; hooks, 1984; Weldon, 2008, 2011). To win control of the national government, the party – which originated in an indigenous movement – expanded its appeal to more groups and a broader range of issues (Anria, 2013; Madrid, 2012). As some indigenous peoples won majority power, more disadvantaged sectors were marginalized. This does not render the MAS any less "indigenous" than civic federations such as CIDOB and CONAMAQ but demonstrates the multiplicities and complexities within the indigenous project (cf. Albró, 2006, pp. 40, 42; Jung, 2008). Indigenous interests and identities are no longer shaped primarily by virtue of their subaltern status. The empowerment of some indigenous Bolivians has rendered visible the hierarchies of power within marginalized groups everywhere.

5

Political Inclusion in Colombia

Colombia is the only country in Latin America with mechanisms of political inclusion targeted explicitly at Afrodescendants and one of the three with reserved seats for indigenous peoples. Both measures originated in the 1991 Constitution, which created two reserved seats for indigenous peoples in the Senate and paved the way for legislation to construct two reserved seats for representatives of "black communities"[1] in the lower house and one seat for indigenous peoples in the same chamber. In 2011, after some twenty years of experience, the Colombian Constitutional Court canceled elections in the reserved seats.[2] Though based on a technicality, the sentence was issued amidst growing criticism of their failure to provide for the effective representation of Afrodescendant and indigenous interests. The Court's decision was challenged and the seats were reinstated in time for the 2014 elections. Yet the ruling was prescient, for the election results were disastrous. The two deputies who won on behalf of "black communities" were not recognized as Afrodescendant and allegedly had ties to drug traffickers, paramilitaries, and politicians jailed for such connections (see Figure 5.1 for photos of María del Socorro Bustamante

---

[1] The term "black communities" refers to a subset of the Afrodescendant population living in rural areas, primarily in the Pacific region. Its meaning and origins are described in greater detail in the text that follows.

[2] The court's sentence required that the government institute a process to consult and secure the consent of indigenous and Afrodescendant communities to legislation regulating the types of parties and organizations able to contest reserved seats (Camacho, 2013; Galvis, 2013). This process, called *consulta previa*, derived from a provision of ILO Convention 169 on the rights of indigenous communities. The right to *consulta previa* was sanctioned by Colombian legislation in 1991 and strengthened in 2009. Government and private sector organizations must heed by a process of consultation, and secure the consent, of indigenous communities prior to the commencement of economic development projects, natural resource extraction, and infrastructural projects that affect them. Law 70 of 1993 extended the right of *consulta previa* to "black communities" (Agrawal et al., 2012, p. 30).

(a)

(b)

FIGURE 5.1. Deputies elected to reserved seats for "black communities," 2014. *Source*: (a) Photo taken by Yomaira Grandett, courtesy of *El Tiempo*, Bogotá, Colombia. (b) Camara de Representantes.

(a) and Moises Orozco Vicuña (b)) ("¿Por qué se indignaron los negros?," 2014; Villamizar, 2014).

What went wrong? The 2014 results were disappointing and depressing. But in light of the way the reserved seats were designed, they are not surprising. Electoral institutions did not create formal constituencies of minority voters to elect their own representatives. Instead, all voters nationwide had the option of casting votes for the reserved seats. Rules on ballot access did little to ensure that organizations fielding candidates for the seats had connections to disadvantaged groups and movements advocating their rights, the structure of the ballot was confusing to voters, and there was no upper limit imposed on the number of votes that could be cast.

This chapter shows how the configuration of electoral institutions created conditions for opportunistic political behavior that undermined the purpose of the constitution. Since minority voters were not grouped into special constituencies, politicians contesting the seats solicited votes nationwide and from all social groups, not just black and indigenous voters. Meanwhile, areas of the country where Afrodescendants and indigenous peoples were geographically concentrated tended to support traditional parties rather than cast votes for representatives of reserved seats (Agudelo, 2000, 2002; Escandón Vega, 2011). The lax ballot access rules enabled corrupt political interests to manipulate the "black community" seats and traditional parties to contest the seats reserved for indigenous peoples (Basset 2011; Gil, 2013; Laurent, 2012b). Meanwhile, confusion induced by the odd structure of the ballot resulted in record numbers of blank and null votes. High numbers of votes were cast in the reserved contests, for few seats, which led to de facto malapportionment across districts. The combination of these factors reduced the legitimacy of reserved seat electoral contests.

Official misdiagnosis of the problem of racial oppression and misconceptions about the best way to combat it characterized Colombian policy from the start. In the early 1990s, Afro-Colombian movements, the state, academics, and nongovernmental organizations (NGOs) made a strategic decision to present the demands of blacks in the same "ethnic" frame that had worked to get rights for indigenous peoples (Hooker, 2005; Paschel, 2010; Wade, 2009, 2011). The "ethnicization" of Afrodescendant rights (Restrepo, 2004) helped secure nominal gains in the short term, especially in a context that was hostile to consideration of "race." But racial inequality differed from indigenous exclusion, and the ethnic framing delayed the state from acknowledging and combatting racism.

The trajectory of indigenous inclusion differed in important ways from that of Afrodescendant inclusion. As this chapter will make clear, indigenous politicians created relatively stable party organizations to advance group interests. These indigenous parties have served as the primary vehicles for the election of indigenous candidates (with some important exceptions). Yet by the end of the period under study, the country's largest indigenous party had abandoned its "indigenous" label, conforming to a broader regional tendency of successful "ethnic" parties to make inclusionary appeals and to solicit support from a heterogeneous constituency, not just one ethnic category (Madrid, 2012). At the same time, mainstream parties began to postulate indigenous candidates in the reserved seats, exacerbating divisions among indigenous movements.

This chapter begins by describing how minority rights were won, paying special attention to the "ethnicization" of black rights during the constituent assembly and follow-up processes. I show that the state's explicit recognition of racial inequality and discrimination as phenomena distinct from ethnic exclusion was slow to develop. The next section focuses on how mechanisms of political inclusion were designed, emphasizing the features of constituency definition, ballot access, and ballot structure. Then, I describe how institutional configurations enabled opportunistic political behavior, first by indigenous parties and then by organizations purporting to represent the interests of Afrodescendants. By the end of the period under study, organizations for both groups had diluted their focus and appeal. The largest indigenous party had evolved into a vehicle for the election of a diverse group of candidates and agendas, while "black community" representatives elected in 2010 and 2014 were criticized for ties to narcotraffickers, paramilitaries, and other groups.

Background: The Achievement of Minority Rights

At the end of the 1980s, the Colombian state suffered from a legitimacy crisis: violence and poverty were both escalating. Believing that the country's centralized and repressive institutions were partly to blame, politicians, public intellectuals, student groups, and other social organizations formed a consensus around the need for massive reform through a constituent assembly. Its goal was to overhaul political institutions to promote national reconciliation, participatory democracy, and pluralism. Delegates designed rules to nourish the expression and consolidation of principled ideas and programs, particularly those held by minorities. To ensure that everyone could participate, the new text eliminated representational thresholds, established low barriers to party registration, a single national district for senate elections, and guaranteed presence for representatives of minority communities. Participants believed that this new mode of doing politics would gradually replace the patronage networks of the past. They also felt that offering different actors a stake in the system would reduce the incentives to resort to organized violence (Paschel, 2010; Van Cott, 2000).

The new constitution advanced the rights of ethnic minorities, particularly indigenous peoples. It included:

- Guaranteed representation: Establishment of a two-seat senatorial district for indigenous peoples; another clause authorized the reservation of up to five seats in the lower house for minorities (two were later allocated to "black communities," one to indigenous peoples, and two to Colombians living abroad (articles 171 and 176).
- Official multiculturalism: The state recognized and protected the ethnic and cultural diversity of the Colombian nation, a clear departure from historic homogenizing national projects (Article 7).
- Creation of new indigenous territories (called ETIs for "entidades territoriales indígenas"): They would have the same legal status as states and municipalities, sharing in fiscal transfers and with the authority to administer public health and education (Articles 286, 288, 329).
- Political autonomy and legal jurisdiction: Indigenous rulers could govern (administer justice, design development programs, public investment, distribute resources, administer natural resources, collaborate in maintenance of public security) in accordance with their own customs (*usos y costumbres*) within their territory, as long as they did not contradict the constitution and other national laws (Articles 246, 330).
- Control over resource exploitation: Mining, electricity, and other projects within indigenous territories should not harm the cultural, social, and economic integrity of the communities and representatives had a right to participate in decision making about resource use (Article 330, para 1) (Constitución Política de la República de Colombia, 2004).

Why were so many indigenous rights recognized in the constitutional text? The global climate made delegates to the constituent assembly and the larger political class receptive to indigenous demands. The last few decades of the twentieth century saw increasing mobilization around indigenous political identities. In the past, many people had militated in politics as peasants or workers. Yet the neoliberal era diminished the political leverage offered by corporatist identities such as "peasant" and "worker," as well as the rights and privileges accruing to these categories. Meanwhile, global agreements and treaties – such as International Labor Organization (ILO) Convention 169 on Indigenous and Tribal Peoples (ratified by Colombia in 1989) – legitimized the category of "indigenous" as the subject of rights. The international human rights regime created a framework to advance new cultural demands as well as old class-based ones (Field, 1996; Jung, 2003, 2008; Laurent, 2005; Sánchez, 2001; Stavenhagen, 2002; Van Cott, 2005; Yashar, 2005).

Colombia's constituent assembly coincided with hemisphere-wide preparations to protest the commemoration of the 500th anniversary of Columbus's "discovery" of the Americas. Anticipation of 1992 fueled indigenous activism and helped generate public sympathy for their cause (Van Cott, 2000, p. 80). Ex-minister Manuel Rodríguez remarked that constituent assembly delegates "felt a sense of historical debt to indigenous peoples."[3]

Indigenous leaders participated directly in the assembly: they were two of seventy voting members. Indigenous groups had originally proposed that their presence in the assembly be guaranteed with reserved seats, an idea rejected by then-president Cesar Gaviria. According to Manuel José Cepeda, who advised the president on the constitution and wrote its first draft, the:

> ... government felt that reservations would end up excluding the indigenous and limiting their base. Since we were trying to write a constitution for the nation, it would be better for indigenous peoples to gain the support of the whole country. And this is what happened! The indigenous were not elected by the indigenous but basically by urban, educated voters. People from the University of the Andes voted for the indigenous candidates! They were the most alternative [candidates].[4]

As we see later, this pattern continued: indigenous representatives tended to draw support from nonindigenous voters, while many indigenous voters opted to support candidates from traditional parties.

Both indigenous delegates in the constituent assembly called for land rights, cultural and political autonomy, respect for customary law, and guaranteed representation in congress (Rappaport & Dover, 1996). Following a peace agreement with the government, a third indigenous former guerrilla leader also participated, but without voting rights. These delegates wore traditional dress during the deliberations and spoke indigenous languages. As a result, what (or whom) had been invisible suddenly became visible on a grand scale.

Some observers perceived that, owing to their small numbers, indigenous peoples did not pose a major challenge to the state. This reduced the risks associated with expanding their rights. As Cepeda noted, "Mexico is one thing,

---

[3] Interview Bogotá, June 13, 2004.
[4] Interview, Bogotá, June 16, 2004.

Guatemala is another, and Colombia a third. They are not a threat. The guerrillas never took up the indigenous cause. Rather, the indigenous are against the guerrillas. They have been victims of everyone. *It was not dangerous to go so far.*" [emphasis added][5]

Afro-Colombians were far more numerous than indigenous peoples but less organized. Prior to the constitutional convention, the black movement lacked resources and was divided in approach. Urban organizations – inspired by the US Civil Rights movement – framed their demands in terms of racial equality and integration. Rural and regionally-focused groups militated for land rights and protection from the extractive practices of large agribusiness corporations (Paschel, 2010, pp. 748–750). The rural groups had begun to organize as peasants, but during the 1980s, they began to frame their demands in cultural terms under the influence of the indigenous movement and their use of ILO Convention 169 on the protection of indigenous and tribal peoples (Agudelo, 2001, pp. 9–10). At the same time, academic studies had been unearthing African-influenced cultural traditions – primarily in the rural Pacific – and emphasizing their importance to the nation through conferences, establishment of a research institute, and newspapers and magazines (Wade, 2009, pp. 168–170).

The black movement failed to elect a delegate to the constituent assembly. Instead, they channeled their demands through Francisco Rojas Birry, an indigenous delegate from the Pacific coast of Colombia with connections to Afrocolombian movements there. Framing black demands as similar to those of indigenous peoples, he proposed that they be granted cultural and political autonomy, collective land rights, and reserved seats in congress. Rojas Birry's committee report called for special rights for ethnic groups including indigenous peoples, *raizales* (residents of the Caribbean islands of San Andrés and Providencia), and "black communities." He noted explicitly that *"black communities" were not the same thing as the "black race"*:

The special rights demanded for them are based on their sociological and anthropological reality. These communities, though they have shared a common history of economic exploitation and acculturation with the black race, have been able to conserve a traditional cultural legacy [and] have been able to conserve a territorial zone that comprises their habitat. The rights defended here are for those communities with a cultural identity, their own authorities and land used collectively. This is the case of the

---

[5] Interview, Bogotá, June 16, 2004. Though such a perspective may have been important in Colombia, it offers a poor guide to the overall variation in group rights in Latin America. As Hooker notes, there is little correlation between group size and the extent to which governments have granted collective rights in the region. Though their population varies cross-nationally, nowhere have Afrodescendants gotten *more* rights than indigenous peoples and in the two countries where some black communities have gotten the same rights as indigenous ones (Honduras and Nicaragua), their size is relatively large (second highest in Honduras) (Hooker, 2005, pp. 292–293).

palenques and black rural communities of the Chocó and some regions of the Pacific. (Rojas Birry, 1991, p. 19)

Not everyone agreed that "black communities" had a distinct cultural identity, however. The issue of whether Afrodescendants were really an ethnic group continued to be controversial. Since emphasizing cultural distinctiveness was the way to gain group rights, however, black movements continued to deploy the ethnic frame.

The constitution treated indigenous peoples and Afrodescendants asymmetrically.[6] Though indigenous peoples were mentioned multiple times, the only mention of Afrodescendant issues came in transitory article 55 (of sixty total), which obliged congress to pass a law recognizing the collective property rights of "black communities" (*communidades negras*) in the rural Pacific who had been occupying vacant/unused land "in accordance with their traditional productive practices." As this suggests, the only Afrodescendants who explicitly gained rights in the constitution were the small fraction of the overall black population whose lifestyles most resembled indigenous peoples.[7]

After the constitution was approved, the government formed a commission of state officials, representatives of "black communities," and academic experts from the Colombian Institute of Anthropology to elaborate a law regulating the collective property titles authorized by transitory article 55. Notably absent were representatives from the urban Afrodescendant organization, Cimarrón, that eschewed an ethnic discourse and framed its demands in terms of racial equality (Paschel, 2010, p. 755). The commission met for almost two years, focusing much of its time on whether Afro-Colombians were really an ethnic group with a distinct cultural identity. Against resistance by some anthropologists who argued that indigenous peoples were ethnic groups but Afrodescendants – who suffered from racism and marginalization – were not, black movements insisted on their cultural distinctiveness, at times bringing maps, drums, and songs to the meetings (Paschel, 2010, pp. 755–760).

The eventual law (Law 70 of 1993) envisioned that collective title would be granted to a community council (*consejo comunitario*) responsible for enforcing locally agreed on rules about the division and use of land. It also allocated

---

[6] The notion of "asymmetric" treatment of indigenous and Afrodescendants comes from Agudelo (2004).

[7] Hoffman notes that "black communities" amount to approximately 540,000 people, a small fraction of the total Afrodescendant population (Hoffmann, 1998, p. 16). Wade (2002) argues that Colombia's Afrodescendants can be divided into three subgroups: (1) a heterogeneous population living, as do 70 percent of Colombians, in urban areas and participating in the majority culture. They tend to be concentrated along the Caribbean coast, particularly in Cartagena, in the upper-central Cauca Valley around the city of Cali, and in other major cities such as Bogotá and Medellín. (2) The "raizales" or residents of the Caribbean islands of San Andrés and Providencia. Raizales speak creole or patois instead of (or in addition to) Spanish, they tend to be Baptist, and consider themselves to be culturally distinct from the mainstream culture. (3) The rural "black communities" living predominantly in the Pacific region.

two seats in the lower house of Congress to representatives of black communities, called for elaboration of a special national development plan, granted presence in the National Planning Council, created a state agency to manage "black" issues. The law required the Education Ministry to create "ethnoeducation" programs to strengthen the cultural identity of black communities, as well as research units to educate everyone on their history and contribution to the nation (República de Colombia, 1993). By 2003, around 4.5 million hectares of land had been allocated to collective title, representing around 4 percent of the total national territory (Hoffmann, 2004, p. 213).

In the mid-1990s, constitutional law and public policy cast black rights as applying to bounded communities maintaining traditional productive practices (Wade, 2002, pp. 7–8). In a sentence issued in 1996 on the reserved legislative seats, the Constitutional Court ruled that *Afrodescendant rights had to be framed in ethnic terms*, because the term "race" implied making "odious racial distinctions" and presupposed "the existence of pure races," an impossibility given the degree of mixture in the country. In the Court's view, granting Afrodescendants collective rights on the basis of race was unacceptable and would take the country back to the "era of complex colonial classifications based in different degrees of blood mixture, which upheld an exclusionary caste system, something utterly incompatible with a constitutional democracy." As a result:

> It should be clear that the collective rights of black communities in Colombia are a function of their status as an ethnic group, bearer of an identity that deserves to be protected and enhanced, not the skin color of its members. (cited in Meertens, 2008, p. 97)

As the ruling makes clear, the state required that Afrodescendants frame their demands in ethnic terms in order to get rights.

Official incentives strengthened culturally and territorially oriented social movement organizations at the expense of those committed to fighting racism. During negotiations over the content of Law 70, the state provided funding for "black community" organizations to consult with their constituencies (Agudelo, 2001). It thus helped institutionalize such movements and granted them privileged access to the government, while limiting their political autonomy and inciting inter-group competition. The Law required groups seeking to take advantage of the new rights to conform to an ethnic model: in addition to a detailed map specifying the boundaries of its community, each council requesting a collective title had to offer oral histories documenting their occupation of the land, estimation of the beneficiaries, and descriptions of their productive activities (Arocha, 2004, p. 168).

An ethnic template shaped the self-understandings of many black activists and their movements. Many leaders assumed African surnames, wore oricha necklaces, and invoked Changó or Elegguá before making a public speech. Community councils became arenas to express and defend ethnic difference (Arocha, 2004, pp. 168–169). Afrodescendant organizations, such as the

Proceso de Comunidades Negras, demanded the "right to difference," alleging that "presenting the situation of Afro-Colombian communities in terms of racial discrimination has little audience" (Wade, 2002, p. 12). Movements benefitting from the "ethnicization of blackness" stood to lose power if official focus shifted to an anti-racism agenda. Many opposed such a shift, though not explicitly.[8]

The ethnic template did not resonate with the self-understanding of the bulk of Afrodescendants, most of whom did not see themselves as members of a distinct ethnic group. For example, when the 1993 census attempted to count blacks ethnically, by asking respondents if they belonged to a "black community," only 1.5 percent answered affirmatively (around 500,000, fewer those who claimed indigenous identity)! Even the government statistical agency concluded in an official document that "many blacks don't consider themselves an ethnic group" (Barbary & Urrea, 2004, p. 5).

Nor was the ethnocultural political agenda widely supported by the Afrodecscendant population, most of which cared about bread and butter issues. Afro-Colombian social movements and political candidates were not popular and earned few votes, even in the Pacific region where Afrodescendants are a majority. As we will see later on, the bulk of the votes for candidates contesting "black community" seats have not come from historically black regions. In those areas, voters tend to opt for traditional parties practicing machine politics, not for politicians with an ethnic agenda. One activist remarked that, for most Afrodescendants, "Black community organizations are strange entities that speak of the environment, Africa, ethnicity, and other elements that Pacific residents don't see as their own issues nor ones connected to their reality" (cited in Agudelo, 2002, p. 185).

While the "ethnicization of blackness" in the Colombian Pacific constituted a "novel historical event" (Restrepo, 2004, p. 711), it offered an inadequate framework to address racial inequality in the country at large. Law 70 and the Supreme Court decision ended up "ruralizing and indigenizing blackness" and prioritizing "ethnic difference over racism" (Wade, 2009, p. 172). As Paschel notes, "The process of constructing the Law of Black Communities led to the reproduction of a specific and geographically limited notion of blacks as rural and from the Pacific Coast that persists today" (Paschel, 2010, p. 759). By focusing on only a small subset of the black population, the affirmative action mechanisms contemplated in Law 70 ended up marginalizing problems of discrimination and racialization experienced by people outside of the rural Pacific (Wade, 2011, p. 22).

Though it ruled on the legality of affirmative action for rural black communities in the 1990s, The Constitutional Court did not take action on racial discrimination until 2005. That year, it ruled against two Cartagena discotheques that had denied entrance to two Afrodescendant sisters (Meertens, 2008).

[8] Interview with Luis Gilberto Murillo, Washington, DC, September 24, 2004.

Discourse on race discrimination and racial equality became more prominent toward the late 2000s in both society and the state, though the ethnic frame did not lose importance. A major turning point came with the 2005 census, when the wording of questions about race and ethnicity changed. The census asked people if, according to their culture, *pueblo*, or physical features, they self-identified or were identified by others as belonging to one of several groups, including the category of "*Negro, mulato, afro-colombiano* or *afrodescendiente*."[9] With this more expansive terminology, some 11 percent of the population identified as Afrodescendant (Del Popolo et al., 2009). Other studies suggest, however, that the official categories are somewhat out of sync with self- and other -perceptions and that, had other terms been used, the size of the black population would be even larger. The recent Project on Ethnicity and Race in Latin America (PERLA) survey, for example, estimates that Afrodescendants make up 19 percent of the Colombian population.[10]

The discursive recognition of racial categories reflected in the census was followed by changes in state policy. In 2007, the government created an Intersectoral Commission for the Advancement of Afrocolombian, *Palenquero*, and *Raizal* Populations in the Interior Ministry and a 2009 publication by the group recognized the existence of racism (Wade, 2011, p. 26). Yet the agency did not abandon the ethnic frame: a bill it submitted to Congress in 2012, the proposed "Law on Equal Opportunities for Afrocolombian Communities," was based on "recognition of the fundamental right to ethnic identity" and the idea of Afrodescendants as an ethnic group.[11] In 2007, the Afrocolombian caucus was launched in Congress, composed of two senators and seven deputies (including both deputies from the reserved seats as well as one white deputy representing the islands of San Andrés and Providencia). Through agreements with the Interior and Justice Ministry, several universities applied small quotas for blacks in university admissions and others offered tuition discounts (Ministerio del Interior y de Justicia de la República de Colombia, n.d.). In 2012, the Interior Ministry presented a bill to Congress that would institute a 10 percent racial quota in military and police academies, financially reward

---

[9] The five groups mentioned by the census included indigenous, *rom* (Roma or gypsy), *raizal* (a native of the Caribbean islands of San Andrés and Providencia), *palenquero* (someone from the runaway slave settlement of San Basilio), or Afrodescendant.

[10] Had the census included the "moreno" category, the size of the group would almost certainly have grown. Estimates on the size of the black population vary depending on the study. They include: around 20 percent of the population (Barbary et al., 2004, p. 75), 26 percent (mentioned in Wade, 2002), 12 percent (the 2010 Latin American Public Opinion Project [LAPOP] survey), and 19 percent (the PERLA study by Edward Telles and collaborators, mentioned in the main text) (Urrea, López, & Vigoya, 2014).

[11] Proyecto de Ley Estatutaria no. 125 of 2012. Retrieved from Congreso Visible www .congresovisible.org (accessed June 3, 2013).

political parties that got Afrodescendants elected, and establish a special loan program for the higher education of black students.[12]

In 2011, Congress approved a law criminalizing racial discrimination and punishing it with prison terms. Introduced by a small evangelical political party (the Movimiento Independiente de Renovación Absoluta, or MIRA), the law was meant to serve as a tool to "promote inclusion and the social changes needed to break the cycle of Afrodescendant poverty."[13] In 2013, the Constitutional Court banned racist speech in universities.[14] These events show that the state's attention to Afrodescendants is no longer limited to "black communities" of the rural Pacific. Official discourse evinced greater acknowledgment of problems of racism and racial inequality. Yet mechanisms of political inclusion were not reformed accordingly. Elections for "black community" seats continued to be held. As we see in the text that follows, they became more and more susceptible to manipulation by corrupt political interests.

Institutional Design

The 1991 Constitution and implementing legislation established a special two-seat Senate district for indigenous peoples and a five-seat special district in the Chamber of Deputies, of which one seat was allocated to indigenous peoples and two to "black communities" (Table 5.1).

Institutional configurations governing access to these seats contributed to the discrediting of mechanisms of inclusion. Rather than creating group-specific constituencies, Colombian institutional engineers enabled *all* voters to opt to support minority candidates. While rules on ballot access attempted to filter out nonindigenous candidates for the reserved senate seats, they were far more permissive in allowing a variety of weakly institutionalized and personalistic groups to contest the "black community" seats. Confusing ballot structure led to an escalation of blank and null votes and failed to ensure any proportionality across special and general races.

---

[12] "Presentan ley para que los afros sean beneficiados," *El Tiempo*, September 26, 2012. Retrieved from www.eltiempo.com/politica/ARTICULO-WEB-NEW_NOTA_INTERIOR-12258027 .html (accessed June 3, 2013).

[13] "Debate en torno al proyecto de ley para la penalización de los actos de discriminación racial. Foro Las penas de la discriminación. Uniandes, septiembre 8 de 2011." Rapporteur's report of the meeting. Retrieved from Congreso Visible www.congresovisible.org/agora/post/debate-en-torno-al-proyecto-de-ley-para-la-penalizacion-de-los-actos-de-discriminacion-racial-foro-las-penas-de-la-discriminacion-uniandes-septiembre-8-de-2011/2349/ (accessed June 3, 2013). MIRA, a small party with three seats in the senate and one in the lower house, was founded (and is led) by lawyer, preacher, and former Bogotá city councillor Carlos Alberto Baena. Baena, who is white, has advocated Afrodescendant rights since his election to Congress in 2010.

[14] See "La Corte pone fin al racismo en las universidades," *Semana*, May 5, 2013. Retrieved from www.semana.com/nacion/articulo/la-corte-pone-fin-racismo-universidades/342366-3 (accessed June 3, 2013).

TABLE 5.1. *Minority Reservations in Colombia*

Legislative Chamber	Group to Which They Apply	Year Adopted	Number of Seats
Senate	Indigenous peoples	1991	2
Lower house	Indigenous peoples	1991, implemented 2001	1
Lower house	"Black communities"	1991, implemented 1994 and after 2001[a]	2

[a] No elections were held for the seats in 1998.
Source: Author.

Rules governing election to reserved seats stayed the same, even as Colombia's electoral system was significantly reformed in 2003, and again in 2009. These reforms created an electoral threshold, required that votes be pooled at the party level, and gave parties the option of closing their lists or offering voters a preference vote (Shugart, Moreno, & Fajardo, 2007). Their goal was to reduce party fragmentation and more closely align the goals of the party with those of individual politicians. By shrinking the number of parties and reducing the incentives to cultivate a personal vote, the reforms contributed to the rationalization of the party system. Between 2002 and 2006, the number of parties with representation in Congress declined from sixty-two to eleven (Escandón Vega, 2011, p. 22). Yet trends in the reserved seats (where the reforms did not apply) went in the opposite direction, especially in the "black community" ones. Fragmentation, malapportionment, and irrationality increased, contributing to the bizarre electoral outcomes of 2014.

Definition of Constituency

There are some restrictions on who can run in Colombia's reserved seats, but any citizen can vote for them. Effectively, the constituency for minority seats (defined as a group that elects a candidate to represent them) forms itself from a national pool. On the day of the election, voters may choose the district in which they cast their vote: the ordinary districts or the special ones for indigenous and Afrodescendant candidates.[15]

In Senate elections, voters may opt to support either a party in the 100-seat ordinary national district or a party contesting the two-seat indigenous district. For lower house races, one indigenous candidate, two Afrodescendant candidates, and two representatives for Colombians living abroad are elected from special

---

[15] This scheme is broadly similar to what holds in neighboring Venezuela. There the country is divided into three virtual districts composed of several states, each one of which elects an indigenous representative to one of three reserved seats. Voters in the states may therefore choose to vote for an indigenous or a "regular" candidate (Constitución de la República Bolivariana de Venezuela, 2004, transitory article 7).

national districts.[16] The other 161 deputies run for seats allocated to the provinces according to population, with each province getting a minimum of two.

Electoral rules in other countries with reserved seats for minorities tend to create group-specific constituencies. By establishing separate voter rolls or drawing single member districts around areas of high minority concentration, such rules attempt to match minority representatives with minority constituencies. In New Zealand, for example, Maoris are registered (optionally) on separate rolls, which elect seven candidates to parliament (Banducci, Donovan, & Karp, 2004). In India, official electoral commissions designate those single-member districts in which only Scheduled Caste and Scheduled Tribe candidates may compete for election, though everyone living in those districts, regardless of their caste membership, will vote for them (Galanter, 1984). In the United States, the Voting Rights Act authorized states to draw the lines of single member districts around areas of high minority concentration to maximize the ability of minority voters to elect a candidate of their choosing. The definition of constituencies by race and ethnicity is designed to promote traditional, principal–agent representation: minority voters authorize representatives to serve their interests and hold them accountable in the next election. Such procedures maximize the chances that representatives will serve as advocates of group interests.

In Colombia and Latin America, the definition of electoral constituencies by race and ethnicity would present practical and ideological problems. Only in the 2000s have the majority of Latin American censuses begun to include questions about race and ethnicity (Del Popolo et al., 2009). The protocol of self-identification used by most censuses tends to lead to undercounting, particularly among Afrodescendants (Telles, 2014a). Group boundaries tend to be fluid, people have mixed and multiple identities, and cultural devaluation of blackness and indigeneity tends to motivate reclassification (passing) (Wade, 1995, 1997). Even in India, where ethnic group identities are more institutionalized, the criteria to classify individuals with multiple and ambiguous identities have been repeatedly challenged in court (Galanter, 1984).

There is principled opposition among politicians to rules that would create constituencies of minority voters, as I mentioned in Chapter 1. In a 2001 ruling on the reserved seats, the Constitutional Court ruled that the constituencies for indigenous and Afrodescendant seats had to be national to "consult the general interest" and "maximize fundamental rights."[17] Yet as we see later, the definition of the constituency as national imposes no upper bound on the number of votes that can be cast there, which has generated de facto malapportionment across districts.

---

[16] In 2011, a new law gave the seat originally reserved for "political minorities" to Colombians living abroad.

[17] Sentence C-169 of 2001.

Ballot Access

Parties contesting regular seats must complete certain requirements established by the National Electoral Council. Before 2003, any party or movement collecting at least 50,000 signatures, having received this same number of votes in the previous election, or having gained a seat in Congress could contest an election. Reforms enacted in 2003, aiming to reduce party fragmentation, stipulated that a party had to receive 2 percent of the nationwide vote in lower house or Senate elections to retain its legal status (in 2009, this threshold was raised to 3 percent) (Scherlis, 2013).

For the reserved seats, rules on ballot access are different, and the threshold requirement does not apply to organizations postulating candidates for election (Giraldo García & López Jiménez, 2007, p. 14). To contest a Senate or lower house seat reserved for indigenous peoples, a candidate must have exercised a leadership position in an indigenous community or organization. To run in the special "black community" districts in the lower house, candidates require the endorsement of a "black community" organization registered with the Interior Ministry.[18] These organizations are not required to demonstrate popular support (such as signatures on a petition) or any organizational capacity (such as presence in a minimum number of provinces). As a result, a large number of groups qualify to – and have actually postulated – candidates in these races.

Whereas the indigenous-led parties that emerged beginning in the early 1990s have relatively stable party organizations and have repeatedly contested elections at multiple levels of government (more on this later), the same cannot be said for groups contesting the "black community" seats. In 2013, the organization *Congreso Visible* attempted to contact all the organizations that had fielded candidates for the seats in the 2006 and 2010 elections. Of the 830 organizations registered with the Interior Ministry, the vast majority existed only on paper (without a functioning telephone), were inactive or had ceased to exist, or were merely the vehicle of a single individual (Camacho, 2013). As we see later, the massive growth in the number of organizations contesting the seats has led to a fragmentation of the vote, with successful candidates elected with only a small percentage of total support. Stricter ballot access rules could have helped avoid this situation.

Ballot Structure

The structure of ballots for national legislative races has confused voters. Let us begin by examining ballots used for election to the Senate. Until 2006, the Senate ballot was designed such that the candidates for the indigenous district were not spatially segregated from those in the ordinary district. All of the candidates' photos appeared together in rows without any indication of who was

---

[18] The law requires that candidates for the seats "be members of such a community and previously sponsored by an organization registered with the Directorate for Black Community Issues in the Interior Ministry" (República de Colombia, 2001).

FIGURE 5.2. 2010 Senate ballot.
Source: Registraduría Nacional del Estado Civil.

running against whom and the ballot spanned multiple pages (eight in 2002).
Due to this structure, former Senate candidate and indigenous leader Antonio
Jacanamijoy argued that, "The special district is not a real special district ....
We want a part of the ballot to say, 'these are the candidates for the indigenous
district.'"[19]

After the 2003 electoral reforms, the ballot was redesigned. For the subsequent elections, the ballot more clearly distinguished between the national
senate district and the indigenous one (see Figure 5.2). But voters could cast a
vote in only one district or the other, and instructions to mark only one, rather
than both, districts were not very prominent. If voters made the error of marking more than one section of the ballot, their vote would be considered null
(Basset 2011).[20]

---

[19] Interview, Bogotá, June 11, 2004.
[20] As an election observer in 2010, Taylor reports that he personally saw ballots marked this way
that were considered null by poll workers (Taylor, 2010).

FIGURE 5.3. 2010 Lower house ballot, Province of Cauca.
Source: Registraduría Nacional del Estado Civil.

Ballots for lower house races were also confusing. Figure 5.3 shows a ballot from the province of Cauca. The ballot is divided into three parts: part A shows the logos of parties seeking the seats to represent the province; part B shows party logos contesting the national indigenous seat; and part C, the parties/organizations contesting the national "black community" seats. Part C is by far the largest part of the ballot, even though only two seats are in dispute. (In Cauca, four seats are in dispute in part A.)

Ballot structure is the likely reason for the large number of blank and null votes cast in the indigenous and Afro virtual "districts." In the 2006 election, the number of blank votes exceeded the number of valid votes cast for the indigenous seats. As a result, no list reached the electoral threshold, which, under the terms of the constitution, was supposed to invalidate the results and require a new election to be held. Most – but not all – indigenous parties protested the convocation of new elections. After several weeks of negotiations, the National Electoral Court decreed that the electoral threshold would not apply in the special reserved districts (Laurent, 2012b, p. 57). In the "black community" districts, numbers of null votes reached a high of some 342,000 in the 2010 elections, but then dropped to some 117,000 in 2014 (Villamizar 2014).

High numbers of spoiled ballots undermined the legitimacy of the reserved seat contests, and the confusing juxtaposition of candidates for different districts on the same ballot may have jeopardized the integrity of the entire electoral process (Basset 2011).[21]

Indigenous Reservations

Indigenous parties benefitted from the dramatic lowering of barriers to entry in the political marketplace created by the 1991 constitution. The creation of a single, national district to elect 100 senators and the reduction of the electoral threshold allowed multiple groups – including indigenous, religious and political minorities, as well as former guerrillas, paramilitaries, and drug traffickers – to form parties and gain seats in Congress. Indigenous candidates and parties, emphasizing general issues and pursuing national campaigns, gathered "votos de opinión" from around the country. (The term "voto de opinión," which means programmatic voting, is used to refer to a nonclientelistic electoral behavior.) Their electoral strategy conformed to the desires of constitution makers who created the single district precisely to encourage senators to champion issues of national concern and not merely the financial interests of their small geographic bases (Botero, 1999, pp. 287–289). Indeed, between 1991 and 2002, around one quarter of senate seats were occupied by nontraditional politicians – indigenous and others – who had run campaigns on national issues and aggregated votes from across the country (Crisp & Ingall, 2002).[22] By 2002, the number of indigenous senators grew to four, including two from the reserved seats and two elected in the ordinary district. Indigenous parties also won seats in the lower house, where there was no reserved seat until 2002 (Table 5.2).[23]

---

[21] Another source of confusion derived from the open list. In contrast to previous elections, when the candidates' faces and names appeared, after 2006 voters saw only party logos (not names of parties) and three-digit numbers designating places on a party list. Voters were asked to mark an X over the logo of their preferred party. If they wanted, they could also mark an X over a three-digit number of the candidate for whom they wanted to cast a preference vote. (Though not all parties offered preference voting, most did.) It is likely that many voters did not remember the number of their preferred candidate and/or were not familiar with party logos (Laurent, 2012b, p. 60). As Steven Taylor (2010) observed: "It was not unusual to see voters on election day calling out to friends or relatives 'what number is whatshisname again?' There is a book one can consult with names and faces, but I don't think most voters were aware of its existence, and sometimes poll workers would offer the book, and others times not. Considering that each party could have up to 100 candidates, it was a fairly thick book" (S. Taylor, 2010).

[22] But the rest of the chamber continued to practice politics in the old ways: they used party machines to court geographically concentrated groups of voters and devoted their legislative careers to procuring pork for them (Crisp & Ingall, 2002).

[23] In the 2002 elections, Jesus Piñacué of the Alianza Social Indígena came in twelfth place nationwide (83,594 votes) in the ordinary district and Gerardo Jumí was elected as the second-place candidate on the list of Antonio Navarro, with whom his party had formed an alliance. Their list came in second place overall with 212,507 votes.

TABLE 5.2. *National Seats Won by Indigenous Candidates Belonging to Indigenous Parties (Unless Noted Otherwise)*

Election Year	Senate	House of Representatives
	No. of indigenous senators (of 102) (reserved district = 2 seats)	No. of indigenous representatives (of 166) (reserved district = 1 seat, starting in 2002)
1991	3	0
1994	2	2
1998	3	2
2002	4 (1 from nonindigenous party)	1 (reserved seat)
2006	2	1 (reserved seat, nonindigenous party)
2010	2	1 (reserved seat, nonindigenous party)
2014	2 (1 from nonindigenous party)	1 (reserved seat)

Source: Laurent (2010, 2012b).

At the same time, the overall proliferation of parties and lists, and the personalistic politics this generated, weakened and contributed to the fractionalization of Colombia's party system (Pizarro, 2001, 2002; Shugart et al., 2007. Combined with longer standing rules permitting parties to field an unlimited number of candidate lists and the historic tendency of parties to grant endorsements (permission to contest an election under the party label) indiscriminately, the constitutional changes ushered in a political free for all. The number of parties and movements with presence in the Senate increased from 23 in 1991 to 62 in 2002 and in the lower house, from 23 in 1991 to 72 in 2002 (Ungar Bleier & Arévalo, 2004). Most of these parties were vehicles for the election of a single senator or deputy and frequently failed to survive longer than one mandate.[24]

The 2003 political reform, discussed earlier, was enacted precisely to combat this situation. The reforms, which required parties to consolidate candidates on a single party list and imposed an electoral threshold, made it more difficult for indigenous and other smaller parties to win outside of the reserved seats (Cepeda, 2003; Pachón & Shugart, 2010). The number of indigenous senators dropped from four to two, and indigenous parties were unable to win seats in regular lower house races (see Table 5.2). As a result, the principal indigenous parties – the Indigenous Social Alliance (ASI) and the Movement of Indigenous Authorities (AICO) – concentrated their efforts on capturing the reserved seats. Competition intensified. By 2010, the number of parties contesting Senate seats

[24] By 2002, only three lists succeeded in electing more than one senator. And the larger parties – the Liberals and Conservatives – actually contained numerous personalistic factions competing as much against one another as against the other parties.

had risen to five (from two in previous elections), and by 2014, 14 parties contested the two seats.[25]

In 2002, elections were held for the first time for the lower house seat reserved for indigenous peoples. Thirty-six candidates grouped into eight different parties registered to contest the seat, and over 200,000 votes were cast in the special district. By 2006 and 2010, the number of indigenous lower house candidates declined to six and eight, respectively, and parties to six and three, respectively, and the number of votes cast also declined (Escandón Vega, 2011, pp. 29–30). In all of these elections, the indigenous district appeared to have diverted votes that, hypothetically, could have been used to elect indigenous candidates contesting ordinary races (Basset, 2011, p. 54).

Who has voted for indigenous candidates? A surprisingly small percentage of voters in indigenous regions have cast their votes for the reserved seats. In the department of La Guajira, where 40 percent of the population is indigenous (compared to 3 percent nationwide), fewer than 2 percent of the electorate cast votes in the reserved contests between 1995 and 2010 (Escandón Vega, 2011, p. 38).[26] In other departments with significant indigenous populations, such as Guainía and Vichada (around 30 percent), the percent of the population who voted in indigenous contests was low, and declined over time to less than 5 percent (Ibid.).

By contrast, in the capital of Bogotá, the share of voters casting votes in the indigenous district (between 0.5 and 3 percent) far exceeded the indigenous share of the city's population (less than one-tenth of 1 percent) (Ibid.). To urban voters fed up with clientelistic parties and politicians, voting for indigenous politicians, who appeared as the most radical alternative, was the ultimate act of protest. As former Senator Gerardo Jumí explained: "People from the center left, democrats, intellectuals, those who did not want to vote for Liberals or Conservatives, voted for indigenous."[27] Senator Jesus Piñacué added that: "Our success has been that there are non-indigenous citizens who understand our goals better than indigenous peoples themselves; so much that they help us get to Congress."[28]

After 2003, some indigenous leaders left indigenous parties and joined the leftist Alternative Democratic Pole party (known as the *Polo*) with the objective of maximizing their chances of gaining a seat in the ordinary contests. Meanwhile, various nonindigenous parties, not only the *Polo* but also the right-wing National Integration Party (Partido de Integración Nacional [PIN]), presented lists to contest the indigenous seats, often led by candidates that lacked close connections to the indigenous movement (Laurent, 2012b,

---

[25] Information from the 2014 elections comes from the Colombian Civil Registry website: www .registraduria.gov.co/congreso2014/preconteo/99SE/DSE9999999_L1.htm (accessed January 30, 2015).

[26] In 1991, the number was higher: 10 percent (Escandón Vega, 2011, p. 38).

[27] Interview, Bogotá, June 24, 2004.

[28] Interview, Bogotá, June 16, 2004.

pp. 58–59). In the 2006 and 2010 elections, the candidate from the *Polo* beat candidates from the indigenous parties to win the reserved lower house seat.

Meanwhile, the Indigenous Social Alliance (Alianza Social Indígena [ASI]), a party with deep roots in the indigenous movement, decided to transform itself into a more inclusive, nonethnic political party, essentially abandoning its project as the partisan expression of an indigenous social movement (Laurent, 2012a). After 2011, the party became known as the *Independent Social Alliance*, seemingly embracing partisan politics. It was an ironic transition given that, twenty years before, the party had presented itself as an *alternative* to traditional parties (Laurent, 2012a, p. 176). On the other hand, party leaders had always insisted that, though the party was born out of the indigenous movement, it had a larger democratic and pluralist political project. Senator Jesus Piñacué said to me in an interview that: "We have the enormous ambition of helping to construct a model of state that respects the other, both in his condition as a member of a group as well as in his condition as an individual citizen."[29]

The decision was not uncontroversial. A dissident wing split off, forming the Indigenous Social Movement (Movimiento Social e Indígena, or MSI), led by a female indigenous leader from Cauca. In the 2010 election for the indigenous Senate seats, she ended up receiving the most preference votes but failed to win a seat, as her party came in fourth place overall (Laurent, 2012b, p. 59).

Both of the primary indigenous parties, ASI and Autoridades Indígenas de Colombia (AICO), grew significantly between 1991 and 2013, fielding candidates for popular election at all levels of government (mayors, governors, provincial assemblies, and city councils) and in every province, not just those with large indigenous populations. In the 1993 local elections, ASI fielded a total of eleven candidates (ten won); AICO, sixteen candidates (eight won). By 2000, ASI was postulating a total of 336 candidates, including 32 for mayor and 3 for governor (that year, the party won 11 mayors' races, 1 governor's race, and 191 seats overall). (In 2000, AICO put forward 196 candidates, 86 of whom won.) In the 2011 local elections, ASI put forward 6,430 candidates in total, and 728 won, among them 59 mayors (including the first Afrodescendant mayor of Cartagena, Terán Dix) and four governors. AICO fielded 3,696 candidates and 288 won, including 24 mayors and 1 governor (Laurent, 2012a, p. 182). A great deal of this growth was facilitated by diluting the parties' original purpose. Many ASI candidates were not indigenous nor did they have any connection to indigenous movements. The party has been the subject of criticism for being a mere party for hire (*repartir avales*) (Laurent, 2012a, quoting ex minister).

[29] Interview, Bogotá, June 16, 2004. He also pointed out that, "The reserved seats are not really to defend indigenous rights because this is very difficult. We are not in the majority. Rather, the idea is to help build a party that at some point can offer a broader *understanding* of what it means to defend indigenous rights."

After the Constitutional Court suspended the reserved seats, indigenous politics was at a crossroads. How indigenous were the main parties and to what extent were the seats a vehicle to represent indigenous interests? As we have seen, the largest indigenous political party had removed the word "indigenous" from its name. Nonindigenous parties, such as the *Polo*, were defeating indigenous parties in the reserved constituencies. What exactly indigenous meant became an open question (Laurent, 2012a, 2012b). As we see later, the "black community" seats also declined as representative mechanisms for Afrodescendant social movements, though to a far greater degree.

Political Behavior in the "Black Community" Seats

Whereas indigenous peoples had been largely excluded from the Colombian government prior to the 1991 Constitution, a small number of prominent Afrodescendants had achieved elective office. (Levels of Afrodescendant presence, however, were nowhere proportional to their population size.) They included Manuel Mosquera Garces, who served as Minister of Education in the 1950s; Diego Córdoba, senator in the 1970s; and Jacobo Pérez, secretary general of the Constituent Assembly (1991).[30] In the 1990s and 2000s, around six seats in the lower house of Congress were occupied by Afrodescendants, and Piedad Corboda, of the Liberal Party from Medellín, held a Senate seat between 1994 and 2010. Cordoba was an outspoken advocate of Afrodescendant rights, women's rights, and human rights; at one point, she was kidnapped by paramilitary organizations.

Elections for the "black community" seats were held for the first time in 1994. For the first and last time, the winners were closely connected to groups advocating Afrodescendant rights. They included Zulia Mena, a leader from the Chocó with a national presence and a member of the commission that wrote the principal piece of legislation advancing the rights of "black communities" (Law 70), and Agustín Valencia, a professor from Calí with Chocoan roots and connections to civic movements (Agudelo, 2000, p. 120). Both deputies were seen as legitimate representatives of the black movement. But their legislative record proved disappointing to activists. Rather than advocate black rights, they fumbled from a lack of political experience and were contaminated by the scandal surrounding allegations that then-president Ernesto Samper had received campaign donations from drug traffickers. Much to the chagrin of supporters, both representatives joined the coalition defending Samper (Agudelo, 2002, pp. 184–185 and fn. 134).

Meanwhile, the Constitutional Court ruled that the legislation creating the black community seats was unconstitutional, on procedural grounds. Since the seats dealt with a constitutional matter, the law needed to be submitted for approval to the Court before its application, which had not been done

[30] Fernando Cepeda, personal communication, October 4, 2005.

(Agudelo, 2002, p. 185). Scholars observed that loss of the two seats provoked little protest or concern, and neither the black movement nor "black communities" of the Chocó mobilized on behalf of their two representatives. There was no election for the seats in 1998, though they were reinstated in 2002.

In 2002, two star black athletes won the seats: María Isabel Urrutia, who had won a gold medal in weightlifting at the Sydney Olympics in 2000 (the only gold medal ever earned by Colombia) and Willington Ortiz, who had been a champion soccer player in the 1970s.[31] Neither deputy had connections to Afro-Colombian social movements or to areas of the country that had benefitted from the Law 70. Over half of Ortiz's votes came from Bogotá and one-third of Urrutia's from the Valle province, areas where both legislators realized their athletic careers (Cunin, 2003; Reyes Gonzáles, 2007).

Once elected, the two deputies attempted to champion black rights. They pushed the president to include, within the National Development Plan, a sub-plan on the development of black communities. Deputy Ortiz presented a bill to Congress to create a quota for Afrodescendants in decision-making positions in the executive branch and worked so that black university students had access to a public fund for scholarships. The quota proposal encountered tremendous resistance in committee, however, with other deputies offering the familiar argument that the quota would lead to a cascade of demands from other groups.[32]

In the 2010 elections, both deputies who won the "black community" seats had alleged connections to paramilitary organizations. Top-vote getter Yahir Acuña's political patron had been identified by military intelligence as part of the political structure of paramilitaries in coastal regions. The deputy himself attracted attention for his meteoric rise: in five years he rose through the city council and the state assembly to be elected federal deputy (Gil, 2013; Misión de Observación Electoral, 2010). Second place winner Heriberto Arrechea said in an interview that he "could not deny" his connection to an ex-senator under investigation for his ties to paramilitary groups.[33] The trajectory of the two deputies echoes larger trends: numerous Colombian politicians were removed from office and jailed in the late 2000s for their connections to paramilitary groups.

By 2014, the seats had become completely divorced from their original purpose of advancing Afrodescendant rights. The two victors, María Del Socorro Bustamante Ibarra and Moisés Orozco Vicuña, both sponsored by the Ebony Foundation of Colombia (Fundación Ébano de Colombia or FUNECO), were

---

[31] As Chapter 2 notes, the athletic backgrounds of Afrodescendant legislators is a broader trend. In 2013, Peru's three Afrodescendant national legislators were all well-known former volleyball players.

[32] Interview with Deputy Willington Ortiz, Bogotá, June 23, 2004.

[33] Retrieved from www.terra.com.co/elecciones_2010/votebien/html/vbn376-afrofranquicias.htm (accessed July 6, 2011).

not recognized as black (see Figure 5.1). Various groups, including politicians who lost the election and Afro-Colombian movements, protested the results in court and the media. Some claimed that Bustamante and Orozco were not qualified because they were not black; others protested that they had done nothing to advance Afrodescendant rights (Villamizar, Duque, & Martínez, 2014). When asked in an interview about allegations she was not eligible to contest the "black community" seat, Bustamante replied: "When I registered as a candidate and filled out the required forms, nowhere did it say that I had to have black skin and a flat nose!"[34] A court order blocked the deputies from being sworn in until the claims could be adjudicated. By the end of 2014, different courts had issued competing judgments on the case and neither Bustamante nor Orozco had assumed a seat.

Notwithstanding the controversy over Bustamante and Orozco, there were more Afrodescendants elected to Congress in 2014 in regular electoral contests than at any time in the past (see Table 5.3). After the elections, there were nine black legislators in the Chamber of Deputies (of 166, some 5 percent of the total) and one in the Senate (of 102, some 1 percent). One deputy was a woman. None of these legislators came from the reserved seats. Table 5.3 lists their party affiliation, showing that all nine were elected from mainstream parties, not group-specific or ethnic parties. In the 2010 elections, five Afrodescendant deputies, and two senators, had been elected in ordinary competition.[35]

The eclipsing of black social movements by political opportunists in the reserved seat contests can be seen in the spectacular growth in the number of candidates and groups in competition, as seen in Table 5.4. In 1994, the first time the seats were contested, twelve candidates competed. In 2006, twenty-seven lists and 69 candidates competed, none of which presented a coherent party platform (Reyes Gonzáles, 2007, p. 140). By 2010, competition had increased to 67 lists and 169 candidates, who received a total of 427,089 votes. This ranked the two-seat "black community" district the eighth highest vote getter among Colombia's thirty-two provinces.

As mentioned earlier, groups competing for the seats are not required to demonstrate any institutional capacity or national presence when they register with the Interior Ministry. The *Congreso Visible* investigation revealed that many are simply names on paper or vehicles to promote a single individual (Camacho, 2013). Unlike the indigenous seats, which motivated the growth of the Indigenous Social Alliance (ASI) and Indigenous Authorities of Colombia (AICO) – real political parties that contested elections at multiple levels on a regular basis since 1991 – the "black community seats" have not led to party formation. Before 2010, almost none of the black organizations had

---

[34] Interview by John Montaño. "Congresista 'afro' dice que no tiene que ser 'negra ni de nariz chata,'" *El Tiempo*, January 20, 2015.
[35] Another two deputies were elected from the reserved seats, bringing the total to seven.

TABLE 5.3. *Afrodescendants in Colombian Congress, 2014*

Senate	Name	Party	
	Edinson Delgado Ruiz	Liberal Party	
Lower house	Name	Party	Province
	Yahir Fernando Acuña	Movimiento Político 100% por Colombia	Sucre
	Julio Gallardo Archbold	Movimiento de Integración Regional	San Andrés
	José Bernardo Florez Asprilla	Partido de la U	Chocó
	Carlos Julio Bonilla Soto	Liberal Party	Cauca
	Nilton Córdoba Manyoma	Liberal Party	Chocó
	Carlos Alberto Cuero Valencia	Centro Democrático	Valle
	Elbert Díaz Lozano	Partido de la U	Valle
	Guillermina Bravo Montaño	Movimiento Independiente de Renovación Absoluta (MIRA)	Valle
	Hernan Sinisterra Valencia	Liberal Party	Valle

Source: afrocolombianosvisibles (2014).

TABLE 5.4. *Organizations and Candidates Contesting "Black Community" Seats*

Election Year	Number of Parties/ Organizations (party list required after 2006)	Number of Candidates	Total Votes Cast
1994	n.a.	12	
2002	n.a.	23	210,572
2006	27	69	136,012
2010	67	169	427,089
2014	29	77	237,061

Source: Registraduría Nacional del Estado Civil.

contested elections outside of the reserved seats and none had won a seat in the "ordinary" races.[36]

---

[36] In 2010, the Afrocolombian National Movement won 10,000 votes in lower house elections in Caquetá province, 1,200 votes in Casanare, and 900 votes in Guainia. The same group won some 14,000 votes in the reserved district. The same year, the Afrocolombian Social Alliance

TABLE 5.5. *Electoral Results for "Black Community" Seats*

Winning Candidate	Party	Number Of Votes Cast for Person	Number Of Votes Cast for Party List (Post 2006)	Party Vote as% of All Votes Cast (Post 2006)
2002 Elections				
María Isabel Urrutia	United Popular Movement (MPU)	40,968		
Willington Ortiz	Not available	30,926		
2006 Elections				
María Isabel Urrutia	Afro-Colombian Social Alliance	n/a (closed list)	7,751	6
Silfredo Morales Altamar	Afrounincca	3,108	6,849	5
2010 Elections				
Yahir Acuña	Afrovides	n/a (closed list)	45,775	9
Heriberto Arrechea	United Popular Movement (MPU)	7,999	26,679	5
2014 Elections				
María del Socorro Bustamante	FUNECO	34,067	58,965	25
Moises Orozco Vicuña	FUNECO	13,249	58,965	25

Sources: National Civil Registry for 2002, 2006, 2014; Misión de Observación Electoral 2010 for 2010. Before 2006, it was not possible to vote for a party list.

As competition for the seats grew in 2006 and 2010, winners were elected with a smaller and smaller portion of the total vote (6 and 5 percent of the total vote in 2006 and 9 and 5 percent in 2010). By 2014, however, the winning list captured one-quarter of the total votes cast, with the bulk of support coming from two states (Bolívar and Valle). Table 5.5 lists the number of votes received by winning candidates and their lists, and the percentage of the vote received by winning lists relative to the total number of votes cast. (Remember that after 2003's changes to the electoral laws, parties were required to put forward a single list, but could choose whether to open the list to preference voting or to close the list).

Who casts votes for the "black community" seats? In the 1990s, it was not black voters. In the 1994 elections, only 12 percent of votes cast in the Pacific

won some 11,636 votes in the national Senate race, well below the threshold required to win a seat. Data from National Civil Registry (Registraduría Civil).

region (Chocó, Valle, Cauca, and Nariño provinces) were cast for the reserved seats. Even though the Chocó was the main area to benefit from Law 70, the principal piece of legislation advancing Afrodescendant rights, only 4,000 people voted for candidates contesting the special district (of a total of around 131,000 votes nationwide) (Agudelo, 2000, p. 122). In the 2000s, an even smaller share of voters cast votes for "black community" seats. In the department of Chocó, where over 60 percent of the population is classified as black, fewer than five percent of voters participated in "black community" elections over the decade (Escandón Vega, 2011, p. 34). Blacks make up around one-quarter of the population in the department of Bolívar, but only some one to two percent of voters cast votes for "black community" seats between 1994 and 2006 (Ibid.). In the city of Cali in 2006, where some one-third of the population is estimated to be Afrodescendant, a mere 2 percent of voters cast votes for the reserved seats (Giraldo García & López Jiménez, 2007, p. 11).

If not for their "designated" representatives, for whom do blacks vote? Historically, the Liberal Party has dominated the Pacific region. It supported the abolition of slavery in 1851 and the elimination of suffrage restrictions in 1931. Prior to that year, only literate and property-owning citizens could vote, resulting in the effective disenfranchisement of many Afrodescendants. Liberal Party administrations increased educational and infrastructural investment. Though black Liberal Party candidates have won elections by appealing, in part, to a racial vote (e.g., in some cases a "lack of blackness" was used to disqualify a competitor), racial affinity is not a sufficient explanation for their success. Rather, politicians maintained patronage networks similar (or more corrupt than) those elsewhere in the country. Votes were exchanged for the construction of public works, school scholarships, jobs, gifts, and social services (Agudelo, 2002, pp. 171–181).

As argued in Chapter 1, patronage networks pose an obstacle to the ability of programmatic political parties to mobilize voters on the basis of race and ethnicity. According to Paula Moreno, former Minister of Culture of Colombia (and the country's first black female minister), representation means the provision of goods: "When you ask someone what representation means for them, and what matters, they say: "What have you done for Tolima [a Colombian province]?" According to voters, doing something for Tolima means increasing its budget and raising its public status through symbolic gestures such as declaring and recognizing folk holidays.[37] The poorer the voter, the more appealing the patronage. Black politicians have been more likely to gain access to power through traditional clientelistic behavior than by advocating ethnic or racial rights.

The appeal of patronage may explain why, ironically, there appears to have been more black support for the reserved seats when nonblack deputies contested them. In the 2014 elections, 8 percent of voters in the department of

[37] Interview, San José, Costa Rica, July 26, 2011.

Bolívar (which is around one-quarter black) cast votes for the black seats, and three-quarters of these voters supported FUNECO, the organization that ended up capturing both seats.[38] Though FUNECO describes itself as a community development organization, media reports connected it to political figures condemned for association with paramilitary and trafficking organizations. FUNECO's patronage politics were more successful at creating constituencies of voters than two decades of ethnic outreach.

Conclusion

Older mechanisms for political inclusion, such as the group rights upheld by the French Estates-General, Zimbabwe's Lancaster House Constitution, Lebanon, Belgium or Bosnia-Herzegovina, derived from political pacts to make representative government *possible*, not to make it *good*. The quotas and reserved seats of the late twentieth and early twenty-first century, by contrast, were introduced to improve the quality of representative democracy. By giving excluded groups a voice in decision making, inclusion would enhance legitimacy and promote greater social equality.

Colombia's experiences show that institutional engineering to promote inclusion can produce unexpected consequences. The reserved seats initially offered a vehicle for indigenous parties and for candidates from black communities of the Colombian Pacific to gain inclusion. Twenty years later, the seats no longer fulfilled their original purposes. The creation of national constituencies and lax rules on ballot access made it possible for politicians with no connection to black movements to win "black community" seats and for nonindigenous parties to contest indigenous reserved seats. Some of the politicians elected to the seats sustained connections to paramilitaries, traffickers, and personalistic and patronage organizations, linkages shared by many others in Colombia's political class.

The important question is: If reserved seats further traditional, patronage, and even criminal, politics, why have them at all? (Gil, 2013) Should the seats be eliminated or should they be reformed? Some observers believe that indigenous parties should contest seats in ordinary races. The requirement to present a single list would compel unity, and the ability of voters to exercise preferences votes would accommodate diversity (Basset 2011).[39] The fact that more blacks get elected outside of the seats than in them suggests they are not needed to promote presence (Ibid.). Others have suggested that the "black community" seats be moved to the Senate, which is the more appropriate institution to channel interests of national concern (Giraldo García and López Jiménez 2007).

---

[38] Data come from the Colombian Civil Registry website, broken down by party and department.
[39] Basset agrees that some affirmative action – such as a lower PR threshold or a legislative allocation (two seats set aside that would go to the top two winners of preference votes) – may be necessary to guarantee a minimum presence.

Colombia's experiences fell short of good representation but were not unequivocally bad. Reserved seats increased the visibility of historically disadvantaged groups, leading to greater public attention to their interests. In other respects, inclusion did not significantly improve their welfare. Competition for the seats incited inter-group conflict and divisions within social movements, but otherwise did not make excluded groups significantly worse off. Reserved parliamentary seats for black communities and indigenous people were simply seats. In Colombia and elsewhere, mechanisms of inclusion may form part of a package of measures to improve social equality and the quality of democracy, but should not be the only or even the most important component.

6

Brazil: Combatting Exclusion through Quotas in Higher Education

Brazil is home to the region's largest Afrodescendant population, longest tradition of race-based organizing, most institutionalized official system of data collection by skin color, and greatest (albeit recent) degree of state attention to racial inequality. Government agencies at all levels have introduced affirmative action programs to expand opportunities for nonwhites. Yet the state has eschewed candidate quotas or reserved seats.[1] Instead, the principal form of affirmative action consists of admissions quotas in public universities aimed at poor Afrodescendants and other economically disadvantaged citizens. Starting in 2001, when the state legislature of Rio de Janeiro abruptly approved a 50 percent "social" quota and then a 40 percent race quota for two state universities, quota policies snowballed around the country. By 2012, when the national congress approved a law mandating quotas by class and race in all federal universities, 71 percent of all public universities already had affirmative action programs (Feres Júnior, Toste Daflon, & Campos, 2012).

As courts in the United States tightened the legal parameters surrounding consideration of race in university admissions, Brazil moved in the opposite direction. The Brazilian government's embrace of race as a category for public policy puts it at odds with its northern counterpart as well as with its own historical tendencies to deny the racialized nature of social inequalities. Official discourse and conventional wisdom denied the salience of race and insisted

---

[1] There have been several proposals to create quotas and reserved seats for Afrodescendants, but by 2014, none had been successful. In 2011, Bahian deputy Luiz Alberto proposed a constitutional amendment to create reserved seats in the federal Chamber of Deputies and all state legislative assemblies, with the number to reflect the population share of *pretos* and *pardos* in each state. The seats would expire at the end of five legislative sessions. Proposta de Emenda à Constituição (PEC) 116/11. Others have endorsed political reforms to create closed lists within Brazil's proportional representation electoral system and quotas stipulating the inclusion of Afrodescendants among the rank-ordered candidates. Some government agencies have introduced quotas for positions in the state bureaucracy.

that discrimination revolved primarily around class. Why did the country suddenly seem to adopt an extreme, rigid form of affirmative action?

Brazil's quota policies may not be such a radical departure from its historic approach to race. Though the Afro-Brazilian movement fought for affirmative action and conceptualized quotas as a way to promote racial inequality, class criteria were actually more pervasive in the laws and policies eventually adopted. More universities have adopted quotas based on social class than on race, and the national law nests racial criteria *within* class criteria to preclude well-off blacks from taking advantage of the policies. Race is not an *independently* valid basis for affirmative action. It should be taken into account only after class.

This chapter accounts for the evolution of affirmative action policy in Brazil. I analyze the transition from the Cardoso era to the Workers' Party administrations, explain the focus on higher education, and explore the relative weight of race- and class-criteria in affirmative action. I explore the policies' use of racial categories and the challenges in targeting beneficiaries by race. In addition, I compare the purposes of university quotas and political quotas. Whereas the latter explicitly address the status hierarchy privileging whiteness by targeting elites, the former focus on redistributing and expanding access to resources in society. In other words, political inclusion is more about recognition, and university quotas are about redistribution.

An important question is whether redistribution alone can combat racialized inequality. At the end of the chapter, I examine briefly the case of Cuba, which offers a test about the extent to which a class-based approach "works" to solve racial inequalities. The Cuban revolution's emphasis on access to education, health care, and employment is reminiscent of the Brazilian approach to race via redistribution of resources. Yet decades after the revolution, though Cuba's Afrodescendants have achieved parity in education, employment, and other social indicators, racism persists. Cuba's lesson for Brazil is that racial inequality cannot be "solved" via universal policies targeted at expanding opportunities. *Racialized status hierarchies must be explicitly and independently addressed*, which is why political inclusion is a potentially valuable policy tool.

What Accounts for Brazil's Policy Change?

In light of Brazil's historical experiences and national ideology, the country's decision to embrace race-based public policies at all is surprising. Though racial status has long been correlated with poverty, income, education, mobility, and access to resources, Brazilians of all colors remained faithful to the idea of racial democracy for decades. Racial democracy maintains that, since Brazil did not experience legal segregation along the lines of the US South or South Africa, race relations are harmonious. Pervasive miscegenation, the numerical preponderance of free blacks, and social recognition of intermediate racial categories helped the country avoid the racial violence of the US South and South Africa (Degler, 1971; Freyre, 1986; Hanchard, 1994; Harris, 1964; Skidmore, 1993b; Tannenbaum, 1946). Though Brazilians are color conscious, and classify one another with hundreds of different phenotypical categories, the state did not enforce binary racial categories and uniform principles of classification. Racial divisions are seen to be less pronounced than in the United States, where the government historically enforced the classification principle of "hypodescent" (according to which mixed people were classified with the subordinate group) (Harris, 1964), and the census upheld a uniform set of racial categories (though these categories have changed over time) (Nobles, 2000).

The Brazilian census counts by "color." Though not interpreted to be the same as race, the terms are often used as synonyms or jointly (as in the common "race/color"). Criteria for classification in Brazil are plural and shifting, and the size of different groups changes, often dramatically, depending on how they are counted (Bailey et al., 2013). For the most part, phenotype, rather than descent-based criteria, tends to prevail, though perceptions of phenotype may vary widely. One implication is that siblings with the same parents can belong to different "racial groups" (Harris, 1964; Telles, 2004). Another implication of the low institutionalization of racial categories is that, though discrimination is pervasive, its dimensions are subtle and flexible. Racism is therefore more easily denied. Most Brazilians insist that social inequalities derived from class discrimination and the legacy of slavery, not racism.

Why did the state suddenly welcome affirmative action after decades of denying racism? In an earlier article (Htun, 2004a), I argued that the presidency of Fernando Henrique Cardoso (FHC, 1995–2002) proved a watershed for the Brazilian state's approach to race. Though social scientists (including the president, a sociologist) had been publishing evidence of racial inequality for decades, and black social movements had been organizing around racism, the state did little besides upholding laws banning discrimination (Htun, 2004a). There was more government action after the return to democracy in 1985, including creation of the Palmares Cultural Foundation and collective titling of land belonging to former *quilombos* (communities formed by runaway slaves). State governments in Rio de Janeiro and São Paulo established agencies to promote Afrodescendant rights and appointed black officials to senior posts (Andrews, 1991; Nascimento & Larkin Nascimento, 2001). Yet there was no official discussion of affirmative action until the FHC administration, which assumed power in 1995.

At that time, the federal government created high-level working groups and launched a National Human Rights Plan specifically to combat racial inequality through affirmative action, among other measures (Htun, 2004a; Reichmann, 1999). In a process accelerated by Brazil's preparation for the World Conference on Racism, held in Durban in 2001, numerous state agencies began to launch affirmative action policies and introduce racial quotas in hiring, including several ministries, the Constitutional Court, and the diplomatic training school (Rio Branco Institute). In 2002, an executive decree created the National Affirmative Action Program (Htun, 2004a). Compared to the changes that came later, during the governments of Lula and Dilma Roussef, these policies seem timid. Yet in light of the hegemony of racial democracy and historical pattern of state inaction, they were revolutionary.

I attributed the Cardoso-era changes to the president's own beliefs, which led to the appointment of key senior officials (such as Paulo Sergio Pinheiro, secretary of state for human rights), and triggered a transformation in official discourse and policy. In addition, I traced the emergence of an "issue network" linking black social movements with white economists in prestigious research institutes, journalists, nongovernmental organizations (NGOs), private foundations, and government officials. The network gained credibility because of the growing visibility of social science studies, conducted by government officials, which evinced the durability of racial inequality. In addition, the Ford Foundation began to target support at groups endorsing affirmative action. This confluence of factors enabled the racial equality issue network to take advantage of the political openings created under the Cardoso presidency to push for more expansive changes. An Afrodescendant caucus began to meet regularly in the national legislature and in 2001, the first-ever meeting of black federal and state legislators was held in Salvador. Finally, the World Conference on Racism motivated soul searching and "imposed a deadline for consensus on change" (Htun, 2004a).

Some of these same factors motivated parallel action by state governments, including the quotas in higher education admissions that later spread throughout the country. In the 1990s, a deputy from the Workers' Party (Carlos Minc) introduced, to the Rio de Janeiro state legislature, several bills to create special slots for low-income students and for disadvantaged ethnic-racial groups in public universities. Minc had worked with social movements, student groups, and university officials to develop his proposals (Peria & Bailey, 2014). None of Minc's bills became law, but they were discussed in the assembly and put the issue of educational quotas on the legislative agenda. Several years later, other politicians seized on Minc's ideas.

In 2000, Governor Anthony Garotinho submitted a bill to the Rio de Janeiro legislature establishing a 50 percent admissions quota for public school students in state universities. It took university officials by surprise.[2] The Progressive Party of Brazil (Partido Progressista [PP]) deputy José Amorim, a politician without connections to the black movement, introduced a bill establishing a 40 percent quota for *negros* and *pardos*. Amorim claimed to have been inspired

---

[2] In an interview, the rector of Rio's state university (Universidade Estadual do Rio de Janeiro [UERJ]) recalled that in a meeting about another issue, Garotinho casually mentioned to her that he would shortly introduce a bill to the state legislature to establish a 50 percent quota in her university. She almost fell out of her chair (interview with UERJ Rector Nilcéa Freire, Rio de Janeiro, July 5, 2002), originally cited in Htun (2004a).

by the World Conference on Racism, held in Durban, South Africa, statistical data on racial inequality, and some national initiatives to combat inequality (Peria & Bailey, 2014). Yet he acted alone in promoting the bill and shepherding its passage through the state assembly. Both bills (the public school and "racial" quotas) were adopted by the state legislature in 2000 and 2001, respectively (Ibid.).[3] Approval of both bills was so rapid as to preclude public debate and input; many members of the black movement did not even know a racial quota was being considered (Htun, 2004a).

Admissions quotas, and particularly the use of racial criteria, proved extremely controversial (as will be discussed more in the text that follows). Many prominent black leaders, including Rio de Janeiro Governor Benedita da Silva[4] and then-deputy Paulo Paim, defended quotas as a way to force people to talk about race, an important goal in light of the historic Brazilian tendency to deny its relevance. Yet some sectors of the Afro-Brazilian movement complained that they were unable to express any criticism without being accused of complicity in racism (Htun, 2004a). Others criticized quota laws' inattention to the financial problems of students after entering the university and use of the category *pardo*, which ignored the work of the movement to consolidate all Afrodescendants under the *negro* label (Peria & Bailey, 2014) (more on the categories used by the law later).

Though policy changes on race were initiated prior to the assumption of power by the Workers' Party, it was under the presidency of Luiz Inácio Lula da Silva (Lula, 2003–2010) and his successor, Dilma Rousseff (2011–present), that affirmative action was institutionalized. The 2000s witnessed the proliferation of affirmative action policies in public universities around the country, the widespread embrace of race as a category in public policy and political discourse, and the establishment of multiple programs directed at expanding opportunities and improving the social status of Afrodescendants. To attract black votes, many of the country's major political parties created "black" or "Afro" wings, such as "Tucanafro" in the Partido da Social Democracia Brasileira (PSDB) and "PMDB Afro" in the Partido do Movimento Democrático Brasileiro (PMDB).

Affirmative Action

What steps did Lula take? One plank of Lula's presidential campaign was "No Racism in Brazil" (*Brasil sem racismo*), which committed the candidate to combating racial inequality through affirmative action. Shortly after assuming office, Lula created a state secretariat for the promotion of racial equality

---

[3] The law's use of the category "negro" reflects the influence of black social movements, differs from past practice, and is discussed in the text that follows.

[4] When Anthony Garotinho resigned as governor in 2002 to run for president of Brazil, his lt. governor assumed his post.

(Secretaria de Políticas de Promoção da Igualdade Racial [SEPPIR]) and signed a law obliging public schools to teach Afro-Brazilian culture and the history of Africa (Feres Júnior et al., 2012, p. 403). He launched the Programa Universidade para Todos (PROUNI) program, which funded tens of thousands of scholarships for low-income students in private universities and adopted a federal policy on the health of the black population, which aimed to combat racism in the public health system, among other goals (Ministério da Saúde 2010). In 2010, he signed into law the Statute of Racial Equality, which set forth principles of racial equality and committed the state to promote affirmative action.

The vast majority of public universities began to adopt affirmative action programs in the 2000s. Most were introduced by universities themselves, though some programs were created by state law.[5] The federal government took additional measures to expand access to higher education. Overall, educational affirmative action programs included:

- Admissions quotas by public school (social). The vast majority of quotas applied to graduates from public schools, widely viewed as a proxy for class.
- Admissions quotas by income (social). Some universities employed income criteria, defined as multiples of the minimum wage, in their quotas.
- Admissions quotas by race/color. Relying largely on the principle of self-declaration, these policies applied quotas to nonwhites, who were classified in different ways, such as by the census categories (*preto* and *pardo*), the newer term *negro*, and, in some cases, the terms *afro-descendente*, *afro-brasileira*, or *raça negra* (Feres Júnior, 2008).
- Bonus points. Some universities, including the prestigious University of São Paulo (USP), State University of Campinas (UNICAMP), and the Federal University of Minas Gerais (UFMG), added points to the entrance exam score of people belonging to socially and/or racially defined categories (Paixão, Monçores, & Rossetto, 2012).
- Scholarships by public school. By 2012, PROUNI (a program created in 2004), designed to enable lower income students to attend private universities, had benefitted more than 900,000 students with full scholarships and some 740,000 with partial ones (Feres Júnior et al., 2012, p. 404). Families with per capita income of less than three minimum wages could qualify. In addition, students with partial scholarships could apply for federal loans to finance the remainder of their tuition through a program called Financiamento Estudantil (FIES).
- Scholarships by race/color. PROUNI applied quotas in the distribution of scholarships for *pretos*, *pardos*, and indigenous peoples according to their share of the population in each state.

---

[5] Of the seventy-three university affirmative action programs studied by Peria and Bailey in 2011, 19 were established by state law, while the rest introduced by university decision (2014).

In addition, some universities added admissions slots that could be filled only by members of determined groups (*acréscimo de vagas*). Left unfilled, the slots remained vacant; they were not redistributed to the general population (Feres Júnior, 2008, p. 45).

Under the presidential administration of Lula's Workers' Party successor, Dilma Rousseff (2011–), two blockbuster Constitutional Court decisions affirmed the legality of race-based affirmative action. The first decision, issued in April 2012, affirmed the racial quotas in university admissions and the second, from May 2012, validated the use of racial criteria by PROUNI. Then, in August of the same year, Rousseff signed a law establishing a 50 percent "social" quota in all federal universities. The social quota required that half of admissions slots be allocated to students from public schools. Within the social quotas, half of slots were to be reserved for students whose families earn less than 1.5 minimum wages, and half for students with families earning above that level. Within each income band, slots were to be reserved for people self-identifying as *preto*, *pardo*, or indigenous, in accordance with their share of the population in each state.

As this brief sketch shows, affirmative action in Brazil focuses on access to higher education, not political inclusion or on support for minority-owned businesses.[6] Why the focus on higher education? Widely recognized as the principal mechanism of social mobility, educational levels are closely correlated with income, meaningful and stable work, and security. Yet enrollment in higher education reflects and magnifies social inequalities. In 2008, 21 percent of whites ages eighteen to twenty-four were enrolled in postsecondary education, compared to merely 8 percent of nonwhites (*pardos* and *pretos*). Though overall enrollment grew considerably over time for both groups – in 1988, only 8 percent of whites and 2 percent of *pardos* and *pretos* were enrolled – the gap between whites and nonwhites has persisted (Paixão et al., 2010, p. 227).

Public higher education is free, and most of the best institutions are public. Demand for admission greatly exceeds supply. Dozens of applicants compete for each slot in the most prestigious fields of study in public university – including medicine, law, dentistry, and engineering. The only criterion for admission to university is one's score on the entrance examination (*vestibular*). Lower and middle-income students tend to lose out in this competition, for two reasons. First, the excellent primary and secondary schools that offer the best training for such exams tend to be private, accessible only to the well off. A majority of university students come from private schools, but the vast majority of Brazilians – 86 percent – go to public schools (Schwartzman, 2008a). Second, success on the *vestibular* usually depends on completing preparatory courses, which are expensive and accessible primarily to well-off students from private schools (Schwartzman, 2008b, 2009).[7]

---

[6] Bills to create candidate quotas and reserved seats have been presented in Congress but as of 2014, not approved.

[7] As we see later, organizations to offer pre-*vestibular* training for poor students, including Afrodescendants, were established in Rio de Janeiro beginning in the early 1990s and later

Intellectual elites graduating from public universities have tended to be the economic elites who are able to pay for good private secondary schools and supplementary preparatory courses, dramatically diminishing the chances for upward mobility on the party of lower and middle classes. Quotas – whether social or racial – have been advanced by advocates as the most efficient mechanism to break this perverse cycle (Guimarães, 2008, p. 184). The small range of variation in Brazilian affirmative action policies stems from the central role of the *vestibular* exam in the admissions process. Effectively, affirmative action programs redistribute the results of the *vestibular*, so that individuals of certain social groups compete against one another for a subset of the total number of admissions slots (Feres Júnior, 2008, p. 45). Advocates of quotas attribute growth in the numbers of *pardos* and *pretos* in higher education in the 1990s and 2000s to the introduction of affirmative action (Paixão et al., 2010, p. 231).

The Growing Dominance of Class over Race

Higher education quotas were consolidated and expanded dramatically under the two Workers' Party administrations. As is clear from the inventory of measures, policies did not employ only racial criteria. Though the black movement fought for affirmative action, in the eventual application, social or class criteria were actually more pervasive. Of the approximately seventy universities practicing some form of affirmative action in 2012 (out of a total of ninety-six public universities in the country), sixty used class criteria – operationalized primarily by a public school background–while forty used race (Daflon et al., 2013).[8] What is more, universities almost always applied social criteria on top of racial ones to preclude well-off blacks from taking advantage of the policies. Evolving policy trends suggest that race-based affirmative action was hijacked by a class-based approach to social inequalities.

The experience of reform in Rio de Janeiro, where admissions quotas were first adopted, illustrates how policies changed to privilege class over race. In Rio, the laws initially treated class and race separately. As described earlier, state laws adopted in 2000 and 2001 in Rio de Janeiro established quotas for public school students and for black students (at 50 and 40 percent, respectively). Initially, the state university applied these quotas in distinct ways: different entrance portals were created for private and public school candidates, and the racial quota was calculated on top of these. A candidate did not have to meet both criteria to qualify (Htun, 2004a, p. 71, fn. 21).

Implementation of the policies – particularly their use of race/color criteria–provoked a backlash. Academics, public intellectuals, and others argued

---

spread throughout the country. Groups offering such courses were important advocates of educational quotas.

[8] Different scholars have produced slightly different numbers but concur on the general trends. Peria and Bailey (2014) analyzed seventy-nine affirmative action programs, of which thirty-nine used racial criteria, while sixty targeted public school students.

that quotas violated constitutional principles of equal rights, imported a binary racial system into Brazil, doing violence to its history and traditions of mixing and fluidity, and were an ill-conceived response to the problem of low quality public schools (Fry et al., 2007; Maggie & Fry, 2004; for analysis of objections, see Feres Júnior 2008). Meanwhile, hundreds of students filed lawsuits claiming their test scores were higher than those of students admitted under racial and public school quotas. There were reports of white students fraudulently self-identifying as black. In addition, quota beneficiaries overwhelmingly included students from elite public schools with competitive admissions processes and not students from "regular" public schools. Combined with the perceived lack of legitimacy of the quotas due to their rapid approval, there was an overwhelming desire to submit affirmative action to reform (Peria & Bailey, 2014).

A working group coordinated by the state's education ministry, which included university officials and representatives from movements advocating the rights of lower income students (particularly Educação e Cidadania de Afrodescendentes e Carentes [EDUCAFRO]), considered different proposals for reform, most of which involved further refinement of the group to benefit from quotas. According to Peria and Bailey, EDUCAFRO members wanted the law to target only the neediest students, including darker skinned blacks who were more likely to be victims of racism and people from very low-income backgrounds (2014).

Since university officials opposed the introduction of systems to verify applicants' racial status (to make sure they were "truly" black) (though such a practice had been used at the National University of Brasília, see Chor Maio & Ventura Santos, 2005), the working group agreed to introduce more stringent criteria to define quota beneficiaries. This would involve eliminating the "*pardo*" category and adding an income qualification, both of which would prevent relatively well-off students from public schools from taking advantage of the quota (Peria & Bailey, 2014). The idea that quotas should benefit only the truly disadvantaged, bypassing middle- and upper income black students, was widely shared (Feres Júnior, 2008). The final proposal, approved by the state legislature in 2003, created a *45 percent quota for low income students* in university admissions, including 20 percent from public schools, 20 percent who self-identified as *negro*, and 5 percent indigenous or disabled.

Affirmative action policies in other states similarly subsumed race to class. Though race was taken into account by a significant number of affirmative action policies adopted before the national law (forty of some seventy), to qualify, black students had to be from public schools (thirty), demonstrate low family incomes (five), or both (one). In only four programs analyzed by Daflon et al. was race alone a valid criterion to qualify for a quota (2013, p. 313).[9]

---

[9] Peria and Bailey's (2014) data reveal similar trends. They identified thirty-nine programs using race, of which twenty-eight required black students to come from public schools and five required documentation of low incomes. In only six of thirty-nine programs (15%) was race alone sufficient to qualify for the quota.

Only the poor and/or the poor *and* black could qualify. The main beneficiaries of Brazil's quotas were therefore public school students (Daflon et al., 2013). This trend reflects recognition of the disadvantage they suffered relative to private school and better-off students in the *vestibular* process as well as entrenched resistance to race-based public policies. Some university administrators have described the inclusion of class criteria as a "conciliatory" measure aimed to gain broader public acceptance while responding to demands of black movements (Ibid., p. 312).[10]

The Invention of *"Negro"*

A notable feature of some of Brazil's affirmative action policies is their use of the category *negro*. The Brazilian state had historically counted nonwhites in the census using other terms: *preto* (black), *pardo* (mixed, not black, not white), and *amarelo* (yellow, for Asian). The intermediate *pardo* category recognized racially mixed individuals. Yet the official classification scheme was perceived to dilute Afro-Brazilian collective identity and was criticized for facilitating whitening (Bailey, 2009; Hanchard, 1994; Nobles, 2000; Telles, 2004). Prior to the 2000 census, some groups mobilized a campaign to convince Afrodescendants of various shades to reject the whitening ideology that had encouraged them to classify as *pardo* and instead declare their color as *preto* (Nobles, 2000). The idea was that promoting a unified, black identity with a clearly demarcated boundary would help expose racism, mobilize blacks to combat it, and make society as a whole more aware of inequality.

Luisa Schwartzman describes these efforts as a new "racial project" produced by an alliance of black movement activists and social scientists. Decades of social science research on racial inequality in Brazil had revealed that both *pretos* and *pardos* lagged whites in terms of basic social indicators such as income and education and that, statistically speaking, both *pretos* and *pardos* were far more similar than either group was to whites (Schwartzman, 2009; Feres Júnior, 2008, p. 64; Hasenbalg, 1979; Henriques, 2001; Paixão et al., 2010; Silva, 1985; Silva & Paixão, 2014; Telles, 2004). Though an earlier generation of social scientists had written of whites (*brancos*) and nonwhites (*não-brancos*), scholars in the 1990s began to write of *brancos* and *negros* in part to ally themselves with the black movement's project to combat racial inequality (Schwartzman, 2009, p. 227; Henriques, 2001). The

---

[10] Some evidence from the state of Rio suggests that nonwhites are losing out in quota policies' emphasis on class. In 2002 and 2003, the years when the state's quota policy applied to public school students and "negros" and "pardos" separately, approximately 11 percent of the entering class of the Darcy Ribeiro Northern Fluminense State University was non-white (a total of forty students in 2002 and sixty in 2003). In 2005, with the application of the new law and its income requirements, the number of nonwhites in the entering class dropped to nineteen, and averaged only thirteen between 2005 and 2009 (approximately 3 percent of all students) (Feres Júnior, 2012, p. 13).

2010 Statute of Racial Equality adopted by the Lula administration codified the new racial project into law. The statute defined the "black population" (*população negra*) as people who declared their color as *preto* or *pardo* (Government of Brazil, 2010), thus moving Brazil one step closer to a binary, U.S.-style racial system.

Rio de Janeiro's quota policies offered Afro-Brazilian movements an opportunity to encourage racial reclassification. The same NGOs that shaped policy design in Rio lobbied other universities around the country to adopt affirmative action. They saw the implementation of university quotas as a chance to promote the integration of *pretos* and *pardos* into a single, *negro* racial group (Peria & Bailey 2014). Due to their influence, many universities and state governments used the term *negro* to refer to quota beneficiaries. Few adopted only the census terms *preto* and *pardo* (Feres Júnior, 2008). A small fraction of programs used the terms *afrodescendente*, *raça negra*, and *afro-brasileira*.

Most policymakers believed that "negro" applied to, and encompassed, people who would normally classify themselves under the *preto* and *pardo* census categories. They also assumed that beneficiaries would know what *negro* meant (*pardo* plus *preto*). But in fact, most of the population used different racial categories and had a different understanding of *negro* than the government and the black movement. Many *pardos* – who were among intended beneficiaries of quotas – did not think the *negro* category applied to them. Students at the State University of Rio de Janeiro surveyed by Luisa Farah Schwartzman tended to believe that *negro* referred only to very dark people (Schwartzman, 2008). The fact that popular understandings of the meaning of *negro* were at odds with elite intentions thwarted the ability of quotas to achieve their intended aims (Schwartzman, 2008, 2009). In fact, few Brazilians tend to identify with the category *negro*. In a 1998 survey, only around 5 percent of the population identified as *negro*, including most who considered themselves to be *pretos* (Feres Júnior, 2008, p. 62). In the 2010 Project on Race and Ethnicity in Latin America (PERLA) survey, merely 6 percent of respondents identified as *negro* in response to an open-ended question about their racial identification (Silva & Paixão, 2014).

The lived reality of Brazil's racial categories differs from statistical trends affirming the gap between whites and nonwhites. Unlike in the United States, being nonwhite in Brazil is not the same as being black. Binary distinctions do not characterize perceptions of inequalities (Schwartzman, 2009). Put another way, *pardos* are not *negro*. *Pardo* means "neither white, nor black" – an option in between the two racial poles. It is a residual category, and not often used in popular discourse (Campos, 2013; Feres Júnior, 2008, p. 63). For many students (and members of the general public), there is a big difference between a *negro* and a light *pardo* (Schwartzman, 2009). As Schwartzman points out, self-classification is informed by many criteria, including family history and dynamics, personal experience with bureaucracy, personal experience with racism and discrimination, and perceptions of policy purpose.

Classification practices shift from person to person and context to context, and are often reflexive, performed *after* engagement with a policy. Some students she interviewed who were light skinned didn't identify as *negro* because they didn't think they had suffered discrimination, and that quotas were for those who had suffered racial discrimination (Ibid.). Critics allege that, as a result of the policies' embrace of the term *negro*, many *pardos*, who are the majority of nonwhites, and have socioeconomic conditions as bad as *pretos*, are ignored in affirmative action policies or forced to be *negros* to qualify (Feres Júnior, 2008).

Are Quotas the Right Move?

Critics claim that, at best, quotas are a distraction from the real reasons for unequal access to higher education and at worst, a mechanism to racialize society and produce fresh divisions. In an open letter to the Supreme Court, a group of intellectuals and other prominent personalities (including former first lady Ruth Cardoso, an anthropologist), charged that the Workers' Party government's policies would induce the "naturalization of race," a discredited notion emanating from nineteenth-century European imperialism (Daher et. al., 2008). They argued that the effects of admissions quotas on social inequality are likely to be trivial, as they affect only the small minority of university students who are enrolled public institutions. Seventy-three percent of university students attend private institutions, many of which are operated as for-profit businesses, and to which the quota law does not apply (Schwartzman, 2013). The potential effect of quotas on the standards of excellence of top public universities could be "serious, and negative," as schools adjust to the influx of unprepared students (Schwartzman, 2008a).

Simon Schwartzman, a prominent education scholar and opponent of quotas, maintains that the principal cause of inequality in higher education is the poor quality of secondary schools. He argues that "the main limitation to access to higher education is not a shortage of admissions slots, nor a lack of funding, and much less any type of discrimination in the selection process. The big obstacle is the secondary school system, which still doesn't prepare students in sufficient numbers to feed the expansion that the higher education system has had" (Schwartzman, 2008b, p. 26). In 2005, fewer than 50 percent of Brazilians of appropriate age were enrolled in secondary school. Secondary school performance is highly correlated with family income and education (though there are racial differences within income bands). Since Brazil offers roughly as many admissions slots in higher education as there are graduates from secondary schools, it is not necessary further to expand the higher education system. Rather, getting people to enroll in, and complete, secondary school is the main challenge the country faces (Ibid.).

An additional challenge revolves around the inadequate training a public secondary school education provides for students entering university, a problem not addressed by the 2012 federal quota law. Simply placing students in university offers no guarantee that they will be able to gain an education and complete their coursework (Schwartzman, 2008a). Poor students have trouble acquiring supplies and supporting themselves while they study, a problem raised in early debates about quotas in Rio de Janeiro (Htun, 2004a). To address some of these concerns, an affirmative action program launched by the São Paulo state government in 2012 requires public school students entering university via quotas to attend a two-year preparatory college and supplies them with a monthly stipend (Schwartzman, 2013).

Critics are right that the quota law's use of racial categories has the potential to solidify racial identities throughout society (though likely only in the longer term). They also have a point that law's focus on elite university admissions does little to address the underlying causes of unequal access to higher education. But critics fail to acknowledge that the law has a potential upside as well: greater diversity among elites. If they induce changes in composition of Brazil's elite, quotas can help to dismantle the status hierarchy privileging whiteness and denigrating blackness. Jonas Zoninsein, a US scholar who defended earlier racial quota policies (before income requirements were introduced), admitted that they were likely to be taken advantage of primarily by better-off blacks. But he argued that they would alter stereotypes, change public impressions of the group, and could therefore help expand opportunities for everyone (Zoninsein, 2004). Affirmative action, Zoninsein wrote, is directed not just at problems of socioeconomic disadvantage but at racism – stigmatization and inferiority – which can lead to lower self-esteem and professional confidence among Afrodescendants (Ibid.).

During the first decade of the 2000s, the meaning of quotas in Brazil as a tool to promote recognition and combat racism was displaced by the emphasis on promoting redistribution and combatting socioeconomic disadvantage. The inequality posed by racial status on its own was inadequate to justify a policy intervention. Only people who suffered from a combination of racial *and* class subordination were entitled to benefit from quotas for university admission. Yet data continue to show that racial status shapes educational outcomes independently of income and family education (Schwartzman, 2008b). The important question is: Are class quotas an adequate tool to address racial hierarchies?

The Class-based Approach to Racial Inequality: Lessons from Cuba

Cuba's experiences pose lessons for Brazil's quest to improve the situation of Afrodescendants. They reveal the potential, and the limitations, of redistributive social programs as mechanisms to combat racialized inequalities. In Cuba, the socialist revolution was effective at improving health, education, and income and expanding blacks' opportunities for work. Yet the Revolution left intact many ingrained prejudices and stereotypes, such as the association of blackness with criminality, the aesthetic valuation of whiteness, and the perception of blacks as inferior and lacking, which continue to harm blacks and deny them equal rights, particularly in the context of market reforms introduced beginning in the 1990s (De la Fuente, 2001, 2013).

Prior to the revolution, gaps in well-being between blacks and whites were pronounced. During the first and second republics (1902–1958), much of the economy and society – particularly at higher echelons – remained segregated, though informally. Racial discrimination persisted and Afrodescendants were excluded from clubs, beaches, bars, and other recreational facilities; the higher ranks of the military and bureaucracy; and prestigious professions (De la Fuente, 2001). There was a significant gap in life expectancy between whites and blacks, and the latter were disproportionately more likely to be imprisoned, unemployed, crowded into shantytowns, and suffering poor living conditions (Domínguez, 1978, pp. 224–225).

The Revolution produced a radical transformation in past patterns of racial inequality and segregation (De la Fuente, 2001; Domínguez, 1978; Sawyer, 2006). An early revolutionary demand, the need to end racial discrimination was mentioned several times by Castro in early 1959, by other communist leaders, the press, and by Afro-Cuban intellectuals. At the same time, black military officers forced the desegregation of parks and clubs. A famous speech by Castro in March, 1959 set the stage for different groups including unions, professional organizations, intellectuals, and religious groups, to launch a massive assault on discriminatory practices and racist ideologies. The government opened access to beaches to everyone; remodeled public parks to end segregation; and, a year later, nationalized private clubs and then private schools. To end racial discrimination in hiring and promote equal opportunities, the state declared that all new employees would be hired only through the Labor Ministry, though it declined to institute numerical racial quotas (De la Fuente, 2001, pp. 259–285). The government spearheaded efforts to promote recognition of African influences on Cuban culture and expand the role of Afrodescendants in popular culture such as beauty contests (Ibid., pp. 285–296).

Data from the 1981 census reveal the profound influence of the Revolution on objective indicators of racial equality. The gap in life expectancy between whites and blacks had closed. Differences in high school and college graduation rates had been eliminated and most occupational sectors had been integrated (though white presence in administrative positions, and black presence in construction, was disproportionately high) (De la Fuente, 2001, pp. 307–312).

In spite of these important gains in health, education, and employment, the cultural status hierarchy privileging whiteness and denigrating blackness remained largely intact. Standards of status and beauty in the media continued to be white (Domínguez, 1978, p. 225). The state has not explicitly promoted such stereotypes, but its inaction has allowed them to persist and even grow (Sawyer, 2006). As a result, racial gaps have increased since the 1990s when the Cuban economy and society began to transform in the wake of the break- up of the Soviet Union and demise of socialism worldwide. Managers in the lucrative tourism sector have sought consciously to hire white employees and to exclude blacks. Low Afrodescendant presence in the tourist industry can be explained only by racism, as before the "special period," blacks were actually disproportionately represented in service jobs. Managers screen prospective employees by the criterion of "good presence," widely understood to mean whiteness. Remittances from Cuban exiles abroad have flowed primarily to white residents of the Island, who used them to found small businesses. Afrodescendant exclusion from this emerging free enterprise system has expanded racial income gaps (De la Fuente, 2001, 2007; Sawyer, 2006).

Afrodescendants are the vast majority of the prison population, more likely to be victimized by the police, and are scarce on television shows (De la Fuente, 2001, pp. 318–322; Sawyer, 2006). The status hierarchy contributes to, and is reinforced by, these trends. De la Fuente notes that, decades after the Revolution launched its assault on racism, "Black was still ugly. Black still meant deficit of culture and refinement, rates of schooling notwithstanding. Black was still associated with violence, rape, robbery, crime. Black continued to be black" (De la Fuente, 2013).

What went wrong? The communist leadership had always believed that racial differences would disappear under socialism. By 1962, the government claimed to have eliminated discrimination by race and sex, and the campaign against racism fizzled, with race rarely mentioned except to note the revolution's success in this area (De la Fuente, 2001, pp. 279–280). As de la Fuente notes, "the official declaration of racism as a solved problem ... precluded any effective public discussion of race in Cuban society and identified this important theme with enemy attempts to create 'divisions' within the Revolution." As a result, "race and racism were turned into taboos, untouchable themes within public discourse" (De la Fuente, 2007, p. 140). It was subversive to speak or write about any race problems (Domínguez, 1978, p. 225).

At the same time, Cuban authorities dismantled and banned those Afrodescendant associations, clubs, and media outlets that could have publicized ongoing discrimination and pressured for additional government intervention (De la Fuente, 2001, pp. 280–285; Domínguez, 1978). The lack of independent organizing in civil society made it impossible to monitor – and contest official claims about – progress toward racial equality. A parallel situation held with the regime's approach to gender. A philosophy emphasizing wage work as the primary means to bring about emancipation, the government's prioritization of state interests over the rights and autonomy of individual women, and the lack of an independent civil society of feminist groups to flag problems and pressure for change, has led to very uneven outcomes on women's rights (Htun, 2007).

Conclusion

The Brazilian government has done much more than the Cuban one to acknowledge and address race as an axis of social difference and hierarchy. What is more, it is a democracy in which civic groups organized around race and other interests can flourish and pressure the government. Yet many Brazilians continue to insist that racial stratification derives primarily, if not exclusively, from class inequality. This position contributed to the decision to nest racial quotas within class ones, rather than giving them an independent basis and justification.

Brazilian authorities should be wary of the Cuban trap of assuming that racial differences will be solved by socioeconomic redistribution, even when poor Afrodescendants are specifically targeted. As de la Fuente notes, "Racism is not simply a question of unequal distribution of resources; it is a cultural and ideological complex that needs to be actively and systematically dismantled" (De la Fuente, 2007, p. 140). The status hierarchy – institutionalized patterns of cultural value that position some groups as superior, good looking, normative, and moral, while casting others as inferior, lacking, ugly, and indecent – is an independent dimension of social justice. The status ordering of society is not caused by, and cannot be reduced, in Marxian fashion, to socioeconomic stratification produced by the division of labor (Fraser, 1997, 2003). Dismantling the status hierarchy involves not just reallocating resources but symbolic readjustment.

Whereas other countries in Latin America have sought to promote diversity from the top down – by introducing quotas and reserved seats in elected office – Brazil adopted a bottom-up approach. The idea is that creating greater numbers of highly educated, dark-skinned people will grow the network of black professionals and higher income earners, which, in turn, will enlarge the pool from which political leaders emerge and are recruited. Does a bottom-up, network-enlarging approach work to promote diversity at the leadership level?

Chapter 3 of this book reported that national governments and political parties worked to expand pools of potential women leaders for years. They offered financial incentives to parties to promote women, provided training to candidates and potential candidates, and organized mentoring programs, among other measures. These gradualist approaches were largely unsuccessful in getting more women to the top (see also Htun, 1997). The stubbornness of the glass ceiling, in spite of the growth of numbers of highly qualified women, strengthened the resolve of advocates, and helped convinced skeptics, to mobilize for gender candidate quotas. Coalitions of women politicians and activists believed that only a top-down, fast track approach could rupture institutionalized sexism in mechanisms of candidate selection (Dahlerup & Friedenvall, 2005). The success of quota laws in increasing women's numbers (in most countries) suggests that they were correct.

The experience of corporate efforts to promote managerial diversity in the United States lends additional support to top-down approaches. Dobbin and Kalev's longitudinal study of 800 companies over 31 years revealed that firms that placed women and minorities in top management teams saw growth in female and minority presence in lower management ranks. They observe that, "in putting a woman or African American at the top, a company signals that it is possible for these groups to succeed, provides a role model to inspire others, and installs someone at the top who believes that talent is widely distributed." Other, more bottom-up approaches, such as horizontal networking among members of disadvantaged groups and diversity training, were far less effective at promoting inclusion in the ranks of senior managers (Dobbin & Kalev, 2013; Dobbin, Kalev, & Roberson, 2013).

Policies to promote diversity in higher education may complement but will not substitute for mechanisms of inclusion in political office. Brazil's university quotas are intended to transform the educational, social, and economic opportunities of Afrodescendants, much as the massive economic growth of the 1960s and 1970s improved the status of middle-class women (Alvarez, 1990). Yet highly educated women with financial power in Brazil, the United States, and other large economies have spent decades frustrated in their attempts to gain access the upper echelons of political power (and the ranks of CEOs). There is little reason to think that Afrodescendant presence in power will match their emerging participation rates in other sectors unless explicit efforts are made to promote diversity in leadership.

7

After Quotas: Women's Presence and Legislative Behavior in Argentina (written with Marina Lacalle and Juan Pablo Micozzi)

What happened after quota laws were adopted? Did women's presence in power improve? Were there changes to legislative behavior and advocacy of women's rights issues? Activists and scholars often justified gender quotas by referring not just to political inclusion but also to political representation. Greater numbers of women elected officials – so the argument goes – leads to more deliberation over gender equality and raises the chances that legal and policy changes expanding rights will be adopted. As Mansbridge puts it: "[The] descriptive representation by gender improves substantive outcomes for women in every polity for which we have a measure" (2005, p. 622). This "story of the critical mass theory" has helped women activists around the world convince policy makers to fix targets, usually 30 percent or higher, for women's presence in politics (Dahlerup, 2006b, pp. 514–517).

Yet analysis of existing research demonstrates that women's political presence is "neither absolutely necessary nor entirely sufficient" for legislative action on women's rights (Beckwith & Cowell-Meyers, 2007; Celis & Childs, 2008; Celis et al., 2008; Childs & Krook, 2006; Reingold, 2008, p. 128). Some women advocate gender equality more forcefully than others; some men are more supportive than some women; and different institutional contexts foster differing amounts of feminist activity (Reingold, 2008). What's more, studies differ in how they conceptualize and measure representative behavior to advance women's rights (which many scholars call "women's substantive representation"). Whereas some conceive it as a *process* of articulating, advocating, and discussing concerns expressed by many women, others view it as an *outcome* that is reflected in changes of laws and policies (Franceschet & Piscopo, 2008). These differences signal a lack of consensus among both scholars and advocates about what it means for women to "make a difference" in political life (Dahlerup, 2006b, p. 517).

Scholars who analyze the *process* of representation tend to focus on activities such as bill initiation, legislator priorities, committee behavior, speeches, and the like. These studies tend to show that women are more likely than men to sponsor feminist legislation, prioritize gender equality issues, and seek to convince other legislators to support gender equality initiatives (see, e.g., Reingold, 2000; Schwindt-Bayer, 2006, 2010; Swers, 2002; Thomas, 1994). However, there is less evidence that women's presence results in positive *outcomes* on women's rights (Childs & Krook, 2006, pp. 523–534; Reingold, 2008, pp. 131–132; Wang, 2013). Some parliaments with few women have taken various initiatives to advance women's rights, while some legislatures with many women have done relatively little (Archenti & Johnson, 2006; Htun, 2002b; Longman, 2006; Tripp, 2006).

Do the changes that women bring to politics stop at *process*, that is, at the level of political discourse and legislative agendas? Or does women's greater presence also help transform policy *outcomes*? Using an original dataset that tracks the fate of some 170,000 bills in the Argentine Congress between 1983 and 2007, this chapter analyzes the relationship between women's presence in power and the introduction and adoption of gender-related legislation. The dataset encompasses three distinct stages in the evolution of women's presence, collinear with the phased implementation of gender quotas in the country: (1) low (pre-quota), (2) uneven (with a quota for just one legislative chamber), and (3) high (quotas for both legislative chambers).

The dataset makes it possible to test different ideas about the relationship between women's presence and legislative behavior on women's rights. Is the relationship linear, that is, does putting more women in Congress lead to a proportional increase in legislative activity? Or do significant changes first occur after women have achieved a "critical mass" of 30 percent of all legislators? Is the high presence of women in one legislative chamber enough to affect behavior, or do women need to reach a critical mass in both chambers? Finally, the chapter analyzes whether women's growing presence triggers a "backlash" that jeopardizes successful advocacy for women's rights. Do growing numbers of women bring about greater efforts by male party leaders and legislators to marginalize and isolate them?

The chapter shows that quotas are revolutionary in some ways but not others. In many countries, they promoted political inclusion by changing mechanisms of candidate selection to bring record numbers of women into elected office. Over time, the quotas became sedimented as common sense, applied by parties without a struggle. Though quotas did not always bring in women with feminist agendas, the Argentine evidence shows that their application coincided with greater legislative attention to women's rights issues. As women's numbers grew, both women and men became increasingly likely to present bills that touched on women. In addition, coalitions of women achieved some legislative victories, such as gender violence and reproductive health laws.

At the same time, quotas failed to modify other institutions that shape inclusion and representation. Some elements of political institutions were modified but others remained intact, a process scholars refer to as "layering"

(Franceschet & Piscopo, 2013, p. 22; Krook, 2009, p. 50; Streeck & Thelen, 2005a). Quotas got women into the legislature but not into the power networks or monopolies where political authority resides. Elite power networks conferring access to resources and high status continued to remain closed to women (Franceschet & Piscopo, 2013). Formal and especially informal practices continued to discriminate (cf. Piscopo & Thomas, 2012). As Franceschet and Piscopo put it, "Quotas alone do not transform the gender hierarchies that structure political careers and power networks" (2013, p. 2).[1]

Statistical evidence presented in this chapter demonstrates that women's growing presence made approval of gender-related legislation less likely, especially when a woman sponsored the bill. As women's numbers increased, the approval rates of bills on gender issues decreased. This pattern, though arithmetically logical since approval rates – even if they stay steady – will appear to decline as the number of bills grows, offers suggestive evidence that women politicians were marginalized by male party leaders and legislators. Our data lend support to the idea that quotas did not alter dominant features of politics, such as the power of party leaders to set agendas, structure committees, and impose partisan discipline at voting time. The structure of gender quotas – which added women to the legislature but divided them across parties – may have reduced women's collective political influence.

Quotas and Women's Presence

Gender quota laws have brought record numbers of women into national legislatures across Latin America. Due to quotas, women made up more than 30 percent of (at least one) national legislative chamber in Argentina, Bolivia, Costa Rica, Ecuador, Mexico, and Nicaragua in 2014. Quotas produced massive growth in women's presence in some countries: in Argentina, women made up a mere 6 percent of the lower house and 3 percent of the Senate before the quota law was adopted in 1991; after the 2013 elections, they had come to occupy 36 and 39 percent of seats, respectively. Women made up 14 percent of Costa Rica's unicameral parliament before the quota law was adopted in 1996; by 2014, this had increased to 33 percent. Not every country saw such gains, however: the effects of quotas have been more minimal in Brazil: women made up 7 percent of the Chamber of Deputies before the 1997 quota law and by 2014, their presence had grown to only 9 percent.[2] In Bolivia and Mexico, quotas have produced progressively greater effects over time as a result of revisions in the details of quota regulations (see Chapter 2 for data on women's presence in Latin American legislatures and countries with quota laws).

---

[1] For an alternative perspective stressing that claims of marginalization and invisibilization of women may be overblown, see Zetterberg (2008).
[2] In Brazil's 2014 elections, women's presence grew to 10 percent of the lower house.

Variation in the results of quotas can be attributed to electoral rules, details of the quota laws, and implementation (Baldez, 2004; Htun & Jones, 2002; Jones, 2009; Schwindt-Bayer, 2009). First, the effectiveness of quotas depends on the electoral system context: they work better in closed-list proportional representation (PR) systems and in larger districts. In closed-list systems, parties present ranked lists of candidates to voters, who in turn choose between competing lists. In larger districts, parties are more likely to elect more than one or two candidates per district, maximizing the chance that parties will elect people ranked third on the party list (the minimum position under the terms of most quota laws). Insofar as it increases party magnitude (the number of seats won by each party per district), district magnitude is a crucial factor (Matland, 2006).

Second, the details of the law matter, as parties tend to comply with quotas in a minimalist manner (Jones, 1998, 2009). If the law fails to contain a placement mandate – requirement that women be included in electable positions in party lists – it will be ineffective, even in a closed-list system. In Costa Rica's first application of a quota law – without a placement mandate – parties ended up placing women in low (merely decorative) positions on party lists. In addition, the law must be carefully constructed to eliminate loopholes. Until it was reformed in 2009, Brazil's law stated that parties had to *reserve* candidacies for women, but did not require that they actually *fill* those positions. Since parties were allowed to field 150 percent more candidates than slots, a party could run an all-male list while technically complying with the gender quota (Htun, 2001). In Ecuador, activists petitioned the courts to modify procedural laws that created a loophole in the quota law, effectively permitting parties to cluster women at the bottom of the party lists instead of alternating them with men (Vega, 2005).

Finally, parties must implement the quota. They have rarely done so voluntarily. Compliance was usually secured under threat of having party lists thrown out in court. Mounting a challenge to noncompliant lists, in turn, has often required special legislation so that third parties – not just the women candidates who were excluded – could initiate lawsuits. In Argentina, networks of women checked party lists to make sure women were included and challenged noncompliant lists in court to get them declared invalid (Durrieu, 1999). Bolivian activists, annoyed at the way party leaders tended to comply with the quota law by counting from the top to the bottom of the list (and minimizing women's chances to get elected), campaigned to get them to count horizontally. By counting across lists, from *titular* to *suplente*, the third slot of each list would correspond to the second titular position (Baldez & Brañez, 2005).

By 2014, Argentina had been applying a gender quota for more than twenty years; Mexico for eighteen, and Costa Rica, sixteen.[3] After a rough start, quotas had significantly reformed candidate selection. As Marcela Durrieu,

---

[3] Quota laws were passed earlier but applied for the first time in legislative elections in Argentina in 1993, Mexico in 1997, and Costa Rica in 1998.

architect of the Argentine quota law said to me in a 2009 interview: "The quota is naturalized. People no longer argue about *whether* women should be included on party lists. Now they argue about *who* they are. It's an enormous change. Young people think there has always been a quota and they think there are quotas everywhere!"[4] As Piscopo and Thomas put it: gender quotas have become a "regular feature of politics" that "party leaders cannot avoid" (Piscopo & Thomas, 2012, p. 10).

Who Are the Beneficiaries of Quotas?

Who do parties nominate to comply with the quota? Though activists helped ensure that women were placed on party lists in the ways specified by the law, they had no control over which women were actually included. It was up to party leaders to decide – the same party leaders whose reluctance to include women motivated the quota movement in the first place. Many observers report that party elites were more interested in loyal candidates than independent feminists. Often (but not always) they recruited women with familial ties to male politicians and party bosses. One Argentine party leader confessed to Jennifer Piscopo that "We filled the quota through marriage" (quoted in Piscopo & Thomas, 2012, p. 13). Candidates recruited for their loyalty generally had little connection to feminist movements and little inclination to fight for change on sexual violence, reproductive rights and the like. Feminist activists I interviewed in different countries complained that feminist women were rarely put on party lists and that the candidates picked by party leaders were often weak, a phenomenon that other scholars have also noted (Hassim, 2009; Schmidt, 2003; Tripp, 2006; Vincent, 2004).

There are gender differences in political trajectories that reduce women's political efficacy relative to men's. Looking at data on the backgrounds of Argentine politicians over five congressional periods, Franceschet and Piscopo found that far fewer women than men had held high-status positions providing access to resources. In particular, men are far more likely than women to have held executive branch positions (chief executive or cabinet minister in federal, provincial, or municipal governments) (51 percent of men versus 27 percent of women). Such positions give people the ability to command patronage networks and control pork via their access to public sector resources. They are frequently the launch pads of powerful political careers (Franceschet & Piscopo, 2013, pp. 16–18). Research from advanced democracies further confirms that men's career trajectories give them access to more financial resources and greater ability to generate name recognition than women (Iversen & Rosenbluth, 2008).

In Argentina, the label *mujer de* ("woman of") is commonly used to refer to women who entered power by virtue of the quota and their familial connections (Franceschet & Piscopo, 2008; Piscopo & Thomas, 2012). The use of the

---

[4] Interview, Buenos Aires, December 9, 2009.

label to malign a legislator's qualifications has led many women defensively to deny being a "*mujer de.*" Rival parties are criticized for filling their lists with "*mujeres de*". In the process, a cleavage has emerged between women who are "dependent tokens" and those who are "independent professionals," thwarting collective action to support bills promoting gender equality (Piscopo & Thomas, 2012, pp. 13–15). Notwithstanding these critiques, careful comparison of the backgrounds of women in the Argentine Congress reveals that they are at least – and usually more – qualified than the men (Ibid.).

The ascension of nonfeminist, conservative, and "token" women has sparked heated debates among activists. Is the physical presence of women important as an end in itself? Or does women's presence matter only if they are strong politicians committed to advancing gender interests? According to one Bolivian observer:

> If women from one day to the next become deputies, they don't assume their role in public responsibly. They aren't participating in major national decisions. I've done training courses for candidates and the women are totally ignorant. Quotas help women get there, but what we need is women who have worked all their lives and are ready to participate for real .... For quotas to have a symbolic effect, the women who are present have to be good. If women are supposed to open up opportunities for other women, they have to be good.[5]

Another activist from the same country concurred: "I'd rather have three good feminists than 60 women who sit there and do nothing."[6]

Other activists believe that the very presence of women, regardless of who they are and what they do, marks progress toward equality. As Colombian quota advocate Beatriz Quintero put it, "Obviously, the beneficiaries of quotas aren't feminists. They might even be against quotas. But when society sees more women in decision making positions, there's a cultural change, even if they aren't feminists or working on women's issues .... We're clear that presence is not the same thing as representation."[7] Former Bolivian minister Gloria Ardaya had a similar view: "Quotas aren't a panacea but they produce a demonstration effect. They help change culture."[8]

To be sure, not all the women who entered power via quotas were antifeminists and unconnected to the women's movement. Some parties – such as Mexico's Partido de la Revolución Democrática (PRD) – have a stronger track record putting feminists on party lists. Even in Argentina, where the "*mujeres de*" phenomenon is prominent, many women politicians have perceived a mandate to emphasize gender equality issues in their legislative careers. Franceschet and Piscopo (2008) attribute the "mandate effect" to the way that the campaign for gender quotas mobilized women in parties and civil society and

---

[5] Jimena Costa, Interview, La Paz, May 13, 2005.
[6] Diana Urioste, Interview, La Paz, May 12, 2005.
[7] Interview, Bogotá, June 7, 2004.
[8] Inteview, La Paz, May 11, 2005.

emphasized the need for parliament to address women's rights. As we see in the text that follows, women's greater presence in the Argentine Congress was associated with increased legislative attention to women's rights on the part of both women *and* men.

Effects of Quotas on Legislative Behavior: Theory and Hypotheses

A considerable amount of research from different countries reveals that women are more likely than men to take action on policy issues regarding women's rights. In Latin America, male and female legislators responding to surveys reported different views and levels of enthusiasm for policy concerning gender issues, although they expressed similar views on the economy, agriculture, foreign policy, and other topics. Schwindt-Bayer's research confirms that more women than men have tended to do constituency service on behalf of women, participate in meetings sponsored by women's groups, give floor speeches on women's rights issues, and sponsor and co-sponsor bills on gender issues (Schwindt-Bayer, 2006, 2010). Franceschet and Piscopo (2008) reported that quota laws in Argentina resulted in an increase in the introduction of women's rights bills, while Micozzi and Lacalle (2010) found that legislative co-sponsorship among women in Argentina's lower house increased following the quota law.

The notion that women are more likely than men to take action on behalf of women's rights generates the first two hypotheses tested in this chapter:

H1: *Women legislators are more likely to introduce bills related to women's rights than their male counterparts.*

H2: *As the presence of women grows in the House and the Senate, the number of women's rights bills submitted will also grow.*

However, conventional wisdom holds that women's advocacy for women's rights is not equally likely in all conditions. Many scholars have suggested that women must reach a "critical mass" – usually about 30 percent of a legislative body – to have an impact on politics (see, e.g., Childs & Krook, 2006; Dahlerup, 2006b; Grey, 2006; Tremblay, 2006). One early formulation held that a specific number of women had to be present to foster the formation of coalitions and advocacy on behalf of women (Thomas, 1994). The value of numbers is partly psychological: being with other women makes each woman feel more comfortable and empowered.[9] Moreover, their combined weight facilitates successful alliances and prompts changes in the organizational culture (Kanter, 1977b). Critical mass theory prompts the next hypothesis:

---

[9] In an interview, I asked then-senator and president of the Partido Revolucionario Institucional (PRI) María de los Angeles Moreno of Mexico how many women would need to be present in a room of ten people for her to feel comfortable raising an issue such as domestic violence. She replied, "Three." Mexico City, July, 1998.

H3: When women occupy 30 percent of the House and Senate seats, the number of women's rights bills introduced will sharply increase.

Yet the idea that women will bring changes to political life only when they reach a critical mass has spawned considerable debate. Critics have claimed that there is no precise threshold that triggers the effects of critical mass since legislative processes are contingent on other variables. Although 30 percent is widely touted, scholars have pointed out that small numbers of women can produce big policy changes while parliaments with many women can end up doing nothing. Whether women take action on women's rights depends on their personal preferences, time in office, political parties, and committee positions – as well as men's reactions and other variables including public opinion, the presence of feminist movements, and international norms. A crucial factor shaping policy activism is the existence of cross-party coalitions of women (*bancadas femeninas*) (Archenti & Johnson, 2006; Beckwith, 2007; Childs & Krook, 2006; Dahlerup, 2006b; Grey, 2006; Tremblay, 2006). As Dahlerup (1988, 2006b) put it, "critical acts" and not "critical mass" further women's rights.

Other scholars suggest that greater numbers of women might produce the opposite effect of that posited by critical mass theories: men who feel threatened by women's presence will work to marginalize and isolate women legislators. Thus an increase in women may produce a backlash that thwarts legislative activity on gender issues (Beckwith & Cowell-Meyers, 2007). Indeed, some research shows that male party leaders have segregated women in less important and less prestigious committees (Heath, Schwindt-Bayer, & Taylor-Robinson, 2005), excluded them from deliberations, and demeaned their words and contributions (Hawkesworth, 2003; Kathlene, 1994). Exclusion of racially- and ethnically-disadvantaged women is even more pronounced. One black Brazilian politician told me that "I was as combative as the white women, but was criticized for being too aggressive and talking too loud .... They even suggested that I straighten my hair."[10]

The gap between women's priorities and their behavior further supports the backlash thesis. Schwindt-Bayer (2010) shows that although women share similar policy priorities and preferences with men, they are less likely to sponsor legislation in areas that are traditional male "domains" (economics, foreign affairs, and budget). She argues that the "gendered legislative environment" marginalizes women. This problem may be particularly acute in a country such as Argentina where party leaders have greater control over individual legislators (Schwindt-Bayer, 2010).

A larger number of women may raise awareness of women's diversity. As they cease to be a marginalized minority and approach parity with men, fissures and subgroups among women will become more evident. Some scholars

---

[10] Interview with Maria José Rocha Lima (Zezé), Brasília, November 14, 2002.

hold that as overall numbers increase, individual women will be less likely to advocate for women on the assumption that their colleagues will take care of those matters (Carroll, 2001; Reingold, 2000). These views suggest a fourth hypothesis:

H4: *The growth in women's presence in the House and the Senate initially increases the number of women's rights bills but as women reach a critical mass, submissions will decline.*

These hypotheses imply that the relationship between women's presence and legislative behavior assumes different shapes. If there is no effect due to critical mass, the relationship is linear: adding more women to the legislature produces a steady increase in bills introduced. If the theory of critical mass is correct, a flurry of representative activity will occur once a certain presence threshold is reached. The backlash theory implies that activity on behalf of women's rights will rise with the numbers of women and then decline after their presence reaches a certain point.

Thus far, this analysis has focused on one dimension of legislative behavior: bill introduction. A frequently studied behavioral measure, bill introduction is an important indicator of representation. It calls attention to women's rights and helps to raise awareness among legislators and the general public. Yet bill introduction does not imply passage into law. Bills must first be put on the agenda and then survive committees and floor votes. The expectation that women's greater numbers will facilitate this process leads to the fifth hypothesis:

H5: *The higher the share of seats held by women in the House and Senate, the greater the chances of approval of gender-related bills.*

However, the backlash hypothesis previously discussed implies that the relationship is not so straightforward. The increased presence of women may trigger a backlash as men seek to defend their historically privileged position. A legislature has many gender hierarchies – like other organizational environments where women suffer discrimination and marginalization (Bjarnegård, 2013; Duerst-Lahti, 2005; Duerst-Lahti & Kelly, 1995; Franceschet & Piscopo, 2008; Hawkesworth, 2003; Piscopo & Thomas, 2012; Schwindt-Bayer, 2010). Power inheres in institutions crafted long ago by fair-skinned, heterosexual men to accommodate their needs and serve their interests (Bailyn, 2003; Hochschild, 1975; Rosser, 2004; Sturm, 2006). Male party leaders and legislators can simply ignore women's rights bills, preventing them from appearing on the committee agenda. The bills may languish and be archived before any action is taken. Or men may unite to defeat a bill. Such conditions would cause a decline in the approval rates of gender-related bills.

Other Hypotheses: The Institutional Context

A great deal of legislative scholarship casts doubt on the idea that the sex of legislators and numbers of women in the assembly should shape legislative behavior. According to these perspectives, other factors – such as party membership – are far more important determinants. Political parties are the central actors in legislative politics: they get representatives elected, organize majorities (and oppositions), and structure the agenda (Cox, 2006; Cox & McCubbins, 1993). Indeed, many scholars agree that party trumps gender as a determinant of legislative behavior (Reingold, 2000).[11] Htun and Power's study (2006) of the Brazilian Congress found party to be a more important determinant of legislator views on gender issues than the sex of the legislator. In her study of the United States Congress, Swers compared bill initiation and committee amendment behavior between men and women from the same party, not across parties (2002). Volden, Weisman, and Wittmer (2010) similarly analyzed how the majority or minority status of men and women affected their ability to keep their sponsored bills alive through later stages of the legislative process.

The importance of party membership varies throughout the legislative process, however. It clearly matters most for voting and agenda setting (Cox & McCubbins, 1993, 2005). But global evidence of partisan effects on bill drafting, patterns of co-sponsorship, and speeches is less conclusive. Factors such as popularity in home districts, career ambitions, territorial origins and even the proximity of offices are influential (Alemán, 2010; Calvo & Leiras, 2010; Crisp, Escobar-Lemmon et al., 2004; Highton & Rocca, 2005; Micozzi, 2009; Rocca & Sanchez, 2008; Rogowski, Sinclair, & Fowler, 2010). This suggests a sixth hypothesis:

H6: *Party membership is more important in determining the approval of a women's rights bill than the actual introduction of a women's rights bill.*

Committee structure and membership are other important influences on legislative behavior. The existence of a women's issues committee and a legislator's membership on it affect the number of women's rights bills introduced and how they are treated. Schwindt-Bayer (2006) found that a woman's tendency to introduce more bills on gender equality was significantly influenced by her membership on a women's issues committee. Yet men have tended to marginalize women on these committees to reserve the work on more powerful committees for themselves (Heath et al., 2005). The association between women legislators and gender-related legislation may reflect sex segregation by committee rather than the autonomous expression of preferences. This implies that:

H7: *Legislators who sit on women's issues committees are more likely to introduce bills related to women's rights.*

A final aspect of the institutional context is bicameralism. Starting with Montesquieu and the Federalists, literature on institutions has shown that the

---

[11] No study has shown gender to be the principal division in legislative activity. Instead, most congressional studies indicate that government/opposition dynamics are the main determinants of legislative behavior.

existence of a second chamber is highly relevant to the legislative process. It may promote consensus (Lijphart, 1999), delay or accelerate collective decisions (Riker, 1992), favor the maintenance of the status quo by adding a veto player (Diermeier & Myerson, 1999; Tsebelis & Money, 1997), or improve the position of overrepresented territorial units (Samuels & Snyder, 2001). Most work on gender-related legislative behavior seems to apply to single chambers. However, Kittilson and Schwindt-Bayer (2010) show that bicameralism, as an institution to safeguard minority rights, can promote women's involvement in politics. Despite including upper houses in their samples, other studies (Jones, 2009; Schwindt-Bayer, 2006) did not theorize the implications of the bicameral format and the relevance of interactions between deputies and senators.

How might bicameralism shape the relationship between women's presence and legislative behavior? Even if one chamber adopts a large amount of legislation on women's rights, the upper house – with its different composition – could block it. There are numerous examples of important gender-related bills that were approved by one chamber but languished or died in the other. The Uruguayan Chamber of Deputies, for example, approved the legalization of elective abortion in 2002 but the Senate defeated the bill in 2004 (abortion was later liberalized for the first trimester in 2011). In Chile, the Chamber of Deputies voted to legalize divorce in 1998, but the Senate stalled for six years – until 2004 (Htun, 2009). Convinced that the other chamber will be unresponsive, women who would otherwise sponsor legislation and advocate for women's rights might deem such actions futile. The possibility that interchamber dynamics shape advocacy on gender issues – at bill introduction and in later stages of the legislative process – suggests that we need to take into account women's presence in both chambers when analyzing bicameral systems.

Background: The Argentine Congress

As shown earlier in the book, Argentina pioneered the use of gender quotas. First applied in the Lower House (30 percent) in 1993, quotas were later extended to the Senate (50 percent) after the introduction of direct popular elections to that chamber in 2001. Focusing on trends over time facilitates the empirical verification of competing theoretical approaches. Since electoral rules did not change dramatically in this period,[12] there is no reason to expect behavioral change due to varying incentives in the electoral system.[13]

---

[12] In 2001, direct election of Senators was introduced (previously, they had been appointed by state legislatures). But there was no change from a few delegates per district to many (as in Colombia), and no dramatic change in the number of parties represented after switching from PR to majoritarian rule or vice versa (as the literature on electoral rules predicts). See Micozzi (2013) for a discussion of behavioral effects related to the adoption of direct elections in the Argentine Senate.

[13] It is accepted that electoral rules influence intraparty dynamics and other aspects of representation. One view holds that single-member-district systems motivate elected officials to focus

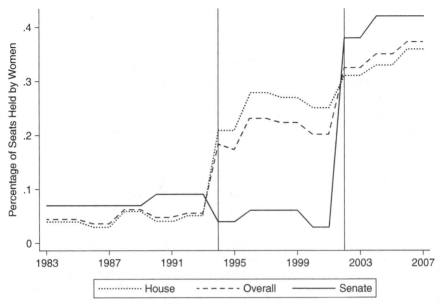

FIGURE 7.1. Women in the Argentine Congress, 1983–2007.

Second, the bicameral structure of the Congress has not changed since the state was formed in 1853. Third, the almost automatic impact of gender quotas on women's presence in the House and the Senate facilitates the use of quotas as a latent variable and a focus on women's share of seats as the main covariate.

The phased implementation of the gender quota law provides the opportunity to evaluate legislative behavior in three dissimilar environments: one without quotas (10 years), one with partial application (7 years in one chamber), and one with implementation in both chambers (6 ½ years). Numbers of women in each chamber differed significantly in these three periods. As shown in Figure 7.1, women's share of seats in the House increased from 6 to 37 percent between the first and second periods. Between the second and third periods, their numbers jumped dramatically in the Senate and continued to climb in the House. After quotas were applied to direct elections to the Senate in

on the needs of a single geographic constituency and the shared interests of the multiple social groups it encompasses. In contrast, PR systems with larger multimember districts make it possible for elected officials to aggregate votes from a smaller number of groups in a larger geographical area (Crisp et al., 2004). As a result, they may specialize in more thematic and social issues, such as gender equality (Grey, 2006). Variation in representative behavior is expected across PR systems depending on the degree to which electoral rules compel the cultivation of individual votes or induce candidates to focus on broad issues of national concern (Carey & Shugart, 1995).

2001, women's presence *in both chambers* exceeded the 30 percent threshold posited by critical mass theory.

In spite of the growth in women's presence shown in Figure 7.1, most of the literature on the Argentine Congress identifies factors other than gender as the principal influences on legislative behavior. For example, studies about roll-call voting have identified coalition membership – specifically the split between government and opposition – as the main predictor of legislative alignments (Jones, 1995, 2002; Jones & Hwang, 2005; Jones, Hwang, & Micozzi, 2009). Given the majority party's control of the agenda, bills that are likely to provoke disagreement tend not to advance to the plenary. Furthermore, individuals who do not support a party decision usually strategically leave the floor rather than vote against the party line (Jones, 1995). As a result, social cleavages – by region, religion, or gender – are rarely brought to bear on voting behavior.

What is more, the Argentine Congress is not a professionalized legislature (Jones et al., 2002). Owing to the structure of incentives generated by the electoral system, the internal organization of the legislature (Alemán, 2006), and federal institutions, legislators have progressive ambition but limited incentives to specialize and develop their legislative expertise (Micozzi, 2009). This reduces the number of legislators who invest time, resources, and energy to become policy specialists on gender-related and other issues. Finally, the power of governors, local leaders, and party bosses regarding candidate selection (De Luca, Jones, & Tula, 2002; Spiller & Tommasi, 2007) leaves little opportunity for a legislator's individualistic behavior, including leadership on gender issues. These features make Argentina a "critical case" for assessing the relationship between women's presence and legislative behavior on women's rights (Eckstein, 1975). If women manage to be effective in this most unlikely setting, where many factors conspire to reduce the influence of gender, women's political inclusion is likely to be able to induce political representation elsewhere.

Analysis and Results

This chapter analyzes the entire set of bills submitted to the Argentine Congress in the first twenty-four years of the current democratic period. This sample permits examination of change over a long period of time, with an enormously large-n, and allows comparison of the fate of bills on women's rights with that of other kinds of bills. Htun, Micozzi, and Lacalle collected information on 172,130 bills b submitted by legislator i in a year t between 1983 and 2007. The data are disaggregated at the bill level with information on content; the sponsor's district, party, and sex; the final status; the committees that worked on the bill; and the committee chair. Other levels of information have also been gathered, such as the total number of

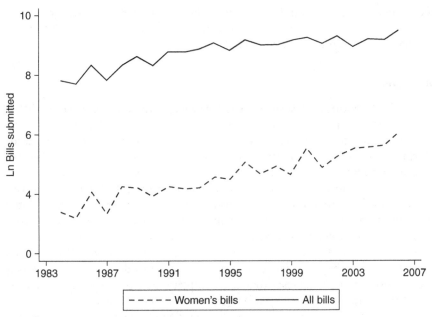

FIGURE 7.2. Trends in bill submission.

bills submitted by a legislator in a given year, their tenure in Congress, and the share of seats held by women in each chamber.[14]

The next step was to identify bills related to women's and gender issues, a difficult endeavor in such a huge sample. To minimize bias and make homogeneous choices, we developed an automated coding scheme that identified women- and gender-related keywords in the title and/or the description of each bill.[15] This method identified 3,272 bills, or 1.8 percent of the whole sample, as "women's rights bills." Around 18 percent of these bills were approved, in contrast with the 28 percent approval rate for other bills.[16]

Descriptive statistics illustrate trends over time in the submission of women's rights legislation. As Figure 7.2 shows, trends in bill submission were positive for both the whole (logged) set of legislation submitted and the logged number of women's rights bills. It could be argued that this growth simply

[14] Official information from the congressional website (www.hcdn.gov.ar).

[15] Keywords were determined by using the literature and consulting with other specialists. After the first wave of coding, the reliability of the criteria were adjusted, resulting in greater than 95 percent accuracy. Options for multiple words were incorporated to minimize spelling-based omissions. The coding scheme can be found in Htun, Lacalle, and Micozzi (2013).

[16] A minuscule portion of the bills identified this way did not seek to advance but rather to restrict women's rights, mostly regarding abortions. Excluding these bills from the sample left a total of 3,230 observations.

reflects increases in the number of seats in both chambers.[17] However, the figure shows that the number of women's rights bills grew at a (slightly) higher rate than the overall number of bills.

Estimations

To test the hypotheses described in the preceding text, we worked at different levels of aggregation. First, to assess the *process* of legislative activity, we focused on patterns of bill submission. These estimations took each legislator *i* at time *t* as the unit of analysis. This means that the year, not the particular congressional period, was used as the temporal cluster, which makes sense since legislators do not behave the same way year in and year out. With this legislator-level approach, the estimations used the number of gender-related bills submitted by year as the dependent variable. Given its nonnegative condition, an event count model was utilized. After testing for overdispersion in regular Poisson models, we realized that a negative binomial model performed better. However, the abundance of zeros in the dependent variable (79 percent of observations) suggests that the complete distribution of the outcome needed to be approximated by mixing two component distributions, one for the zero-outcome portion of the equation and the other for the positive values. Thus, the zero-inflated negative binomial model (Atkins & Gallop, 2007) appeared to suit the data structure better.

To assess the relationship between the introduction of women's rights bills and other types of bills, estimations were computed utilizing the total number of bills submitted annually per legislator as the predictor of zero values. We then estimated the expected number of gender-related bills as a function of the sponsor's sex, the weighted shares of women in the House and the Senate,[18] partisanship, chamber of origin, membership in a committee for women's issues, and indicators of institutional power such as committee chairmanship and congressional tenure. To avoid bias, errors were clustered at the legislator level.

Linear, critical mass, and backlash approaches have different implications for the relationship between women's presence and legislative behavior. Different models were estimated to discover the approach that best characterized the nature of increases in bill submission. The main independent variable – the share of seats held by women in both chambers – was specified in three different ways: as a simple linear variable; as a dummy variable that equals 1 if the weighted share of seats held by women is greater than 0.3, as suggested by critical mass theory, and 0 otherwise;[19] and as a quadratic variable added

---

[17] The House added three deputies in 1991, and in 1995 the Senate added a third member per province bringing the size to seventy-two.

[18] Percentage of seats held by women in each chamber, weighted by the relative size of the chamber.

[19] We did not test the critical mass hypothesis at other threshold levels.

TABLE 7.1. *Process Models*

Variables	Model 1 Linear	Model 2 Critical Mass	Model 3 Quadratic
Female	1.065***	1.113***	1.077***
	(0.125)	(0.125)	(0.121)
Share of Women	1.457***		0.121
	(0.412)		(1.528)
Threshold		0.282***	
		(0.104)	
Sq. Share of Women			3.203
			(3.741)
Peronist Party	−0.146	−0.160	−0.152
	(0.116)	(0.116)	(0.117)
Radical Party	−0.343***	−0.374***	−0.347***
	(0.126)	(0.125)	(0.126)
Center-Left Parties	−0.0562	−0.0890	−0.0847
	(0.248)	(0.254)	(0.255)
Senate Bill	0.286	0.315	0.300
	(0.230)	(0.223)	(0.228)
Women's Committee	0.597***	0.576***	0.593***
	(0.111)	(0.113)	(0.110)
Committee Chair	0.366**	0.375**	0.368**
	(0.151)	(0.156)	(0.151)
Tenure	0.0424***	0.0459***	0.0431***
	(0.0158)	(0.0159)	(0.0159)
Constant	−1.246***	−1.038***	−1.152***
	(0.136)	(0.120)	(0.177)
Linear Combination			3.324
			(2.299)
Number of Bills	−0.138***	−0.140***	−0.139***
	(0.0223)	(0.0226)	(0.0225)
Constant	2.069***	2.109***	2.080***
	(0.158)	(0.158)	(0.159)
Observations	5,935	5,935	5,935

Robust standard errors in parentheses ***$p < 0.01$; **$p < 0.05$; *$p < 0.1$.

to the continuous main covariate to test the curvilinear effects implied by the backlash hypothesis.

The analysis in Table 7.1 confirms many of the theoretical predictions. All three estimated models demonstrate that being a woman makes a legislator more likely to submit women's rights bills, as anticipated by hypothesis 1 (see the positive and highly significant coefficients to *Female* in models 1 to 3). Greater numbers of women in Congress also increases the expected number of women's rights bills. The results confirm the linear hypothesis (H2) that growth in the presence of women increases the number of women's rights bills introduced: *Share of Women* is positive and highly significant (model 1). The results also support the critical mass hypothesis (H3). As model 2 shows, the coefficient for *Threshold* is positive and highly significant. These coefficients support the intuition that boosting women's presence is likely to improve processes of legislative behavior regarding women's rights. Our results do not confirm the backlash hypothesis (H4): the coefficients for the linear and quadratic *Share of Women* (along with their linear combinations) in model 3 do not achieve significance or go in the direction expected. With all else equal, there is no upper limit on the effect of having more women in Congress with regard to the introduction of women's rights bills.

Addressing the question of which theory best explains the relationship between women's presence and legislative behavior – linear or critical mass – required an additional step. Evaluating the goodness of fit of models 1 and 2, and seeing how the Akaike information criterion (AIC) and Bayesian information criterion (BIC) tests performed, led to the conclusion that the linear model better explains the data's performance. The results of this estimation were used to compute predicted values.

Another interesting finding about the prediction of outcomes with the value of zero is that as the total number of bills submitted increases, the likelihood that a women's rights bill will *not* be submitted decreases. In other words, the more bills a legislator submits, the less likely she or he will be *not* to submit a women's rights-related bill. Very productive legislators – both men and women – tend to devote time and effort to delivering gender-related legislation (see the negative and significant coefficients of *Number of Bills* in models 1 to 3). This implies that regardless of gender, individual legislators who have strong concerns tend to promote women's rights in Congress.

The results reveal that, as expected, membership in a women's issues committee is positively and significantly associated with bill submissions on women's rights issues (H7). Partisanship tends to be mostly insignificant, although Radical Party membership was associated with a lower likelihood of submitting a women's rights related bill (models 1 to 3). While the legislator's committee of origin is insignificant, variables measuring institutional power – including possible committee chairmanship and legislative tenure – have positive and significant effects on likelihood of introducing women's rights bills.

Figure 7.3 presents the predicted probabilities anticipated by hypotheses 1 and 2. As the share of women in both chambers increases, the expected number of women's rights bills introduced by both male and female legislators grows. However, both the slope and the intercept of these subgroups are distinct, supporting the view that women tend to be more active than men on women's rights issues. On average, keeping continuous variables at the mean and specifying a male Peronist, senator, committee chair in a totally male Congress, this subject will submit less than one-half of a women's-rights-related bill. Growth in numbers of women in Congress to 27 percent of the total results in

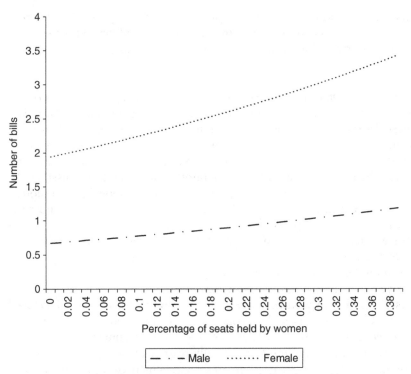

FIGURE 7.3. Predicted number of women's rights bills submitted by year, share of seats held by women in Congress, and gender of legislator.

a doubling of his chances of drafting a women's rights bill. When 40 percent of all legislators are female, his predicted number of women's rights bills is 1.3.

The picture would be different if a woman with the same attributes were specified. The woman legislator would never be likely to write fewer than two gender-related bills per year, even if she was the only female member of Congress. With women occupying one-third of all congressional seats, this female legislator is likely to submit around three targeted bills per year, and when women's share reaches 40 percent, she will introduce 3.5 women's rights bills annually.

At first glance, these predicted figures do not seem large. An average of three bills per capita submitted by 40 percent of 329 legislators, however, adds up to 395 gender-related bills per year. Though these numbers are hypothetical, they reveal the degree to which women's greater presence in positions of power is likely to affect legislative behavior on behalf of women's rights.[20] In

---

[20] It should be noted that the model was also computed using the interaction between the share of seats held by women and being a woman. Although the coefficients didn't change much, the linear combination of each constitutive term and the interaction was statistically insignificant, and was therefore removed from the equation.

summary, the analysis contained compelling evidence to support the idea that higher numbers of women in both chambers positively influenced the submission of women's rights bills, especially by women legislators.

Outcomes

The models confirmed that women's increased presence improves the *process* of representation on behalf of women's rights. What about changes in policy *outcomes*? To test the relationship between presence and outcomes, we calculated the chances of bill approval as a main function of having a woman sponsor, the share of seats held by women, partisanship, institutional power (committee chairmanship and legislative tenure), and total bill submissions. To analyze the fit of each theoretical model, we ran different pooled probit models with clustered standard errors at the legislator-year level. For each hypothesis the estimations were computed first by utilizing the full sample of bills (specifying the women-related content on the right hand side of the equation), and then by restricting the sample to the 3,230 women-related bills. The results of these seven models are presented in Table 7.2.

Negative results across models show that the analyses robustly disprove the hypotheses. A bill with women-related content along with women's increased presence in Congress caused the probabilities of approval to drop *in every single model*. The first three models test the linear argument over the full sample, then use an interaction,[21] and finally restrict the analysis to the set of women-related bills. As women's share in Congress increases, overall approval rates decrease, especially if the bill has women-related content (model 1) – and even more if it was sponsored by a woman (model 2). In the sample of women's rights bills (model 3), as women's presence rose, approval rates declined, regardless of the sponsor's sex.

Models 4 and 5 tested the backlash argument and returned similar results. The linear combination of the continuous and squared share of women in Congress, along with the women-related content of a bill, negatively affects the chances of approval.[22] Models 6 and 7 show similar dynamics for the critical mass hypothesis. Goodness of fit across estimations does not reveal substantive differences. As a result, it is difficult to specify the precise shape of the relationship between women's presence and the probability of bill approval. Although taking a more nuanced approach could affect the results, it is clear that women's increased presence in the House and in the Senate is negatively associated with the probability of approval of women-related bills.

The models support the notion that party membership counts more for the approval of a bill than for its introduction. Conventional wisdom holds that membership in a large national party, such as the Peronists or the Radicals

---

[21] The linear combination of the interaction is strongly negative and significant.
[22] We have no good explanation for why the overall chances of bill approval decline as women's presence increases. This relationship requires further research.

TABLE 7.2. *Outcome Models*

Variables	Model 1 Linear Full	Model 2 Linear Full with Interaction	Model 3 Linear Restricted Sample	Model 4 Quadratic Full	Model 5 Quadratic Restricted Sample	Model 6 Threshold Full	Model 7 Threshold Restricted Sample
Women's Rights Bill	-0.365***	-0.043		-0.362***		-0.362***	
	(0.031)	(0.065)		(0.031)		(0.031)	
Female	0.039	0.039	0.085	0.040	0.074	0.042*	0.072
	(0.025)	(0.025)	(0.066)	(0.025)	(0.066)	(0.024)	(0.066)
Share of Women	-0.261***	-0.243**	-1.334***	-0.926**	1.213		
	(0.097)	(0.098)	(0.274)	(0.377)	(1.209)		
Sq. Share of Women				-2.925***	-5.935**		
				(0.908)	(2.820)		
Threshold						-0.085***	-0.331***
						(0.024)	(0.066)
Female * Women's Share		-1.307***					
		(0.256)					
Peronist Party	0.213***	0.213***	0.135*	0.220**	0.146*	0.217***	0.142*
	(0.029)	(0.029)	(0.078)	(0.029)	(0.077)	(0.029)	(0.077)
Radical Party	0.116***	0.116***	0.053	0.121***	0.071	0.119***	0.079
	(0.029)	(0.029)	(0.087)	(0.029)	(0.087)	(0.029)	(0.086)
Center Left Parties	-0.175***	-0.175***	-0.499**	-0.499**	-0.465**	-0.153**	-0.439*
	(0.063)	(0.063)	(0.230)	(0.063)	(0.230)	(0.064)	(0.230)
Women's Committee	-0.165***	-0.166***	-0.045	-0.167***	-0.16	-0.168***	-0.052
	(0.031)	(0.031)	(0.085)	(0.032)	(0.084)	(0.031)	(0.084)
Committee Chair	0.267***	0.267***	0.091	0.264***	0.086	0.267***	0.093
	(0.027)	(0.027)	(0.075)	(0.027)	(0.075)	(0.027)	(0.075)

(continued)

TABLE 7.2 (*continued*)

Variables	Model 1 Linear Full	Model 2 Linear Full with Interaction	Model 3 Linear Restricted Sample	Model 4 Quadratic Full	Model 5 Quadratic Restricted Sample	Model 6 Threshold Full	Model 7 Threshold Restricted Sample
Tenure	0.003	0.003	0.009	0.002	0.008	0.002	0.007
	(0.003)	(0.003)	(0.010)	(0.003)	(0.01)|0.	(0.003)	(0.01)|0.
Number of Bills	0.0007***	0.0007***	0.0000	0.0008***	0.0000	0.0007***	0.0000
	(0.0002)	(0.0002)	(0.0003)	(0.0002)	(0.0003)	(0.0002)	(0.0003)
Constant	−0.756***	−0.760***	−0.759***	−0.838***	−0.952***	−0.785***	−0.931***
	(0.031)	(0.031)	(0.098)	(0.041)	(0.127)	(0.027)	(0.085)
Linear Combination		−1.547***		−3.175***	−7.417***		
		(0.234)		(0.533)	(2.050)		
Observations	172,070	172,070	3,230	172,070	3,230	172,070	3,230

Robust standard errors in parentheses ***$p < 0.01$; **$p < 0.05$; *$p < 0.1$.

(the only parties that have had majorities over time), is associated with greater chances of getting a bill approved. This means that the less popular center-left delegation has lower chances of getting bills passed. These results also show that the sex of a legislator does not affect the chances of a bill being passed and that when it comes to a vote, party-level factors do not discriminate between men and women.

In summary, the data do not support hypotheses predicting that women's presence boosts the chances for approval of women-related legislation. Instead, the findings show that with the rise in the number of women legislators, the productivity of Congress as a whole declines, particularly for women-related bills.

Conclusion

The analysis presented in this chapter affirms the importance of evaluating how political inclusion influences the behavior of the legislature as a whole, not merely the actions of women representatives. As women's presence in the Argentine Congress has grown, both women *and* men have introduced more women-related bills. This suggests that there is more discussion of gender-related concerns and more consciousness-raising, as well as more space in the legislative agenda for issues related to women's rights. The most dramatic gains came after 2002, when gender quotas were applied to elections for the Senate and women's presence exceeded a critical mass in both chambers. Bicameralism matters: for women's presence to be associated with significant change, numbers of women cannot be dramatically different in the two chambers.

On the other hand, the chance that a women's rights-related bill would actually be approved by Congress were greater when women were fewer in number. As women's presence has grown and the *process* of representation has improved, the chances of successful *outcomes* have shrunk. The huge increase in women's presence secured as a result of gender quotas has made the passage of any individual piece of women-related legislation less likely. To a certain extent, this is the arithmetical result of the inflation in bill submission. Yet it may also be evidence of the marginalization of women within the legislature (cf. Franceschet & Piscopo, 2008; Piscopo & Thomas, 2012; Schwindt-Bayer, 2010). As women's presence has grown, male politicians may have worked harder to reduce their influence by pushing them into less important committees and preventing their bills from reaching the floor.

The research revealed that partisan and institutional factors continue to shape patterns of bill approval. Though gender quotas bring more women into Congress, they do not change party dominance of the legislative agenda, committee structures, or the incentives for legislators to specialize in public-good policy issues. As former deputy Virginia Franganillo put in in an interview: "The quality of representation is not something you can resolve with a law."[23] In fact, gender quotas are designed to maintain these institutional mechanisms and the power of party leaders. Candidate quota laws that require parties to add individual women to party lists and legislative delegations serve to divide women through the party system. (In contrast, a policy of reserved seats for a women's party would not.) Women do not enter power as a group but as individual members of different parties who owe their position to party leaders. Though party dominance has little impact on the process of bill introduction, it produces enduring influence on the patterns of bill approval. The inclusion of women has thus far failed fundamentally to change those institutions that exert the most decisive effects on legislative outputs.

8

Conclusion

The demands of Latin America's marginalized social groups for greater access to power gained traction in the 1990s and the first two decades of the 21st century. Women, whose presence in power lagged their participation at the middle and bottom of parties, civic organizations, unions, and the private sector, mobilized across parties to demand national laws imposing gender candidate quotas on political parties in legislative elections. Boosted by regional trends toward multiculturalism and global norms of ethnic and racial equality, movements of indigenous peoples and Afrodescendants claimed rights to recognition and autonomy, guarantees of political inclusion, and access to higher education.

Many advocates of gender quotas and ethnic reservations expected they would improve not just the inclusion of Latin America's marginalized social groups but also their political representation, and produce better policy outcomes. This book has shown that the process was not so simple. Inclusion is not the same as representation. In fact, in the Latin American countries studied in this book, group inclusion was produced through institutional mechanisms that *precluded* group representation, at least along formal, principal–agent lines. Women, Afrodescendant, and indigenous representatives have been elected not by constituencies constructed from their category but by voters as a whole. Women did not enter power on behalf of women, but divided across parties and accountable to party leaders. Indigenous and Afrodescendant representatives elected to reserved seats were not accountable to voters from those groups. The activists and movements who worked to achieve inclusion had little control over who was elected, allegedly to represent them.

This conclusion considers the implications of the story of political inclusion in Latin America for our understanding of gender, gender equality, race, and ethnicity. I propose a way to think about the relationship between inclusion and representation and urge scholars to look beyond the legislature for mechanisms to represent disadvantaged groups. Finally, I affirm the value of inclusion. Quotas and reservations may disappoint the activists who fought for them by failing to deliver good representation, and by elevating non feminists, corrupt politicians, and party hacks. They may derive from a misdiagnosis of the best way to promote policy change. They may further elite racial projects and inadequate solutions to underrepresentation. Nonetheless, mechanisms of inclusion help to diversify the ranks of political leaders. They help to erode gender and racial biases. And they signal that everyone counts as a citizen.

Gender and Gender Equality

In the normative traditions of the West, the institution of gender helped segregate social and political life into separate spheres for men and women. The domain of the public – encompassing wage work, political decision making, cultural production, and intellectual life – was a man's world. The private sphere – where activities surrounding the maintenance and reproduction of life occurred – was occupied primarily by women. Men's work involved political leadership and decision making; women's work revolved around care for children, the sick, and the elderly, the home, and nutrition (Okin, 1991, 2008; Pateman, 1989; Rosaldo, 1974). In the nineteenth century, the *exclusion* of women from politics was widely seen as a sign of modernity and civilization (Towns, 2010).

Quotas reversed the gender system's historic marginalization of women from politics. By making sure that women were at least physically present in the formal arenas where governmental decisions are (supposed to be) made, quotas eroded the gender system's crude segregation of the social world. Yet once in power, women confronted more gender-based obstacles. Political institutions and organizations are gendered on the inside as well as on the outside. Historically constructed by men and designed around their habits and needs, national legislatures and political parties functioned by rules and were permeated by practices that were biased against many women's bodies, backgrounds, and schedules. Consequently, many women were frustrated trying to exercise effective representation and reach other political goals, and many aspects of gendered hierarchies of power remained intact. As former Argentine Senator Beatriz Raijer put it, "having a position does not mean having power."[1] Political institutions are not unique in this respect: other large organizations are similarly gendered (Acker, 1990; Kanter, 1977a). Quotas eroded gender-based exclusion in the political sphere, but this peeled away only the first layer of the onion. For women (and other marginalized groups)

---

[1] Interview, Buenos Aires, August 2000.

to exercise effective and not just nominal power, more profound institutional change is needed.

The gender system puts women (and sexual minorities) at a disadvantage in numerous ways besides political exclusion. Gender inequality "is not one homogeneous phenomenon, but a collection of disparate and interlinked problems" (Sen, 2001). Women suffer unequal access to health care and other basic services, are more likely to be victims of violence and abuse, perform a disproportionate, and uncompensated, share of child and elder care, encounter discrimination in the labor market, are more likely to be affected by civil wars, natural disasters, and climate change, and receive fewer, and more uneven, government support services, among other injustices (Fuchs, 1990; Goldin, 1990; Lewis, 1992; Mettler, 1998; Orloff, 1993; Pedersen, 1993; World Bank, 2011).

Contrary to the expectations of many activists, governments, and international organizations, adding more women to power did not trigger a massive change on the multiple dimensions of gender oppression. It has been far easier to place more women into positions of leadership than to alter the gender structure of society. The most pervasive changes following in the wake of quotas have been more quotas (cf. Hassim, 2009). In many countries, women brought into power with quotas succeeded in introducing similar policies to the executive and legislative branches, lower levels of government, and the boards of civil society organizations. They have also strengthened national legislative quotas by increasing percentage thresholds (with several countries at 50 percent) and widening the domain of quota laws' application (such as to single-member district elections) (Piscopo, 2015). Quotas begat quotas.

By applying gender quotas, otherwise discriminatory regimes could make progress on political inclusion quickly and independently of other constraints on women's lives. Rwanda is the most extreme example. Thanks to the Constitution (2003) and electoral legislation (2007), the country has both reserved seats for women (twenty-four) and a candidate quota (30 percent) for parties contesting the fifty-three parliamentary seats elected through closed-list proportional representation. In 2014, Rwanda had the highest level of women's parliamentary presence in the world: women occupied 64 percent of seats in the lower house and 38 percent in the (largely appointed) Senate. Yet the country ranked 76 in the United Nation's Development Programme (UNDP)'s gender inequality index in 2012 (and would be much lower if women's parliamentary presence were not a component of the index), political liberties are limited, civil society muzzled, and women's status suffers in other key respects. Critics allege women's high presence in power constitutes a democratic "alibi" for Rwanda's otherwise authoritarian government (Hassim, 2009; Longman, 2006).

Meanwhile, countries such as the United States and Brazil have relatively few women in power but strong feminist movements, which historically pushed for progressive policies. Owing to its single-member district electoral system, high incumbency rates, and competitive primaries to pick candidates for popular election, the United States has fewer women in national elected office relative to other advanced democracies. After the 2014 elections, after which women's presence hit an historic high, the United States still ranked 71st in the world.[2] Yet the US feminist movement pushed for early action on violence against women, equal opportunity in the workplace, and the liberalization of laws on abortion. US women have made dramatic gains in the workforce, and in 2011 held more than half of all managerial and professional positions, considerably more than in other advanced economies.[3]

Numbers of women in national elected office in Brazil have historically been among the lowest in Latin America, never exceeding ten percent of the Chamber of Deputies. Yet the country is home to one of the most robust feminist movements in the region and has adopted progressive legislation in many areas. Brazil was the first country in the world to introduce women's police stations to receive victims of violence, the first Latin American country to require the public health system to attend to abortions in those cases permitted by law, and the first to implement a large-scale family planning program designed by feminists (Htun, 2002b).

Comparative research on the correlates of progressive policy affirms that women's presence in elected office is neither necessary nor sufficient for women's rights. Htun and Weldon's analysis of policies to combat violence against women in seventy countries identified autonomous feminist movements and international norms, not women legislators, as the principal drivers of comprehensive governmental approaches (Htun & Weldon, 2012). Our study of family law emphasized secular political institutions as the most prominent correlate of egalitarian policy. Women's presence in parliament had only a small association with sex equality (Htun & Weldon, forthcoming 2015). When it comes to legislation mandating equal treatment in the workplace, the role of feminist movements and international conventions such as Convention on the Elimination of All Forms of Discrimination Against Women (CEDAW) outweighed that of women in government. Nor was women's parliamentary presence the main factor associated with expansive social welfare policies such as parental leave and child care (Htun & Weldon, 2014). Our research affirms the

---

[2] Women made up 19 percent of the lower house and 20 percent of the Senate, and these numbers reflected considerable growth over the previous decade. In 2003, women made up 14 percent of the lower house and 13 percent of the Senate. Even with these lower numbers, the United States ranked 57th at that time, illustrating how quickly political inclusion improved elsewhere.

[3] In other respects, however, the United States lags other advanced democracies. It is unique in offering no national paid maternity or parental leave policy, and other social welfare benefits are weak. Women's rights is not one issue but many issues. Countries can be progressive in some areas and regressive in others (Htun, 2003a; Htun & Weldon, 2010).

findings of case studies arguing that women in parliament affect policy primarily through their alliances with women's social movements and by leveraging international norms on women's rights.

Racial and Ethnic Politics

In a recent manifesto, Juan Pablo Luna, Victoria Murillo, and Andrew Schrank criticize the way that a generation of Latin Americanist social scientists have begun to apply "alien theories and methods" to local contexts. They call for a return to empirically grounded theories in the tradition of Guillermo O'Donnell, Albert Hirschmann, and Fernando Henrique Cardoso. Only by "taking the region on its own terms," they say, will we grasp current developments and contribute more broadly to comparative social science (Luna, Murillo, & Schrank, 2014, pp. 4–5).

When it comes to the study of race and ethnicity, political scientists need to heed this advice and avoid unreflective application of concepts such as "ethnicity," "ethnic group," and "ethnic party" to Latin America. They should be reluctant to rely on large, cross-national datasets that contain counts of ethnic groups and estimates of ethnic diversity. As this book has shown, the criteria to sort people by race and ethnicity are not the same across regions. Rather than descent or perceptions of descent, Latin Americans tend to apply racial and ethnic labels according to a plurality of criteria, including physical appearance, socioeconomic status, context, and mood. Chapter 2 reported that depending on the method of counting, the size of the region's racial and ethnic groups varies significantly. As a result of such flux, it is not surprising that categorical ethnic and racial distinctions are less accurate predictors of socioeconomic stratification than objective assessments of skin color (Telles, 2014b).

Ethnic and racial categories used in Latin American policy and scholarly discourse originated in racial projects formulated by elites, from the top down. As Chapter 2 described, the term "Afrodescendant" emerged among international development agencies and was then adopted by scholars. The category "negro" or black is widely used among activists and among U.S. scholars its meaning as a mark of Afrodescendancy is taken for granted. In line with these trends, the Brazilian government legally reclassified people denoted by the census as "preto" and "pardo" as the "população negra" (black population) in 2010. But the term is rarely chosen by citizens to identify themselves. As the PERLA survey on Brazil revealed, only six percent of the sample chose to identify as "negro" in response to an open-ended question about self identification (Silva and Paixão, 2014: 191).

Race-based public policies are attempting to render orderly a complex reality of racial identity and identification. Though color is clearly correlated with low social status and discrimination, potential beneficiaries of such policies have not always come forward in the ways anticipated by authorities. As

Chapter 6 showed, state governments and university administrations in Brazil faced challenges applying educational quotas that required sorting students by race. The practice was contested as a matter of principle (Feres Júnior, 2008; Fry & Maggie, 2004; Maggie & Fry, 2004). In addition, there were discrepancies between the groups that policymakers thought the categories included, on the one hand, and the understanding of students about whether the category applied to them (Schwartzman, 2009). The gap between elite policy projects and racial discourse on the ground would be even greater in other countries, where there is even less stability in practices of racial and ethnic categorization than in Brazil (Telles & Flores, 2014).[4]

Advocates of political inclusion for indigenous peoples and Afrodescendants have tended to propose reserved seats in parliament, the way that virtually all other democracies have institutionalized ethnic or racial guarantees of inclusion (Htun, 2004b). Reserved seats are logically appropriate for groups that want to form their own parties or steer clear of existing parties. But reserved seats may not be the best way to promote the political presence of most of Latin America's racial and ethnic minorities (or majorities). Most indigenous and Afrodescendant elected officials owe their positions to mainstream parties, not group-specific ones, and tend to get elected from parties across the spectrum (see Chapter 2). Even Bolivia's Movimiento al Socialismo (MAS), responsible for the historically high presence of indigenous legislators at the national level, is not a group-specific party but a multiethnic, populist one (Anria, 2013; Madrid, 2012). Since race and ethnicity tend to cross cut the party system, quotas in parties may be a better mechanism to promote inclusion of members of disadvantaged racial and ethnic groups (but they will not solve the challenge of promoting change without reifying racial and ethnic categories). Rather than copying remedies for inclusion pioneered in other regions, Latin Americans should adopt policies tailored for the particularities of racial and ethnic formation in their own countries.

Rethinking the Inclusion-to-Representation Link

The vast majority of the literature on the "substantive" representation of women and minorities, including Chapter 7 of this book, has analyzed the ways that the legislative participation of women and minorities induces, or

---

[4] Lack of consensus over racial and ethnic categories has probably not precluded a country from adopting quotas or reservations for disadvantaged ethnic and racial minorities. Chapter 5 documented Colombia's stumbling attempts to apply reserved seats by race, anticipation of which did not deter policy adoption. Objections to the government's reification of racial categories failed to obstruct the introduction of university racial quotas in Brazil.

FIGURE 8.1. Inclusion and representation as joint outcomes.

fails to induce, representative activity advancing their rights. The hypothesized causal relationship runs from presence to behavior:

Political presence → legislative behavior

Other analyses have sought to identify the conditions under which women and minorities can serve as effective legislators to advocate on behalf of their communities. These include the presence of parliamentary caucuses, strategies of issue disaggregation, the strength of Left parties, and an engaged civil society (Beckwith & Cowell-Meyers, 2007; Celis et al., 2008; Htun, 2003a; Wang, 2013). In this approach, the causal relationship between presence and behavior is contingent on contextual factors:

Contextual factors → effective political presence → legislative behavior

In both of these perspectives, the presence of disadvantaged groups generates, or enables, legislative behavior to advance their rights.

Latin America's experiences offer grounds to think about the relationship between presence and behavior, or inclusion and representation, in other ways. This book described the coalitions of social movements and politicians that mobilized to pressure for gender quotas. Though less of a focus here, these same groups lobbied legislators to take action to promote women's rights in other areas such as violence against women, equality in the workplace, and parental leave. The same holds for Afrodescendant and indigenous rights. Those forces that organized around guarantees of inclusion also sought action on other initiatives, including changes to educational curricula, land rights, natural resource policy, health care, and economic opportunities, among other issues.

Societal and transnational pressures compelled countries to introduce mechanisms of inclusion *and* influenced legislators to advocate women and minority rights. As this suggests, political inclusion and representation were not the beginning and the end points of a causal process. Rather, they were *joint products* of other factors.

In Figure 8.1, the primary causal relationships run from left to right. Civic mobilization in transnational and domestic contexts simultaneously brought about improvements in political presence *and* greater representative behavior to advance the rights of disadvantaged groups. Greater presence of women and other disadvantaged groups was one outcome of a broader process of claims making and state response.

Representation beyond the Legislature

Some representatives are better than others. Dovi argues that legislators who possess mutual relationships with other members of disadvantaged groups are more likely to promote the goals of democratic inclusion than are legislators who have no connection (Dovi, 2002). For example, a woman or Afrodescendant legislator with no connection to the women's or Afrodescendant movements is still eligible for a candidate quota slot or a reserved parliamentary seat. But she is less likely to be aware of the concerns of the broader group, and therefore less likely to improve democratic deliberation by contributing perspectives informed by the range of experiences of group members (Ibid.).

As Chapter 5 on Colombia showed, institutional engineering can put into power people who share a social identity but otherwise have little connection to others working to promote the well-being of the group. Some Afrodescendant legislators elected in reserved seats allegedly had ties to violent, undemocratic paramilitary groups and no connection to the black movement. In 2014, legislators elected to the seats were not even recognized as black. Over time, the presence of legislators whose behavior violated the goals of democratic inclusion undermined the purpose of institutional engineering. Disconnected from group representation, group inclusion lost its legitimacy.

This book showed that there is no feasible statutory way to prevent these outcomes. It is hypothetically possible to craft group-specific constituencies of women, Afrodescendants, or indigenous peoples able to authorize and hold accountable their representatives. But segregating the electorate is a problematic practice for a liberal democracy. In Latin America, such a move would be ethically and bureaucratically challenging in light of the ambiguity of racial and ethnic boundaries and the more universal tendency of women to cross-cut partisan, economic, and ideological divisions.

How can a polity promote group representation with the institutional mechanisms available to liberal democracies? Is it possible to furnish incentives to champion the perspectives and preferences of marginalized citizens? The answer is to look beyond the legislature for sources of representation. By organizing across lines of internal difference, communicating, and mobilizing around shared interests in civil society, disadvantaged groups can form constituencies to hold politicians and the political system accountable.

Democratic theorists have identified vehicles of group representation and accountability outside of the legislature including self-authorized representatives such as social movements (Strolovitch, 2007; Urbinati & Warren, 2008; Weldon, 2011); the construction of deliberative "minipublics" with decision-making authority (Fung, 2006); the creation of specialized government agencies (such as gender machineries) (McBride & Mazur, 2011); a public rendering of accounts, such as in the ancient Greek practice of "euthynai," wherein officials responded to public comments and questions (Rehfeld & Schwartzberg, 2013); citizen councils (Fung, 2003); participatory budgeting (Wampler, 2010); deliberative polling (Fishkin, 1991); and other mechanisms of participatory democracy (Fung & Wright, 2003). Analysis of policy outcomes reveals that some of these instruments – particularly autonomous social movements – may be more effective advocates of group interests than legislative presence (Dryzek, 1996; Htun & Weldon 2012; Weldon, 2002, 2011).

The reason for the gap between inclusion and representation is not just bad representatives. The problem inheres in the constraints of representative electoral democracy. Constituencies of disadvantaged groups can rarely be engineered from above. Rather, they must grow from below through processes of civic mobilization, deliberation, and interest articulation. Rather than seeking further modification of electoral institutions, advocates of group representation would be better off seeking the parallel mobilization, within civil society, of disadvantaged groups. An engaged civil society can help resolve the deficits of a diverse legislature. Though legislative presence is important and desirable, it is not a quick fix for enduring challenges of inequality, marginalization, and lack of representation.

Inclusion and Society's Status Hierarchies

Political inclusion does not, on its own, deliver political representation. It is nonetheless a valuable objective. The mere presence in power of members of disadvantaged and historically excluded groups helps to erode status hierarchies, those "institutionalized patterns of cultural value that pervasively deny some members [of society] the recognition they need to be full, participating partners in social interaction" (Fraser, 2003, p. 49). Status hierarchies constitute some groups as normative and valuable and others as inferior, deficient, or unworthy (Ibid., pp. 29–30). They are manifest in norms of beauty, assumptions about intelligence, aesthetics of print and digital media, the composition of political leaders, and other cultural institutions.

The political exclusion of women, Afrodesendants, and indigenous peoples in Latin America upholds gendered and racialized status hierarchies. The presence in power of some groups supports beliefs that they are better looking, smarter, more interesting and more competent, and lead more worthy lives than those others who are absent. As Mansbridge put it, a monopoly on political decision making by members of one social group – white, male, heterosexual, for example – reinforces the notion that only members of that group should rule and are fit to rule (Mansbridge, 1999a, p. 649).[5] The media is complicit in

---

[5] Concepts about the ideal features of rulers come to be modeled on the group's characteristics and experiences, such as military service, height, and other manly virtues. The informal norms and

processes of exclusion. A person who watched only TV in Brazil and Mexico, and never walked on the street, for example, would get the impression that all Brazilians and Mexicans are fair-skinned and fair-haired (Telles, 2014a).

Status hierarchies are matters of justice, for they have the potential to distort processes of recognition that are essential to the flourishing of human selves (Taylor, 1992). People suffer harm if the dominant social images of them projected by popular culture and the news media are "confining or demeaning or contemptible." Nonrecognition or misrecognition can imprison someone in a "false, distorted, or reduced mode of being." For these reasons, recognition is a "vital human need" (Kymlicka, 1995; Taylor, 1992, pp. 25–26). Though Charles Taylor proposed that it was "authentic" individual and group identities that merited recognition,[6] others have alleged that the focus on identities elides the internal complexity and hierarchies within "identity" groups, "mask[ing] the power of dominant groups and reinforc[ing] intragroup domination" (Fraser, 2000, p. 112, see also Appiah, 1997). For these reasons, Nancy Fraser alleges, we should conceptualize equal recognition as a matter of relative social *status*. In her view, the politics of recognition should direct our attention to the cultural values and norms that privilege some groups and subordinate others. Equal recognition involves dismantling status hierarchies that reinforce demeaning, disparaging, constraining, and other negative ideas about certain social groups.

When they succeed at placing members of disadvantaged groups in visible positions of power, policies to promote political inclusion begin to weaken stereotypes that reinforce discrimination. As Phillips puts it, presence in power conveys information about "... who does and who does not count as a full member of society" (2012, p. 517). In India, the greater presence in power of Dalits (formerly known as untouchables) helped reduce caste bias and changed public attitudes about disadvantaged groups (but did not alter policy outcomes or lead to greater development in Dalit communities) (Jensenius, 2014). According to feminists advocating parity in France, the presence of women as representatives of the nation demonstrates that the universal human being is embodied as feminine as well as masculine (Scott, 2004). Men are no longer seen as the norm from which women are the deviation or "other." Rather, being a woman, having a woman's body, and enduring women's life experiences is recognized as part of the *universal* human condition.

In a society that values equality and diversity, political inclusion looks good, and exclusion looks bad. I participated in the inaugural session of the Fourth

---

practices surrounding the act of ruling – such as how and when to speak, where to be and when, and what to talk about – come to be based on how members of that group act and what they do.

[6] Taylor's approach, and much of the political discourse it inspired, emphasized the formative conditions of individual and group identities. If dominant social norms and practices demean some groups, individual members will suffer harm, and the group as a whole will be unable to develop an autonomous sense of collective identity. For individuals and groups to develop fully, cultural and social norms need to incorporate appropriate recognition of authentic group identities.

Regional Conference of Afrodescendant Women in Latin America, which took place in the Hall of Former Presidents (Sala Expresidentes) of the Costa Rican National Assembly in July, 2011. Portraits of all the country's former presidents, white and male, hung on the walls, while the meeting's participants, mostly women and mostly black, talked about their desire for greater political presence, among other issues. The physical surroundings embodied the exclusion this particular meeting was convened to combat, and the homogeneity of the portraits did not pass unnoticed. During her presentation, Matilde Ribeiro, the former minister of state for racial equality in Brazil, declared: "The number of blacks in the Brazilian Congress is shameful .... I would like to see photos of our black colleagues on the walls of these legislative chambers!"

Some scholars view instruments of inclusion as shallow, mere accessories adorning political elites trying to expand their power, gain votes, and look good. They express suspicions about the transformative potential of quotas and reservations, arguing that they serve as democratic distractions for authoritarian governments, offer mechanisms for entrenched elites to place lackeys in positions of power, or undermine themselves over time, when weak beneficiaries confirm negative stereotypes about members of the broader category (Hassim, 2009; Longman, 2006; Tripp, 2006).

It is understandable to be disappointed with quotas and reservations as instruments of democratic renewal. As reported here, the institutionalization of inclusion in many countries has not achieved the expected results of promoting good representation, insuring the presence of legislators committed to gender and racial justice, and bringing about policy change. Many women on party lists are not feminists. Many indigenous and Afrodescendant legislators are party hacks.

It may be normatively problematic to expect representatives who are members of marginalized groups to devote their political careers to advocating the rights of their category. Most legislators from such groups are likely already to suffer disadvantage outside and within the halls of Congress. They don't need additional responsibilities. Legislators should be free to behave in a manner responsive to internal convictions and as they are compelled in order to continue in their positions. Many desire to defend the rights of marginalized groups, and actually end up doing so. Yet we should not require them to. *Taking action against injustice, discrimination, and inequality is the responsibility of the entire political class.* Inclusion may help remind them of this responsibility, but should not absolve them of it.

Before giving up on inclusion, we may want to check our expectations. We need to clarify what the point of instruments of inclusion is. They are not so much a tool to represent interests than a way to combat gendered and racialized status hierarchies. Diversity in leadership helps to break down social biases. The visible presence of people of darker skin and non-European features in power communicates a message of recognition, broadens the criteria of what is considered desirable and normative, and expands and alters the

Mexico (1998, 2000 [2], 2001): Interviews with politicians, government officials, lawyers, activists, academics, journalists; observation of political meetings; participation in seminars, panels, and workshops at academic institutions and NGOs

Peru (1997, 2000): Interviews with politicians, government officials, lawyers, activists, academics; participation in seminars at NGOs; participant observation in political meetings

In addition, I made shorter trips to attend conferences and workshops with politicians, government officials, activists, and scholars. These included a 2011 trip to Costa Rica to participate in the Fourth Regional Conference of Afrodescendant Women, two trips to Nicaragua in 1996 and 1998 to participate in regional meetings on women and politics, and a 1999 trip to Venezuela for a workshop on women's leadership. I participated in several conferences and seminars in Washington, DC with women leaders and activists in Latin America organized by the Inter-American Dialogue and the Inter-American Development Bank.

II. Partial list of people interviewed and position or organization at time of interview

Argentina

Mabel Bianco, president of the Foundation for Women's Studies
Haydee Birgin, president of Latin American Team for Justice and Gender
Elisa Carrió, federal deputy
Pimpi Colombo, Buenos Aires city legislator
Malena Derdoy, Defense Department official
Chiche Duhalde, federal deputy
Marcela Durrieu, former federal deputy
Virginia Franganillo, former federal deputy
Natalia Gherardi, lawyer at Latin American Team for Justice and Gender
María Florentina Gomez Miranda, former federal deputy
María José Lubertino, UCR and former city assembly constituent
Diana Maffia, Buenos Aires city legislator
José Luis Manzano, former Interior Minister
Juliana Marino, Buenos Aires city legislator
Marta Oyhanarte, Buenos Aires city legislator
Gustavo Martínez Pandiani, foreign ministry official
María del Carmen Pasarín, foreign ministry official
Beatriz Raijer, senator
Marcela Rodriguez, law professor
Susana Sanz, National Women's Commission official
Esther Schiavoni, president of National Women's Council
Carmen Storani, president of National Women's Council
Ana María Suppa, former Buenos Aires city legislator and director of city women's agency

Bolivia
Antonio Araníbar, United Nations Development Program
Rafael Archondo, United Nations Development Program
Gloria Ardaya, former minister
Issac Avalos, CSUTCB executive director
José Bailaba, national deputy
Esther Balboa, former vice presidential candidate
Carlos Bohrt, senator
Pamela Callá, anthropologist
Oscar Camara, Director of Social Control of Business
Victor Hugo Cardenas, former vice president
Teresa Canaviri, government official
Leandro Chacalluca, national deputy
María Eugenia Choque, Center for Aymara Studies
Nilda Copa, Bartolina Sisa Women's Federation
Jimena Costa, political scientist
Roberto de la Cruz, El Alto city councillor
José Luis Exeni, National Electoral Court
Ximena Florez, national deputy
Moises Guarachi, land and territory secretary of CSCB
Freddy Herrera, taxi drivers' union
Rafael Loayza, political scientist and advisor to Tuto Quiroga
Sergio Mendinacelli, former member of constituent assembly
Ines Miranda, national deputy
Dunia Mukrani, Women's Coordination
Alicia Muñoz, senator
Pedro Nuni, CIDOB vice president
Padre Obermeyer, German priest
Rosario Paz, feminist activist
Pedro Portugal, director of Pukara
Tata Elias Quelca, CONAMAQ executive director
Felipe Quispe, general secretary of CSUTCB, president of MIP, and former
   presidential candidate
Salvador Romero, president of National Electoral Court
Elizabeth Salguero, national deputy
Saya Afro-Boliviana staff members
Gloria Tillca, national deputy
Pilar Uriona, Women's Coordination
Diana Urioste, Women's Coordination

Brazil
Luis Alberto, federal deputy
João Almino, director of Rio Branco Institute
Branca Moreira Alves, UNIFEM
Dyana Dias de Azevedo, CFEMEA

Leila Linhares Barsted, CEPIA
Iara Bernardi, federal deputy
Eva Blay, former senator
Angela Borba, PT women's secretariat
Nigel Brooke, Ford Foundation
Aldir Cabral, federal deputy
Gilda Cabral, CFEMEA
Sonia Corrêa, IBASE
Iáris Ramalho Cortês, CFEMEA
Delaine Martins Costa, IBAM
Rosiska Darcy D'Oliveira, president of National Women's Council
Denise Dora, THEMIS
David Fleischer, political scientist
Marcio Fortes, federal deputy
Nilceia Freire, UERJ rector
Denise Frossard, prosecutor
Tatau Godinho, CUT
Ricardo Henriques, IPEA
Rosana Heringer, Candido Mendes University
Ana Jensen, PSDB
Luis Paulo, PSDB
Maria do Carmo Lara, federal deputy
Elizabeth Leeds, Ford Foundation
Gilmar Machado, federal deputy
Cesar Maia, mayor of Rio de Janeiro
Hildézia Alves de Medeiros, CACES
Guacira Cesar de Oliveira, CFEMEA
Paulo Paím, federal deputy
Hildete Pereira, IPEA
Dulce Maria Pereira, Palmares Foundation
Paulo Sergio Pinheiro, Secretary for Human Rights
Jacqueline Pitanguy, CEPIA and former National Women's Council President
Maria José Rocha Lima (Zezé), former Bahian state deputy
Edna Roland, speaker of World Conference on Racism
Carmelina dos Santos Rosa, ministry of justice official
Gilberto Saboia, head of Brazilian delegation to World Conference on Racism
Wania Sant' Anna, Rio de Janeiro secretary of human rights
Ivair dos Santos, ministry of justice official
Schuma Schumaher, REDEH
Vera Soares, feminist activist
Eduardo Suplicy, senator
Marta Suplicy, federal deputy
Marcos Tenório, chief of staff to Marta Suplicy and then Iara Bernardi

Dojival Viera, Ministry of Education official, director of Diversity in the University
Zito, mayor of Duque de Caxias

Chile
Andrés Allamand, former national deputy
Ximena Diaz, Women's Studies Center
Isabel Duque, ISIS
Pía Guzmán, national deputy
Soledad Larraín, former SERNAM minister
Adriana Muñoz, national deputy
Fernanda Otero, RN official
Lily Perez, national deputy
Maria Antoinetta Saa, national deputy
Lucía Santa Cruz, Liberty and Development Institute
Carolina Schmidt, SERNAM minister
Rosalba Todaro, Women's Studies Center
Alejandra Valdes, Comunidad Mujer
Teresa Valdes, FLACSO
Soledad Weinstein, ISIS

Colombia
Aura Vanessa Aguilar, president of sports league
Lorenzo Almendra, national representative
Natalia Ángel, law professor
Jaime Arocha, anthropologist
Gina Benedetti, former mayor of Cartagena
César Caballero, director of National Administrative Department of Statistics
María Cristina Calderón, lawyer for Pro-Família
Fernando Cepeda, former ambassador to UN, OAS, UK, France, Canada
Manuel José Cepeda, Constitutional Court judge
Martha Chaverra, National Direction of Ethnicities
Carlos Gaviria, senator
Antonio Jacanamijoy, senate candidate
Zulema Jattin, national representative
Gerardo Jumí, national representative
Magdalena León, sociologist
Claudia Mejía, Sisma Mujer
Reginaldo Montes, national representative
Paula Moreno, former Minister of Culture
Gabriel Mujuy, former federal deputy
Luis Gilberto Murillo, former governor
Willington Ortiz, national representative
Gina Parody, national representative

Jesus Piñacué, senator
Beatriz Quintero, National Women's Network
Chucho Ramírez, director of indigenous affairs at Interior Ministry
Olga Lucía Reyes, official at National Administrative Department of Statistics
Dilia Robinson, ministry of education official
Manuel Rodríguez, former minister and member of Law 70 committee
Judith Sarmiento, presidential advisor on gender equality
Elisabeth Ungar, political scientist
Ariel Uribe, National Direction of Ethnicities
María Isabel Urrútia, national representative
Magdala Velasquez Toro, historian

Mexico
Isabel Arvide, journalist
Patricia Espinosa, president of National Women's Institute
Amalia García, senator
Sandra Herrera, PAN women's secretariat
Cecilia Loría, director of Causa Ciudadana
Patricia Mercado, presidential candidate
Malu Mícher, PRD women's secretariat
María de los Angeles Moreno, senator
Beatriz Paredes, senator
Cecilia Romero, senator
Margarita Zavala, PAN women's secretariat

Peru
Maruja Barrig, feminist activist and consultant
Violeta Bermudez, CLADEM
Cecilia Blondet, Institute for Peruvian Studies
Monica de las Casas, CLADEM
Carlos Iván Degregori, Institute for Peruvian Studies
Lourdes Flores, congresswoman
Beatriz Merino, congresswoman
Rocío Palamino, Grupo Impulsor Nacional
Miriam Schenone, Minister for Women
Giulia Tamayo, Grupo Impulsor Nacional
Nancy Tolentino, Women's Ministry official
Virginia Vargas, Flora Tristan Center for Peruvian Women
Ana Vasquez, Grupo Impulsor Nacional
Roxana Vasquez, CLADEM
Rocío Villanueva, Defensoría del Pueblo
Victoria Villanueva, Movimiento Manuela Ramos
Ana María Yañez, Movimiento Manuela Ramos

Appendix 2

Mechanisms of Inclusion

What can be done to reverse historical patterns and promote the political inclusion of historically excluded groups? Countries have approached this problem in two ways: by adopting particular electoral regulations and, less commonly, through modification of electoral rules. *Electoral regulations* are provisions designed specifically to increase the political presence of members of a particular group, such as candidate quotas in political parties, the reservation of a fixed number of parliamentary seats, and the creation of majority–minority districts (districting) (Krook & Moser, 2013, p. 34). *Electoral rules* govern the translation of votes into seats, and variation in their configurations – including proportional representation or plurality rule, the size of districts, and ballot structure – influence the electoral prospects of women, ethnic minorities, and other historically excluded groups (Moser & Scheiner, 2012; Norris, 2004; Reynolds, 2011).

This appendix lists the variety of electoral regulations that take the form of reserved parliamentary seats, candidate quotas, and legislative allocations. The arguments of this book should be relevant to these experiences. I focus on statutory mechanisms, not voluntary arrangements adopted by political parties. Some statutory mechanisms, such as the over-representation of certain regions, are not included. Nor do I include non group-specific policies such as low-threshold PR or redistricting.

Worldwide Policies to Promote Inclusion, circa 2013

Country	By Ethnicity, Race, or Nationality	By Gender
Afghanistan	10 of 249 seats reserved for Kuchis (4%)	Electoral law states that women must hold at least twice as many seats as there are provinces, currently 27%, including three women for the ten seats reserved for the Kuchi.

(continued)

Country	By Ethnicity, Race, or Nationality	By Gender
Albania		30% of party electoral lists; one of top three spots on list must be of different sex.
Angola		30% of party electoral lists
Argentina		30% of party electoral lists; at least one woman for every two men
Armenia		20% of party electoral lists and on at least every tenth position; applies to 69% of seats
Bangladesh		13% of seats
Belgium	49 seats for Flemish, 29 for French, and 1 for German speakers in Senate (100% reserved); half of cabinet ministries reserved for French speakers and half for Dutch speakers; lower house of parliament divides into French and Dutch cultural councils when dealing with regional and cultural issues.	50% of party electoral lists
Bhutan	10 of 150 seats reserved for representatives of Buddhist groups (nominated) (7%)	
Bolivia	7 seats in lower house for originary peoples	50% of party electoral lists
Bosnia- Herzegovina	3 member presidency (Bosniak, Croat, Serb); in 42-member National House of Representatives, 28 seats are allocated to the Federation of Bosnia and Herzegovina and 14 seats to the Republika Srpska; the 15-member House of Peoples consists of 5 Bosniaks, 5 Croats, and 5 Serbs	33% of party electoral lists; a woman must be one of top candidates on list; two among first five candidates, and three among top eight.
Brazil		30% of party electoral lists
Burkina Faso		30% of party electoral lists

Country	By Ethnicity, Race, or Nationality	By Gender
Burundi[a]	60% of seats reserved for Tutsis, 40% for Hutus, and 3 for Twa of a total of 100 lower house seats; Senate of 49 is divided equally between Hutus and Tutsi.	One in four on party electoral lists; co-optation of additional seats to reach 30% representation
China	15% seats reserved for minority groups	For the 2008 election, Congress declared women's seat share would be no less than 22%.
Colombia	2 seats reserved for "black communities" and 1 for indigenous peoples of 166 (2%) in lower house; 2 of 102 seats reserved for indigenous peoples in Senate (2%)	30% of party lists
Costa Rica		50% of electable positions on party lists
Croatia	5 of 153 seats in unicameral assembly reserved for ethnic minorities (3%) (an additional 6 seats reserved for Croatian diaspora)	
Cyprus	24 seats reserved for Turks (unfilled) and 1 seat each for Maronite, Roman-Catholic and Goumenian minorities of 80 in national assembly (34%)	
Djibouti		10% of seats
Dominican Republic		33% of party lists
East Timor		One out of every four candidates on electoral lists
Ecuador		50% of party electoral lists
Egypt		Parties must nominate at least one woman as part of district candidate lists.
Eritrea		30% of seats
Ethiopia	22 of 117 upper house seats (Council of the Federation) reserved for representatives of minority nationalities (19%)	

(continued)

Country	By Ethnicity, Race, or Nationality	By Gender
Fiji	23 and 19 of 71 seats reserved for Fijians and Indo-Fijians, respectively	
France		50% of candidates; parties and groups cannot present numbers of candidates that differ by more than 2%.
Guyana		33% of party electoral lists
Haiti		30% in all elected and appointed positions
Honduras		40% of party electoral lists
India	79 seats reserved for Scheduled Castes and 41 for Scheduled Tribes of 543 in the Lok Sabha (lower house of parliament); Prime Minister has the right to appoint up to 2 Anglo-Indians to the same chamber (22%)	
Indonesia		At least one in every three candidates on party electoral lists
Iran	5 of 290 seats reserved for Zoroastrians, Jews, and Christians (2%)	
Iraq		No fewer than one out of the first three candidates; no fewer than two of the first six candidates on the list must be a woman and so forth.
Ireland		30% of candidates
Jordan	9 seats for Christians, 6 for Bedouins, and 3 for Circassians of 110 (22%)	10% of seats
Kenya		33% of seats
Kiribati	1 of 41 seats for Banabans (2%)	
Kosovo[b]	20 of 120 seats reserved for minorities (17%)	
Kyrgystan		30% of party electoral lists

Country	By Ethnicity, Race, or Nationality	By Gender
Lebanon	Of 128 national assembly seats: Maronites (34), Sunnis (27), Shiites (27), Greek Orthodox (14), Greek Catholics (8), Druzes (8), Armenian Orthodox (5), Alaouites (2), Armenian Catholics (1), Protestants (1), Christian Minorities (1) (100% reserved)	
Macedonia		One out of every three positions on party electoral lists
Mauritania		30% to 50%; where three candidates are to be elected, the lists must include at least one female candidate placed first or second; otherwise each group of four candidates on the list must include two women.
Mauritius	8 of 70 seats are filled by the "best losers" representing the four constitutionally recognized ethnic communities (Hindus, Muslims, Chinese, and Franco-Mauritian/Creole Christians).	
Mexico	28 indigenous-majority districts	40% of candidates
Montenegro	5 of 81 seats reserved for Albanians (6%)	
Morocco		9% of seats
Nepal		At least 33% for entire assembly; 50% on party electoral lists for seats allocated under PR
New Zealand	7 of 120 seats reserved for Maoris in unicameral parliament (6%)	
Niger	8 of 83 seats reserved for Tuaregs in unicameral parliament (10%)	10% of seats
North Korea		20% of candidates

(*continued*)

References

Abou-Zeid, Gihan. (2006). The Arab region: Women's access to the decision-making process across the Arab nation. In Drude Dahlerup (Ed.), *Women in politics: Electoral quotas, equality and democracy* (pp. 168–193). London: Routledge.

Acker, Joan. (1990). Hierarchies, jobs, bodies: A theory of gendered organizations. *Gender & Society*, 4(2), 139–158.

afrocolombianosvisibles. (2014). Afronota: Bancada Afro 2014–2018. Retrieved from http://afrocolombianosvisibles.blogspot.com/search?updated-max=2014-10-20T04:24:00-07:00

Agrawal, Nina, André, Richard, Berger, Ryan, Escarfuller, Wilda, & Sabatini, Christopher. (2012). *Political representation and social inclusion: A comparative study of Bolivia, Colombia, Ecuador, and Guatemala.* New York: Americas Society.

Agudelo, Carlos Efrén. (2000). *Comportamiento electoral en poblaciones negras.* Algunos elementos para el análisis. *Documentos de Trabajo CIDSE-Univalle*, pp. 2–35.

(2001). Nuevos actores sociales y relegitimación del estado. Estado y construcción del movimiento social de comunidades negras en Colombia. *Análisis Político*, 43(May–August), 3–31.

(2002). Etnicidad negra y elecciones en Colombia. *Journal of Latin American Anthropology*, 7(2), 168–197.

(2004). La Constitución Política de 1991 y la inclusión ambigua de las poblaciones negras. In Jaime Arocha (Ed.), *Utopía para los excluidos: El multiculturalismo en África y América Latina* (pp. 179–203). Bogotá: Universidad Nacional de Colombia.

Albó, Xavier. (2002). *Pueblos indios en la política.* La Paz: Centro de Investigación y Promoción del Campesinado (CIPCA).

(2008). *Movimientos y poder indígena en Bolivia, Ecuador y Perú.* La Paz: Centro de Investigación y Promoción del Campesinado (CIPCA).

Albró, Robert. (2006). The culture of democracy and Bolivia´s indigenous movement. *Critique of Anthropology*, 26(4), 387–410.

Alemán, Eduardo. (2006). Policy gatekeepers in Latin American legislatures. *Latin American Politics and Society*, 48(3), 125–155.

(2010). Unified government, bill approval, and the legislative weight of the president. *Comparative Political Studies*, 43(4), 511–534.

Alvarez, Sonia E. (1990). *Engendering democracy in Brazil: Women's movements in transition politics.* Princeton, NJ: Princeton University Press.

Amenta, Edwin, Caren, Neal, Chiarello, Elizabeth, & Su, Yang. (2010). The political consequences of social movements. *Annual Review of Sociology*, 36, 287–307.

Ames, Barry. (1995). Electoral strategy under open-list proportional representation. *American Journal of Political Science*, 39(2), 406–433.

Anderson, Benedict. (1991). *Imagined communities: Reflections on the growth and spread of nationalism.* New York and London: Verso.

Andrews, George Reid. (1991). *Blacks and whites in São Paulo, Brazil, 1888–1988.* Madison: The University of Wisconsin Press.

(2004). *Afro-Latin America, 1800–2000.* New York: Oxford University Press.

Angosto Ferrández, Luis Fernando. (2011). La competencia por la representación indígena en las elecciones venezolanas (2004–2010). *Cuestiones Políticas*, 27(46), 13–54.

Anria, Santiago. (2009). *Informal institutions and party organizations: A case study of MAS-IPSP in urban areas of La Paz and El Alto.* M.A. thesis, Simon Fraser University.

(2013). Social movements, party organization, and populism: Insights from the Bolivian MAS. *Latin American Politics and Society*, 55(3), 19–46.

Appiah, Anthony. (1997). Race, culture, identity: Misunderstood connections. In Anthony Appiah & Amy Gutmann (Eds.), *Color conscious: The political morality of race (pp. 30–105).* Princeton, NJ: Princeton University Press.

Aragón, Jorge. (2012). *Participación y representación política indígena: Perfil electoral y orientaciones políticas de la población indígena en el Perú.* Lima: Jurado Nacional de Elecciones/Dirección Nacional de Educación y Formación Cívica Ciudadana.

Archenti, Nélida, & Johnson, Niki. (2006). Engendering the legislative agenda with and without the quota. *Sociología, Problemas, e Práticas*, 52, 133–153.

Arocha, Jaime. (2004). Ley 70 de 1993: Utopía para afrodescendientes excluidos. In Jaime Arocha (Ed.), *Utopía para los excluidos: El multiculturalismo en África y América Latina* (pp. 159–178). Bogotá: Universidad Nacional de Colombia.

Assies, Willem, & Salman, Ton. (2005). Ethnicity and politics in Bolivia. *Ethnopolitics*, 4(3), 269–297.

Atkins, David C, & Gallop, R. J. (2007). Rethinking how family researchers model infrequent outcomes: A tutorial on count regression and zero-inflated models. *Journal of Family Psychology*, 21(4), 726–735.

Auyero, Javier. (2001). *Poor people's politics: Peronist survival networks and the legacy of Evita.* Durham: Duke University Press.

Bachelet, Michelle. (2007). Mensaje No. 860-355: Mensaje de S.E. la Presidenta de la república con el que inicia un proyecto de ley que establece participación política equilibrada de hombres y mujeres. Santiago, Chile (October 26, 2007).

(2009). *Al pais le hace bien que haya más mujeres en la política.* Retrieved from www.datoanuncios.org/?a=20870.

Bailey, Stanley. (2009). *Legacies of race: Identities, attitudes, and politics in Brazil.* Stanford, CA: Stanford University Press.

Bailey, Stanley R, Loveman, Mara, & Muniz, Jeronimo O. (2013). Measures of "race" and the analysis of racial inequality in Brazil. *Social Science Research*, 42(1), 106–119.

Bailyn, Lotte. (2003). Academic careers and gender equity: Lessons learned from MIT1. *Gender, Work & Organization*, 10(2), 137–153.

Baldez, Lisa. (2002). *Why women protest: Women's movements in Chile.* Cambridge: Cambridge University Press.

(2004). Elected bodies: The adoption of gender quotas in Mexico. *Legislative Studies Quarterly*, 29(2), 231–258.

Baldez, Lisa, & Brañez, Patricia. (2005). ¿Cuánto hemos avanzado las mujeres con las cuotas? El caso Boliviano. In Magdalena León (Ed.), *Nadando contra la corriente: Mujeres y cuotas políticas en los países andinos* (pp. 141–168). Bogotá: United Nations Development Fund for Women, United Nations Population Fund.

Banducci, Susan, Donovan, Todd, & Karp, Jeffrey. (2004). Minority representation, empowerment, and participation. *Journal of Politics*, 66(2), 534–566.

Barbary, Olivier, Ramírez, Héctor Fabio, Urrea, Fernando, & Viáfara, Carlos. (2004). Perfiles contemporáneos de la población afrocolombiana. In Olivier Barbary & Fernando Urrea (Eds.), *Gente negra en Colombia: Dinámicas sociopolíticas en Cali y el Pacífico* (pp. 69–112). Medellín: Centro de Investigaciones y Documentación Socioeconómicas, Facultad de Ciencias Sociales y Económicas de la Universidad del Valle.

Barbary, Olivier, & Urrea, Fernando. (2004). Introducción. In Olivier Barbary & Fernando Urrea (Eds.), *Gente negra en Colombia: Dinámicas sociopolíticas en Cali y el Pacífico* (pp. 21–65). Medellín: Centro de Investigaciones y Documentación Socioeconómicas, Facultad de Ciencias Sociales y Económicas de la Universidad del Valle.

Barragan, Rossana. (2008). Oppressed or privileged regions: Some historical reflections on the use of state resources. In John Crabtree & Laurence Whitehead (Eds.), *Unresolved tensions: Bolivia past and present* (pp. 83–103). Pittsburgh: University of Pittsburgh Press.

Basset, Yann. (2011). "Las Circunscripciones Especiales: Unas instituciones obsoletas?" *Análisis Político* 72 (May-August): 43–59.

Beckwith, Karen. (2007). Numbers and newness: The descriptive and substantive representation of women. *Canadian Journal of Political Science*, 40(1), 27–49.

Beckwith, Karen, & Cowell-Meyers, Kimberly. (2007). Sheer numbers: Critical representation thresholds and women's political representation. *Perspectives on Politics*, 5(03), 553–565.

Benhabib, Seyla. (1992). *Situating the self: Gender, community and postmodernism in contemporary ethics.* New York: Routledge.

(2002). *The claims of culture: Equality and diversity in the global era.* Princeton, NJ: Princeton University Press.

Bih-Er, Chou, Clark, Cal, & Clark, Janet. (1990). *Women in Taiwan politics.* New York: Lynne Rienner.

Bird, Karen. (2001). Liberté, egalité, fraternité, parité ... and diversité?: The difficult question of ethnic difference in the French parity debate. *Contemporary French Civilization*, 25(2), 271–292.

(2002). *Who are the women? Where are the women? And what difference can they make? The effects of gender parity in French municipal elections.* Paper presented at the Annual Meeting of the American Political Science Association, Boston.

Bjarnegård, Elin. (2013). *Gender, informal institutions and political recruitment: explaining male dominance in parliamentary representation.* New York: Palgrave Macmillan.

Bjarnegård, Elin, & Pär Zetterberg. (2014). Why are representational guarantees adopted for women and minorities? Comparing constituency formation and electoral quota design within countries. *Representation*, 50(3), 307–320.

Blofield, Merike H., & Haas, Liesl. (2005). Defining a democracy: Reforming the laws on women's rights in Chile, 1990–2002. *Latin American Politics and Society*, 47(3), 35–68.

Botero Jaramillo, Felipe. (1998). El senado que nunca fue. La circunscripción nacional después de tres elecciones. In Andrés Davila & Ana María Bejarano (Eds.), *Elecciones y democracia en Colombia, 1997–1998* (pp. 285–335). Bogotá: Ediciones Uniandes.

Bourdieu, Pierre, & Wacquant, Loïc. (1999). On the cunning of imperialist reason. *Theory, Culture, and Society*, 16(1), 41–58.

Brubaker, Rogers. (2004). *Ethnicity without groups*: Cambridge, MA: Harvard University Press.

Brubaker, Rogers, Loveman, Mara, & Stamatov, Peter. (2004). Ethnicity as cognition. *Theory and Society*, 33(1), 31–64.

Bruhn, Kathleen. (2003). Whores and lesbians: Political activism, party strategies, and gender quotas in Mexico. *Electoral Studies*, 22(1), 101–119.

Brusco, Valeria, Nazareno, Marcelo, & Stokes, Susan Carol. (2004). Vote buying in Argentina. *Latin American Research Review*, 39(2), 66–88.

Buvinić, Mayra. (2004). Introduction: Social inclusion in Latin America. In Mayra Buvinić, Jacqueline Mazza & Ruthanne Deutsch (Eds.), *Social inclusion and economic development in Latin America* (pp. 3–31). Baltimore: Inter-American Development Bank via the Johns Hopkins University Press.

Cabrero, Ferran, Pop, Álvaro, Morales, Zully, Chuji, Mónica, & Mamani, Carlos. (2013). *Ciudadanía intercultural: Aportes desde la participación política de los pueblos indígenas en Latinoamérica Programa Global de Apoyo al Ciclo Electoral.* Quito, Ecuador: Programa de las Naciones Unidos para el Desarrollo.

Caldwell, Kia Lily. (2007). *Negras in Brazil: Re-envisioning black women, citizenship, and the politics of identity.* New Brunswick: Rutgers University Press.

Calvo, Ernesto, & Leiras, Marcelo. (2010). *Compañero, correligionario, comprovinciano: Initial notes on the nationalization of legislative collaboration.* Paper presented at the 106th Meeting of the American Political Science Association, Washington, DC.

Calvo, Ernesto, & Murillo, Maria Victoria. (2004). Who delivers? Partisan clients in the Argentine electoral market. *American Journal of Political Science*, 48(4), 742–757.

Camacho, Paola. (2013). Afrocolombianos sin representación en el Congreso. Retrieved from www.congresovisible.org/agora/post/afrocolombianos-sin-representacion-en-el-congreso/5107/

Cameron, John D. (2010). *Is this what autonomy looks like? Tensions and challenges in the construction of indigenous autonomy in Bolivia.* Paper presented at the Annual Meeting of the Latin American Studies Association, Toronto, ON, Canada.

Campos, Luis Augusto. (2013). O Pardo como dilema político. *Insight Inteligência, Outubro-novembro-dezembro*, 80–91.

Cárdenas, Víctor Hugo. (2011). Participación política indígena y políticas públicas para pueblos indígenas en Bolivia. In Beatriz Cajías de la Vega (Ed.), *Participación política indígena y políticas públicas para pueblos indígenas en América Latina* (pp. 17–64). La Paz: Fundación Konrad Adenauer.

Carey, John M., & Shugart, Matthew Soberg. (1995). Incentives to cultivate a personal vote: A rank ordering of electoral formulas. *Electoral Studies*, 14(4), 417–439.

Carroll, Susan J. (Ed.). (2001). *The impact of women in public office*. Bloomington: Indiana University Press.

Catalyst. (2013). 2013 Catalyst Census: Fortune 500 Women Board Directors.

Caul, Miki. (1999). Women's representation in parliament: The role of political parties. *Party Politics*, 5(1), 79–98.

Celis, Karen, & Childs, Sarah. (2008). The descriptive and substantive representation of women: New directions. *Parliamentary Affairs*, 61(3), 419–425.

Celis, Karen, Childs, Sarah, Kantola, Johanna, & Krook, Mona Lena. (2008). Rethinking women's substantive representation. *Representation*, 44(2), 99–110.

Cepeda, Fernando. (2003). *La reforma política en Colombia. Reforma política para la ampliación de la democracia* (pp. 15–39). Bogotá: Consejo Gremial Nacional.

Central Intelligence Agency. (2011). The world fact book. Retrieved from www.cia.gov/library/publications/the-world-factbook/

Chandra, Kanchan. (2004). *Why ethnic parties succeed: Patronage and ethnic head counts in India*. New York: Cambridge University Press.

(2005). Ethnic parties and democratic stability. *Perspectives on Politics*, 3(2), 235–252.

(2006). What is ethnic identity and does it matter? *Annual Review of Political Science*, 9, 397–424.

Chien, Tuan-sheng. (1950). *The government and politics of China*. Cambridge, MA: Harvard University Press.

Childs, Sarah, & Krook, Mona Lena. (2006). Should feminists give up on critical mass? A contingent yes. *Politics & Gender*, 2(4), 522–530.

Chor Maio, Marcos, & Ventura Santos, Ricardo. (2005). Política de cotas raciais, os "olhos da sociedade" e os usos da antropologia: O caso do vestibular da Universidade de Brasília (UNB). *Horizontes Antropológicos*, 11(23), 181–214.

Constitución Política de la República de Colombia. (2004). *Constitución Política de Colombia*. Bogotá: Editorial Temis.

Constitución de la República Bolivariana de Venezuela. (2004). *Constitución de la República Bolivariana de Venezuela*. Caracas: Imprenta Nacional.

Cope, R. Douglas. (1994). *The limits of racial domination: Plebeian society in colonial Mexico City, 1660–1720*. Madison: University of Wisconsin Press.

Cox, Gary W. (2006). The organization of democratic legislatures. In Barry Weingast & Donald Wittman (Eds.), *The Oxford handbook of political economy* (pp. 141–161). New York: Oxford University Press.

Cox, Gary W., & McCubbins, Mathew D. (1993). *Legislative leviathan: Party government in the House*. Berkeley: University of California Press.

Cox, Gary W., & McCubbins, Mathew D. (2005). *Setting the agenda: Responsible party government in the U.S. House of Representatives*. Cambridge: Cambridge University Press.

Crenshaw, Kimberlé. (1991). Mapping the margins: Intersectionality, identity politics, and violence against women of color. *Standford Law Review*, 43(6), 1241–1299.

Crisp, Brian F., Escobar-Lemmon, Maria C., Jones, Bradford S., Jones, Mark P., & Taylor-Robinson, Michelle M. (2004). Vote-seeking incentives and legislative representation in six presidential democracies. *Journal of Politics*, 66(3), 823–846.

Crisp, Brian F., & Ingall, Rachael E. (2002). Institutional engineering and the nature of representation: Mapping the effects of electoral reform in Colombia. *American Journal of Political Science*, 46(4), 733–748.

Cunin, Elisabeth. (2003). La política étnica entre alteridad y esterotipo. Reflexiones sobre las elecciones de marzo de 2002 en Colombia. *Análisis Político*, 48(January–April), 77–93.

Daflon, Verônica Toste, Feres Júnior, João, & Campos, Luiz Augusto. (2013). Race-based affirmative actions in Brazilian public higher education: An analytical overview. *Cadernos de Pesquisa*, 43(148), 302–327.

Daher, Adel, et. al. (2008). Manifesto: Cento e treze cidadãos anti-racistas contra as leis raciais. *Revista Época*. Retrieved from http://revistaepoca.globo.com/Revista/Epoca/0,,EDR83466-6014,00.html

Dahlerup, Drude. (1988). From a small to a large minority: Women in Scandinavian politics. *Scandinavian Political Studies*, 11(4), 275–297.

(2002). Using quotas to increase women's political representation. In Azza Karam (Ed.), *Women in parliament: Beyond numbers* (Updated from 1998 ed., pp. 91–106). Stockholm: International IDEA.

(2006a). Introduction. In Drude Dahlerup (Ed.), *Women, quotas, and politics* (pp. 3–31). New York: Routledge.

(2006b). The story of the theory of critical mass. *Politics & Gender*, 2(4), 511–522.

(2008). Gender quotas-controversial but trendy: On expanding the research agenda. *International Feminist Journal of Politics*, 10(3), 322–328.

Dahlerup, Drude, & Friedenvall, Lenita. (2005). Quotas as a fast track to equal representation for women. *International Feminist Journal of Politics*, 7(1), 26–48.

Darcy, Robert, Welch, Susan, & Clark, Janet. (1994). *Women, elections, and representation* (2nd ed.). Lincoln: The University of Nebraska Press.

Degler, Carl. (1971). *Neither black nor white: Slavery and race relations in Brazil and the United States*. Madison: The University of Wisconsin Press.

De la Fuente, Alejandro. (2001). *A nation for all: Race, inequality, and politics in twentieth-century Cuba*. Chapel Hill: University of North Carolina Press.

(2007). Race, culture, and politics. In Marifeli Pérez-Stable (Ed.), *Looking forward: Comparative perspectives on Cuba's transition* (pp. 138–162). Notre Dame, IN: University of Notre Dame Press.

(2013). A Lesson from Cuba on Race. *New York Times*. Retrieved from http://opinionator.blogs.nytimes.com/2013/11/17/a-lesson-from-cuba-on-race/

De Luca, Miguel, Jones, Mark P., & Tula, María Inés (2002). Back rooms or ballot boxes?: Candidate nomination in Argentina. *Comparative Political Studies*, 35(4), 413–436.

Diermeier, Daniel, & Myerson, Roger. (1999). Bicameralism and its consequences for legislative organization. *American Economic Review*, 89(5), 1182–1196.

Do Alto, Hervé, & Stefanoni, Pablo. (2009). *El Mas, un partido en tiempo heterogéneo.* La Paz: PNUD-Idea Internacional.

Dobbin, Frank, & Kalev, Alexandra. (2013). *Do affirmative action and equal opportunity work? Evidence from private sector workplaces.* Paper presented at Conference on Contested Responses to Gender Inequalities, Yale Law School and Yale Women's Faculty Forum, New Haven, CT, April 26–27, 2013.

Dobbin, Frank, Kalev, Alexandra, & Roberson, QM. (2013). The origins and effects of corporate diversity programs. In Quinetta M. Roberson (Ed.), *The Oxford handbook of diversity and work* (pp. 253–281). Oxford Library of Psychology. New York: Oxford University Press.

Domínguez, Jorge I. (1978). *Cuba: Order and revolution.* Cambridge, MA: Belknap Press of Harvard University Press.

(1980). *Insurrection or Loyalty: The Breakdown of the Spanish-American Empire.* Cambridge, MA: Belknap Press of Harvard University Press.

Dovi, Suzanne. (2002). Preferable descriptive representatives: Will just any woman, black, or Latino do? *American Political Science Review,* 96(4), 729–743.

Downs, Anthony. (1957). *An economic theory of democracy.* New York: Harper and Row.

Dryzek, John. (1996). Political inclusion and the dynamics of democratization. *American Political Science Review,* 90(3), 475–487.

Duerst-Lahti, Georgia. (2005). Institutional gendering: Theoretical insights into the environment of women officeholders. In Sue Thomas & Clyde Wilcox (Eds.), *Women and elective office: Past, present, and future* (2nd ed., pp. 230–243). New York: Oxford University Press.

Duerst-Lahti, Georgia, & Kelly, Rita Mae. (1995). *Gender power, leadership, and governance.* Ann Arbor: University of Michigan Press.

Durrieu, Marcela. (1999). *Se dice de nosotras.* Buenos Aires: Catálogos Editora.

Eaton, Kent. (2007). Backlash in Bolivia: Regional autonomy in Bolivia as a reaction against indigenous mobilization. *Politics & Society,* 35(1), 71–102.

(2011). Conservative autonomy movements: Territorial dimensions of ideological conflict in Bolivia and Ecuador. *Comparative Politics,* 43(3), 291–310.

Eckstein, Harry. (1975). Case study and theory in political science. In Fred Greenstein & Polsby Nelson (Eds.), *Strategies of inquiry,* Vol. 7 (pp. 79–135). Reading, MA: Addison-Wesley.

Escandón Vega, Marcela Patricia. (2011). *Circunscripciones especiales indígenas y afro (1991–2010): Cuestionamientos a la representación identitaria en el Congreso de Colombia.* Bogotá: Universidad de los Andes, Facultad de Ciencias Sociales-CESO, Departamento de Ciencia Política.

Espeland, Wendy Nelson, & Sauder, Michael. (2007). Rankings and reactivity: How public measures recreate social worlds. *American Journal of Sociology,* 113(1), 1–40.

Esping-Andersen, Gösta. (2009). *The incomplete revolution: Adapting welfare states to women's new roles.* Cambridge, UK: Polity Press.

Farthing, Linda. (2009). Thinking left in Bolivia: Interview with Álvaro Garcia Linera. Retrieved from http://boliviarising.blogspot.com/2009/08/thinking-left-in-bolivia-interview-with.html. Accessed October 1, 2009.

Fearon, James D. (2003). Ethnic and cultural diversity by country. *Journal of Economic Growth*, 8(2), 195–222.

Feres Júnior, João. (2008). Ação afirmativa: Política pública e opinião. *Sinais Sociais*, 3(8), 38–77.

(2012). Inclusão no ensino superior: Raça ou renda? In Marcelo Giardino (Ed.), *Democratização da educação superior no Brasil: Avanços e desafios*: Cadernos do pensamento crítico Latino-Americano: Grupo Estratégico de Análise da Educação Superior no Brasil da FLASCO Brasil.

Feres Júnior, João, Toste Daflon, Verônica, & Campos, Luiz Augusto. (2012). Ação afirmativa, raça e racismo: Uma análise das ações de inclusão racial nos mandatos de Lula e Dilma. *Revista de Ciencias Humanas*, 12(2), 399–414.

Fernando, André. (2011). Participação política e políticas públicas para os povos indígenas no Brasil. In Beatriz Cajías de la Vega (Ed.), *Participación política indígena y políticas públicas para pueblos indígenas en América Latina* (pp. 65–139). La Paz: Fundación Konrad Adenauer.

Ferree, Karen E., Powell, G. Bingham, & Scheiner, Ethan. (2013). How context shapes electoral rule effects. In Mala Htun & G. Bingham Powell, Jr. (Eds.), *Report of the task force on electoral rules and democratic governance*. Washington, DC: American Political Science Association.

Field, Les W. (1996). State, anti-state, and indigenous entities: Reflections upon a Páez Resguardo and the new Colombian Constitution. *Journal of Latin American Anthropology*, 1(2), 98–119.

Fishkin, James S. (1991). *Democracy and deliberation: New directions for democratic reform* (Vol. 217). New York: Cambridge University Press.

Franceschet, Susan. (2005). *Women and politics in Chile*. Boulder, CO: Lynne Rienner.

(2010). Continuity or change? Gender policy in the Bachelet administration. In Silvia Bortzutzky & Gregory B. Weeks (Eds.), *The Bachelet Government: Consensus and Change in the Post-Pinochet Chile* (pp. 158–180). Gainseville: University Press of Florida.

Franceschet, Susan, & Piscopo, Jennifer. (2013). Federalism, decentralization, and reproductive rights in Argentina and Chile. *Publius, the Journal of Federalism*, 43(1), 129–150.

Franceschet, Susan, & Piscopo, Jennifer M. (2008). Gender quotas and women's substantive representation: Lessons from Argentina. *Politics & Gender*, 4(3), 393–425.

Fraser, Nancy. (1997). *Justice interruptus: Critical reflections on the "postsocialist" condition*. New York: Routledge.

(2000). Rethinking recognition. *New Left Review*, 3, 107–120.

(2003). Social justice in the age of identity politics: Redistribution, recognition, and particpation. In Nancy Fraser & Axel Honneth (Eds.), *Redistribution or recognition? A political-philosophical exchange* (pp. 7–109). New York: Verso.

(2007). Feminist politics in the age of recognition: A two-dimensional approach to gender justice. *Studies in Social Justice*, 1(1), 23–35.

Freyre, Gilberto. (1986). *The masters and the slaves* (Samuel Putnam, Trans.). Berkeley: University of California Press.

Friedman, Elisabeth. (2000). *Unfinished transitions: Women and the gendered development of democracy in Venezuela*. University Park: Pennsylvania State University Press.

Fry, Peter, & Maggie, Yvonne. (2004). Cotas raciais – Construindo um país divido? *Econômica*, 6(1), 153–161.

Fry, Peter, Maggie, Yvonne, Chor Maio, Marcos, Monteiro, Simone, & Ventura Santos, Ricardo (Eds.). (2007). *Divisões perigosas: Políticas raciais no Brasil contemporâneo*. Rio de Janeiro: Civilização Brasileira.

Fuchs, Victor R. (1990). *Women's quest for economic equality*. Cambridge, MA: Harvard University Press.

Fung, Archon. (2003). Recipes for public spheres: Eight institutional design choices and their consequences. *Journal of Philosophy*, 11(3), 338–367.

(2006). Varieties of participation in complex governance. *Public Administration Review*, 66(s1), 66–75.

Fung, Archon, & Wright, Erik Olin. (2003). *Deepening democracy: Institutional innovations in empowered participatory governance*. London: Verso.

Galanter, Marc. (1984). *Competing equalities: Law and the backward classes in India / Marc Galanter*. Berkeley: University of California Press.

Galvis, Miguel Antonio. (2013). La Corte Constitucional Colombiana recortó derechos políticos de minorias étnicas. *Comunidad El Pais*. Retrieved from http://lacomunidad.elpais.com/minorias-etnicas/2013/5/5/la-corte-constitucional-colombiana-recorto-derechos-politicos-de

García Bedolla, Lisa. (2007). Intersections of inequality: Understanding marginalization and privilege in the post-civil rights era. *Politics & Gender*, 3(2), 232–248.

Gil, Laura. (2013). Circunscripciones especiales. *El Tiempo*. Retrieved from www.eltiempo.com/opinion/columnistas/lauragil/ARTICULO-WEB-NEW_NOTA_INTERIOR-12862314.html

Giraldo García, Fernando, & López Jiménez, José Daniel. (2007). *Mecanismos de participación política electoral afrodescendiente en Colombia. Estudios sobre la participación política de la población afrodescendiente: La experiencia en Colombia*. San José: Inter-American Institute of Human Rights.

Giraud, Isabelle, & Jenson, Jane. (2001). Constitutionalizing equal access: High hopes, dashed hopes? In Jytte Klausen & Charles S. Maier (Eds.), *Has liberalism failed women? Assuring equal representation in Europe and the United States* (pp. 69–88). London: Palgrave.

Glendon, Mary Ann. (1989). *The transformation of family law*. Chicago: University of Chicago Press.

Goetz, Anne Marie. (2003). Women's political effectiveness: A conceptual framework. In Anne Marie Goetz & Shireen Hassim (Eds.), *No shortcuts to power: African women in politics and policy making*. London: Zed Books.

Goldin, Claudia. (1990). *Understanding the gender gap: An economic history of American women*. Oxford: Oxford University Press.

(2006). *The quiet revolution that transformed women's employment, education, and family*. National Bureau of Economic Research Working Paper no. 11953.

Graham, Richard, Skidmore, Thomas, Helg, Aline, & Knight, Alan (Eds.). (1990). *The idea of race in Latin America, 1870–1940*. Austin: University of Texas Press.

Grey, Sandra. (2006). Numbers and beyond: The relevance of critical mass in gender research. *Politics & Gender*, 2(4), 492–502.

Guimarães, Antonio Sérgio Alfredo. (2008). Novas inflexões ideológicas no estudo do racism no Brasil. In Jonas Zoninstein & João Feres Júnior (Eds.), *Ação afirmativa no ensino superior brasileiro* (pp. 175–192). Rio de Janeiro: IUPERJ.

Guinier, Lani. (1994). *The tyranny of the majority: Fundamental fairness and representative democracy.* New York: The Free Press.

Gustafson, Bret. (2008). By legal means or otherwise: The Bolivian right regroups. *NACLA Report on the Americas,* 41(1), 20–25.

(2009a). Manipulating cartographies: Plurinationalism, autonomy, and indigenous resurgence in Bolivia. *Anthropological Quarterly,* 82(4), 985–1016.

(2009b). *New languages of the state: Indigenous resurgence and the politics of knowledge in Bolivia.* Durham: Duke University Press.

(2011). Power necessarily comes from below: Guaraní autonomies and their others. In Nicole Fabricant & Bret Gustafson (Eds.), *Remapping Bolivia: Resources, territoriality and indigeneity in plurinational state* (pp. 268–308). Santa Fe: SAR Press.

Haas, Liesl. (2000). *Legislating equality: Institutional politics and the expansion of women's rights in Chile.* PhD dissertation, University of North Carolina.

Habermas, Jürgen. (1996). *Between facts and norms: Contributions to a discourse theory of law and democracy.* Cambridge, MA: MIT Press.

Hanchard, Michael George. (1994). *Orpheus and power: The movimento negro of Rio de Janeiro and São Paulo, Brazil, 1945–1988.* Princeton, NJ: Princeton University Press.

Hancock, Ange-Marie. (2007). When multiplication doesn't equal quick addition: Examining intersectionality as a research paradigm. *Perspectives on Politics,* 5(1), 63–79.

Harris, Marvin. (1964). *Patterns of race in the Americas.* New York: Walker and Company.

Hasenbalg, Carlos. (1979). *Discriminação e desigualdades raciais no Brasil.* Rio de Janeiro: Graal.

Hassim, Shireen. (2009). Perverse consequences: The impact of quotas for women on democratisation in Africa. In Ian Shapiro, Susan C. Stokes, Elisabeth Jean Wood, & Alexander S. Kirshner (Eds.), *Political representation* (pp. 211–235). New York: Cambridge University Press.

Hawkesworth, Mary. (2003). Congressional enactments of race-gender: Toward a theory of raced-gendered institutions. *American Political Science Review,* 97(4), 529–550.

Heath, Roseanna Michelle, Schwindt-Bayer, Leslie A., & Taylor-Robinson, Michelle M. (2005). Women on the sidelines: Women's representation on committees in Latin American legislatures. *American Journal of Political Science,* 49(2), 420–436.

Henriques, Ricardo. (2001). *Desigualdade racial no Brasil: Evolução das condições de vida na década de 90. IPEA texto para discussão no. 807.* Brasília and Rio de Janeiro: Instituto de Pesquisa Econômica Aplicada (IPEA).

Hero, Rodney E., & Wolbrecht, Christina. (2005). Introduction. In Christina Wolbrecht & Rodney E Hero (Eds.), *The politics of democratic inclusion* (pp. 1–14). Philadelphia: Temple University Press.

Highton, Benjamin, & Rocca, Michael S. (2005). Beyond the roll-call arena: The determinants of position taking in congress. *Political Research Quarterly,* 58(2), 303–316.

Hinojosa, Magda. (2012). *Selecting women, electing women: Political representation and candidate selection in Latin America.* Philadelphia: Temple University Press.

Hirshfield, Laura E, & Joseph, Tiffany D. (2012). 'We need a woman, we need a black woman': Gender, race, and identity taxation in the academy. *Gender and Education,* 24(2), 213–227.

Hochschild, Arlie Russell. (1975). Inside the clockwork of male careers. In Florence Howe (Ed.), *Women and the power to change* (pp. 47–80). Berkeley: Carnegie Commission on Higher Education.

Hoetink, Harmannus, & Hooykaas, Eva M. (1971). *Caribbean race relations: A study of two variants* (Vol. 337). London: Published for the Institute of Race Relations by Oxford University Press.

Hoffmann, Odile. (1998). Políticas agrarias, reformas del estado y adscripciones identitarias: Colombia y México. *Análisis Político,* 34(May–August), 3–24.

(2004). Espacios y región en el Pacífico sur: Hacia la construcción de una sociedad regional? In Olivier Barbary & Fernando Urrea (Eds.), *Gente negra en Colombia. Dinámicas sociopolíticas en Cali y el Pacífico* (pp. 195–224). Medellín: Cidse-Ird-Colciencias.

Hola, Eugenia, Veloso, Paulina, & Ruiz, Carolina. (2002). *Percepciones de los lideres políticos y sociales sobre la ley de cuotas: Contenidos y factibilidad.* Santiago, Chile: Servicio Nacional de la Mujer.

Holmsten, Stephanie S., Moser, Robert G., & Slosar, Mary C. (2010). Do ethnic parties exclude women? *Comparative Political Studies,* 43, 1179–1201.

Hooker, Juliet. (2005). Indigenous inclusion/black exclusion: Race, ethnicity and multicultural citizenship in Latin America. *Journal of Latin American Studies,* 37(2), 285–310.

Hooks, Bell. (1984). *Feminist theory from margin to center.* Boston: South End Press.

Horowitz, Donald L. (1985). *Ethnic groups in conflict.* Berkeley: University of California Press.

Htun, Mala. (1997). *Moving into power: Strategies to expand women's opportunities for leadership in Latin America and the Caribbean.* Washington, DC: Inter-American Development Bank.

(1998a). *Women's rights and opportunities in Latin America: Problems and prospects.* Women's Leadership Conference of the Americas Issue Brief. Washington, D.C.: Inter-American Dialogue.

(1998b). *Women's political participation, representation and leadership in Latin America.* Women's Leadership Conference of the Americas Issue Brief. Washington, D.C.: Inter-American Dialgoue.

(2001). *Women's leadership in Latin America: Trends and challenges.* Paper presented at Politics Matters: A Dialogue of Women Political Leaders, Inter-American Development Bank, Washington, DC.

(2002a). Mujeres y poder politico en Latinoamérica. In Myriam Méndez-Montalvo & Julie Ballington (Eds.), *Mujeres en el parlamento: Más allá de los números* (pp. 19–43). Stockholm: International IDEA.

(2002b). Puzzles of women's rights in Brazil. *Social Research: An International Quarterly,* 69(3), 733–751.

(2003a). *Sex and the state: Abortion, divorce, and the family under Latin American dictatorships and democracies.* New York: Cambridge University Press.

(2003b). Women and democracy. In Jorge Dominguez & Michael Shifter (Eds.), *Constructing democratic governance in Latin America* (2nd ed., pp. 118–136). Baltimore: Johns Hopkins University Press.

(2004a). From 'racial democracy' to affirmative action: Changing state policy on race in Brazil. *Latin American Research Review* (1), 60–89.

(2004b). Is gender like ethnicity? The political representation of identity groups. *Perspectives on Politics*, 2(3), 439–458.

(2005). Women, political parties and electoral systems in Latin America. In Julie Ballington & Azza Karam (Eds.), *Women in parliament. Beyond numbers. A new edition* (pp. 112–121). Stockholm: International IDEA.

(2007). Gender equality in transition polities: Comparative perspectives on Cuba. In Marifeli Pérez-Stable (Ed.), *Looking forward: Comparative perspectives on Cuba's transition* (pp. 119–137). Notre Dame, IN: University of Notre Dame Press.

(2009). Life, liberty, and family values: Church and state in the struggle over Latin America's social agenda. In Frances Hagopian (Ed.), *Religious pluralism, democracy, and the Catholic Church in Latin America* (pp. 335–364). Notre Dame, IN: University of Notre Dame Press.

Htun, Mala, & Jones, Mark P. (2002). Engendering the right to participate in decision-making: Electoral quotas and women's leadership in Latin America. In Nikki Craske & Maxine D. Molyneux (Eds.), *Gender, rights and justice in Latin America* (pp. 69–93). London: Palgrave.

Htun, Mala, & Ossa, Juan Pablo. (2013). Political inclusion of marginalized groups: Indigenous reservations and gender parity in Bolivia. *Politics, Groups, and Identities*, 1(1), 4–25.

Htun, Mala, & Piscopo, Jennifer. (2010). *Presence without empowerment? Women and politics in Latin America and the Caribbean.* New York: Social Science Research Council.

(2014). Women in politics and policy in Latin America and the Caribbean. Conflict Prevention and Peace Forum (CPPF) Working Papers on Women in Politics, No. 2. Social Science Research Council.

Htun, Mala, & Power, Timothy J. (2006). Gender, parties, and support for equal rights in the Brazilian congress. *Latin American Politics and Society*, 48(4), 83–104.

Htun, Mala, & Weldon, S. Laurel. (2010). When do governments promote women's rights? A framework for the comparative analysis of sex equality policy. *Perspectives on Politics*, 8(1), 207–216.

(2012). The civic origins of progressive policy change: Combating violence against women in global perspective, 1975–2005. *American Political Science Review*, 106(3), 548–569.

(2014). *Progressive policy change on women's social and economic rights.* Background paper for Progress of the World's Women.

(Forthcoming 2015). Religion, the State, Women's Rights, and Family Law. *Politics and Gender*.

n.d. *States and the Logic of Gender Justice*. Unpublished book manuscript.

Hughes, Melanie. (2011). Intersectionality, quotas, and minority women's political representation worldwide. *American Political Science Review*, 105(3), 604–620.

Hylton, Forrest, & Sinclair, Thomas. (2007). *Revolutionary horizons: past and present in Bolivian politics*. New York: Verso.

Inglehart, Ronald, & Norris, Pippa. (2003). *Rising tide: Gender equality and cultural change around the world*. New York: Cambridge University Press.

Inter-Parliamentary Union. (2013). Women in National Parliaments. Available from Inter-Parliamentary Union Women in National Parliaments. Retrieved from www.ipu.org/wmn-e/world.htm

Ishiyama, John. (2009). Do ethnic parties promote minority ethnic conflict? *Nationalism and Ethnic Politics*, 15(1), 56–83.

Ishiyama, John, & Breuning, Marijke. (2011). What's in a name? Ethnic party identity and democratic development in post-communist politics. *Party Politics*, 17(2), 223–241.

Iversen, Torben, & Rosenbluth, Frances. (2008). Work and power: The connection between female labor force participation and female political representation. *Annual Review of Political Science*, 11, 479–495.

Jaquette, Jane S. (1994). *The women's movement in Latin America: participation and democracy*. Boulder, CO: Westview Press.

Jensenius, Francesca Refsum. (2014). *Consequences of representation: Electoral quotas for India's ex-untouchables*. Unpublished manuscript.

Jenson, Jane, & Valiente, Celia. (2003). Comparing two movements for gender parity: France and Spain. In Lee Ann Banaszak, Karen Beckwith & Dieter Rucht (Eds.), *Women's movements facing the reconfigured state* (pp. 69–93). New York: Cambridge University Press.

Johnson, Brian B. (2010). Decolonization and its paradoxes: The (re)envisioning of health policy in Bolivia. *Latin American Perspectives*, 172(37), 139–159.

Johnson, Ollie. (1998). Racial representation and Brazilian politics: Black members of the national Congress, 1983–1999. *Journal of Inter-American Studies and World Affairs*, 40, 97–118.

Jones, Mark P. (1995). *Electoral laws and the survival of presidential democracies*. Notre Dame, IN: The University of Notre Dame Press.

(1998). Gender quotas, electoral laws, and the election of women: Lessons from the Argentine provinces. *Comparative Political Studies*, 31(3), 3–21.

(2002). Explaining the high level of party discipline in the Argentine Congress. In Scott Morgenstern & Benito Nacif (Eds.), *Legislative politics in Latin America*. New York: Cambridge University Press.

(2005). The desirability of gender quotas: Considering context and design. *Politics & Gender*, 1(4), 645–652.

(2009). Gender quotas, electoral laws, and the election of women: Evidence from the Latin American vanguard. *Comparative Political Studies*, 42(1), 56–81.

Jones, Mark P., & Hwang, Wonjae. (2005). Party government in presidential democracies: Extending cartel theory beyond the U.S. Congress. *American Journal of Political Science*, 49(2), 267–282.

Jones, Mark P., Hwang, Wonjae, & Micozzi, Juan Pablo. (2009). Government and opposition in the Argentine Congress, 1989–2007: Understanding inter-party dynamics through roll call vote analysis. *Journal of Politics in Latin America*, 1(1), 67–96.

Jones, Mark P., Saiegh, Sebastian, Spiller, Pablo T., & Tommasi, Mariano. (2002). Amateur legislators–professional politicians: The consequences of party-centered electoral rules in a federal system. *American Journal of Political Science*, 46(3), 656–669.

Jordan-Zachery, Julia S. (2007). Am I a black woman or a woman who is black? Some thoughts on the meaning of intersectionality. *Politics & Gender*, 3(2), 254–263.

Joseph, Tiffany D, & Hirshfield, Laura E. (2011). 'Why don't you get somebody new to do it?'Race and cultural taxation in the academy. *Ethnic and Racial Studies*, 34(1), 121–141.

Jouannet, Andrés. (2011). Participacíon política indígena en Chile: El caso Mapuche. In Beatriz Cajías de la Vega (Ed.), *Participación política indígena y políticas públicas para pueblos indígenas en América Latina* (pp. 93–133). La Paz: Fundación Konrad Adenauer.

Jung, Courtney. (2003). The politics of indigenous identity: Neoliberalism, cultural rights, and the Mexican Zapatistas. *Social Research*, 70(2), 433–462.

(2008). *The moral force of indigenous politics: Critical liberalism and the Zapatistas.* New York: Cambridge University Press.

Kanter, Rosabeth Moss. (1977a). *Men and Women of the Corporation* (Vol. 5049). New York: Basic Books.

(1977b). Some effects of proportions on group life: Skewed sex ratios and responses to token women. *American Journal of Sociology*, 82(5), 965–990.

Kathlene, Lyn. (1994). Power and influence in state legislative policymaking: The interaction of gender and position in committee hearing debates. *American Political Science Review*, 8(3), 560–576.

Kaup, Brent. (2010). A neoliberal nationalization: Constraints on natural gas led development in Bolivia. *Latin American Perspectives*, 37(3), 123–138.

Kittilson, Miki Caul. (2001). Political parties and the adoption of candidate gender quotas: A cross-national analysis. *Journal of Politics*, 63(4), 1214–1229.

Kittilson, Miki Caul, & Schwindt-Bayer, Leslie. (2010). Engaging citizens: The role of power-sharing institutions. *Journal of Politics*, 72(4), 990–1002.

Knight, Alan. (1990). Racism, revolution, and indigenismo: Mexico, 1910–1940. In Richard Graham (Ed.), *The idea of race in Latin America, 1870–1940* (pp. 71–113). Critical Reflections on Latin America Series. Austin: University of Texas Press.

Kohl, Benjamin. (2010). Bolivia under Evo Morales: A work in progress. *Latin American Perspectives*, 37(3), 107–122.

Krasner, Stephen D. (1984). Approaches to the state: Alternative conceptions and historical dynamics. *Comparative Politics*, 16(2), 223–246.

Krook, Mona Lena. (2008). La adopción e impacto de las leyes de cuotas de género: una perspectiva global. In Marcela Ríos Tobar (Ed.), *Mujer y política: El impacto de las cuotas de género en América Latina* (pp. 27–59). Santiago: Editorial Catalonia.

(2009). *Quotas for women in politics: Gender and candidate selection worldwide.* New York: Oxford University Press.

(2010). Women's representation in parliament: A qualitative-comparative analysis. *Political Studies*, 58(5), 886–908.

Krook, Mona Lena, & Moser, Robert G. (2013). Electoral rules and political inclusion. In Mala Htun & G. Bingham Powell Jr. (Ed.), *Political science, electoral rules, and democratic governance*. Washington, DC: American Political Science Association.

Krook, Mona Lena, & O'Brien, Diana Z. (2010). The politics of group representation: Quotas for women and minorities worldwide. *Comparative Politics*, 42(3), 253–272.

Kymlicka, Will. (1995). *Multicultural citizenship: A liberal theory of minority rights*. Oxford: Clarendon Press.

Laserna, Roberto. (2010). Mire, la democracia boliviana en los hechos. *Latin American Research Review*, 45(Special Issue), 27–58.

Laurent, Virginie. (2005). *Comunidades indígenas, espacios políticos y movilización electoral en Colombia, 1990–1998*. Bogotá: Instituto Colombiano de Antropología e Historia (ICANH).

(2010). Con bastones de mando o en el tarjetón: Movilizaciones políticas indígenas en Colombia. *Colombia Internacional*, No. 71, 35–61.

(2012a). Dos décadas de movilización electoral indígena en colombia. *Una mirada a las elecciones locales de octubre de 2011 política y territorio. Análisis de las elecciones subnacionales en Colombia, 2011*. Bogotá: Programa de las Naciones Unidas para el Desarollo (PNUD).

(2012b). Mulitculturalismo a la colombiana y veinte años de movilización electoral indígena: Circunscripciones especiales en la mira. *Análisis Político*, 25(75), 47–65.

Lawless, Jennifer L., & Fox, Richard L. (2005). *It takes a candidate: Why women don't run for office*. New York: Cambridge University Press.

Lee, Taeku. (2008). Race, immigration, and the identity-to-politics link. *Annual Review of Political Science*, 11, 457–478.

León, Magdalena, & Holguín, Jimena. (2005). La cuota sola no basta: El caso de Colombia. In Magdalena León (Ed.), *Nadando contra la corriente: Mujeres y cuotas políticas en los países andinos*. Bogotá: United Nations Development Fund for Women, United Nations Population Fund..

Levitsky, Steven. (2003). *Transforming labor-based parties in Latin America: Argentine Peronism in comparative perspective*. New York: Cambridge University Press.

Levitsky, Steven, & Murillo, María Victoria. (2009). Variation in institutional strength. *Annual Review of Political Science*, 12, 115–133.

Lewis, Jane. (1992). Gender and the development of welfare regimes. *Journal of European Social Policy*, 2(3), 159–173.

Lijphart, Arend. (1977). *Democracy in plural societies: A comparative exploration / Arend Lijphart*. New Haven, CT: Yale University Press, 1977.

(1995). Self-determination versus pre-determination of ethnic minorities in power-sharing systems. In Will Kymlicka (Ed.), *The rights of minority cultures* (pp. 275–287). Oxford: Oxford University Press.

(1986). Proportionality by non-PR methods: ethnic representation in Belgium, Cyprus, Lebanon, New Zealand, West Germany, and Zimbabwe. In Bernard Grofman & Arend Lijphart (Eds.), *Electoral laws and their political consequences* (pp. 113–123). New York: Agathon Press.

(1999). Constitutional choices for divided societies. *Journal of Democracy*, 15(2), 96–109.

Locatelli, Piero. (2014). Brancos serão quase 80% da Câmara dos Deputados. *Carta Capital: Politica*, August 10, 2014.

Longman, Timothy. (2006). Rwanda: Achieving equality or serving an authoritarian state? In Gretchen Bauer & Hannah E. Britton (Eds.), *Women in African parliaments* (pp. 133–150). Boulder, CO: Lynne Rienner.

Loveman, Mara. (2014). *National colors: Racial classification and the state in Latin America*. New York: Oxford University Press.

Lubertino Beltrán, María José. (1992). Historia de la 'Ley de Cuotas.'. *Cuotas mínima de participación de mujeres: El debate en Argentina* (pp. 9–43). Buenos Aires, Argentina: Fundacion Friedrich Ebert.

Lucas, Kevin, & Samuels, David. (2010). The Ideological "Coherence" of the Brazilian Party System, 1990–2009. *Journal of Politics in Latin America*, 2(3), 39–69.

Lucero, José Antonio. (2008). *Voices of struggle: The politics of indigenous representation in the Andes*. Pittsburgh: University of Pittsburgh Press.

Luna, Juan Pablo, Murillo, Maria Victoria, & Schrank, Andrew. (2014). Latin American political economy: Making sense of a new reality. *Latin American Politics and Society*, 56(1), 3–10.

Madrid, Raúl. (2008). The rise of ethnopopulism in Latin America. *World Politics*, 60(3), 475–508.

(2012). *The rise of ethnic politics in Latin America*. New York: Cambridge University Press.

Maggie, Yvonne, & Fry, Peter. (2004). A reserva de vagas para negros nas universidade brasileiras. *Estudos Avançados*, 18(50), 67–80.

Mahoney, James, & Thelen, Kathleen. (2010). A theory of gradual institutional change. In James Mahoney & Kathleen Thelen (Eds.), *Explaining institutional change: Ambiguity, agency, and power* (pp. 1–37). Cambridge: Cambridge University Press.

Mainwaring, Scott. (1999). *Rethinking party systems in the third wave of democratization: The case of Brazil*. Stanford, CA: Stanford University Press.

Mainwaring, Scott, & Scully, Timothy. (1995). *Building democratic institutions: Party systems in Latin America*. Stanford, CA: Stanford University Press.

Mamdani, Mahmood. (1996). *Citizen and subject*. New York: Cambridge University Press.

(2001). *When victims become killers: Colonialism, nativism, and the genocide in Rwanda*. Princeton, NJ: Princeton University Press.

Manning, Jennifer E. (2014). *Membership of the 113th Congress: A Profile*. Washington, DC: Congressional Research Service.

Mansbridge, Jane. (1999). Should blacks represent blacks and women represent women? A contingent 'yes'. *Journal of Politics*, 61(3), 628–657.

(2003). Rethinking representation. *American Political Science Review*, 97(4), 515–528.

(2005). Quota problems: Combating the dangers of essentialism. *Politics & Gender*, 1(4), 622–637.

(2011). Clarifying the concept of representation. *American Political Science Review*, 105(3), 621–630.

Martínez Casas, Regina, Saldívar, Emiko, Flores, René D., & Sue, Christina A. (2014). The different faces of *Mestizaje*: Ethnicity and race in Mexico. In Edward Telles (Ed.), *Pigmentocracies*. Chapel Hill: University of North Carolina Press.

Marx, Anthony W. (1998). *Making race and nation: A comparison of the United States, South Africa, and Brazil*. New York: Cambridge University Press.

Marx, Jutta, Borner, Jutta, & Caminotti, Mariana. (2007). *La legisladoras: Cupos de género y política en Argentina y Brasil*. Buenos Aires: Siglo XXI Editora Iberamericano, Programa de las Naciones Unidas para el Desarollo (PNUD), Instituto Tortuato di Tella.

Matland, Richard E. (2006). Electoral quotas: Frequency and effectiveness. In Drude Dahlerup (Ed.), *Women, quotas, and politics* (pp. 275–292). New York: Routledge.

Matland, Richard E., & Studlar, Donley T. (1996). The contagion of women candidates in single-member district and proportional representation electoral systems: Canada and Norway. *Journal of Politics*, 58(3), 707–733.

Mazur, Amy. (2001). Drawing lessons from the French Parity Movement. *Contemporary French Civilization*, 25(2), 201–219.

McBride, Dorothy, & Mazur, Amy. (2011). Gender machineries worldwide. *Background Paper, World Development Report 2012*. Washington, DC: The World Bank.

Meertens, Donny. (2008). Discriminación racial, desplazamiento y genero en las sentencias de la Corte Constitucional. El racismo cotidiano en el banquillo. *Universitas Humanística*, 37(66), 83–106.

Mettler, Suzanne. (1998). *Dividing citizens: Gender and federalism in New Deal public policy*. Ithaca, NY: Cornell University Press.

Micozzi, Juan Pablo. (2009). *The electoral connection in multi-level systems with non-static ambition: Linking political careers and legislative performance in Argentina*. PhD dissertation, Rice University.

(2013). Does electoral accountability make a difference? Direct elections, career ambition, and legislative performance in the Argentine Senate. *Journal of Politics*, 75(1), 137–149.

Micozzi, Juan Pablo, & Lacalle, Marina. (2010). *The more women at work, the sooner we win? Gender quotas and legislative productivity in the Argentine Congress*. Paper presented at the 68th Annual MPSA National Conference, Chicago.

Miller, Francesca. (1991). *Latin American women and the search for social justice*. Hanover, NH: University Press of New England.

Ministério da Saúde. (2010). Política nacional de Saúde integral da População negra. uma política para o SUS / Ministério da Saúde, Secretaria de Gestão Estratégica e Participativa, departamento de Apoio à Gestão Participativa. – 2. ed. – Brasília: Editora do Ministério da Saúde, 2013.

Ministerio del Interior y de Justicia de la República de Colombia. (n.d.). *Acuerdos, resoluciones o convenios con instituciones de educación superior*. Retrieved from www.siswer.com/documentos/negritudes/LISTADOCONVENIOSUNIVERSIDADES.pdf

Misión de Observación Electoral. (2010). Informe de observación electoral: Elecciones de congreso (14 de Marzo del 2010) *Hombres y mujeres al servicio de la democracia*.

Moi, Toril. (2001). *What is a woman? and other essays*. Oxford: Oxford University Press.

Mokrani, Dunia, & Uriona, Pilar. (2009). *Informe de coyuntura: Mujeres y pueblos indígenas en la ley de régimen electoral transitorio*. La Paz: Coordinadora de la Mujer.

Montville, Joseph V. (1990). *Conflict and peacemaking in multiethnic societies*. New York: Free Press.

Mörner, Magnus. (1967). *Race mixture in the history of Latin America*. Boston: Little, Brown, and Company.

Moser, Robert. (2008). Electoral systems and the representation of ethnic minorities: Evidence from Russia. *Comparative Politics*, 40(3), 273–292.

Moser, Robert, & Holmsten, Stephanie. (2008). *The paradox of representation: Can PR elect more women and minorities?* Paper presented at the annual meeting of the MPSA National Conference, Palmer House Hilton, Chicago.

Moser, Robert G., & Scheiner, Ethan. (2012). *Electoral systems and political context: How the effects of rules vary across new and established democracies.* New York: Cambridge University Press.

Mujeres Presentes en la Historia, Movimiento de. (2007). *Argumentación de las propuestas de las mujeres hacia la asamblea constituyente.* La Paz: Movimiento de Mujeres Presentes en la Historia.

Nascimento, Abdias do, & Larkin Nascimento, Elisa. (2001). Reflexões sobre o movimento negro no Brasil, 1938–1997. In Antonio Sérgio Alfredo Guimarães & Lynn Huntley (Eds.), *Tirando a máscara: Ensaios sobre o racismo no Brasil* (pp. 203–236). São Paulo: Editora Paz e Terra.

Nash, Jennifer C. (2008). Re-thinking intersectionality. *Feminist Review*, 89(1), 1–15.

Navia, Patricio. (2008). Legislative candidate selection in Chile. In Peter M. Siavelis & Scott Morgenstern (Eds.), *Pathways to power: Political recruitment and candidate selection in Latin America* (pp. 92–118). University Park: The Pennsylvania State University Press.

Nobles, Melissa. (2000). *Shades of citizenship: Race and the census in modern politics.* Stanford, CA: Stanford University Press.

Norris, Pippa. (2004). *Electoral engineering: Voting rules and political behavior.* Cambridge: Cambridge University Press.

Novillo Gonzáles, Monica. (2011). *Paso a paso. Así lo hicimos. Avances y desafíos en la participación política de las mujeres.* La Paz: Coordinadora de la Mujer.

Okin, Susan Moller. (1991). Gender, the public and the private. In David Held (Ed.), *Political theory today.* Stanford, CA: Stanford University Press.

(2008). *Justice, gender, and the family.* New York: Basic Books.

Orloff, Ann Shola. (1993). Gender and the social rights of citizenship: The comparative analysis of gender relations and welfare states. *American Sociological Review*, 58(3), 303–328.

Pachón, Mónica, & Shugart, Matthew Soberg. (2010). Electoral reform and the mirror image of interparty and intraparty competition: The adoption of party lists in Colombia. *Electoral Studies*, 29(4), 648–660.

Paixão, Marcelo, & Carvano, Luis M. (2008). *Relatório anual das desigualdades raciais no Brasil, 2007–2008.* Rio de Janeiro: Laboratório de Analise Econômicas, Sociais e Estatísticas em Relações Raciais (LAESER) at the Federal University of Rio de Janeiro.

Paixão, Marcelo, Monçores, Elisa, & Rossetto, Irene. (2012). Ações afirmativas por reserva de vagas no ingresso discente nas Instituições de Ensino Superior (IES): um panorama segundo o Censo da Educação Superior de 2010. In Marcelo Giardino (Ed.), *Democratização da educação superior no Brasil: Avanços e desafios.* Cadernos do pensamento crítico Latino-Americano: Grupo Estratégico de Análise da Educação Superior no Brasil da FLASCO Brasil.

Paixão, Marcelo, Rossetto, Irene, Montovanele, Fabiana, & Carvano, Luiz M. (2010). *Relatório anual das desigualdades raciais no Brasil, 2009–2010: Constituição Cidadã, seguridade social e seus efeitos sobre assimetrias de cor ou raça.* Rio de Janeiro: Editora Garamond.

Paschel, Tianna S. (2010). The right to difference: Explaining Colombia's shift from color-blindness to the law of black communities. *American Journal of Sociology*, 116(3), 729–769.

Pateman, Carole. (1989). *The disorder of women: Democracy, feminism, and political theory*. Stanford, CA: Stanford University Press.

Paulson, Susan, & Callá, Pamela. (2000). Gender and ethnicity in Bolivian politics: Transformation or paternalism? *Journal of Latin American Anthropology*, 5(2), 112–149.

Paxton, Pamela, & Hughes, Melanie M. (2013). *Women, politics, and power: A global perspective* (2nd ed.). Thousand Oaks, CA: SAGE.

Pedersen, Susan. (1993). *Family, dependence, and the origins of the welfare state: Britain and France, 1914–1945*. New York: Cambridge University Press.

(2004). *Eleanor Rathbone and the politics of conscience*. New Haven, CT: Yale University Press.

Peria, Michelle, & Bailey, Stanley R. (2014). Remaking racial inclusion: Combining race and class in Brazil's new affirmative action. *Journal of Latin American and Caribbean Ethnic Studies*, 9(2), 156–176.

Phillips, Anne. (1995). *The politics of presence*. New York: Clarendon Press; Oxford University Press.

(2012). "Representation and Inclusion." *Politics & Gender*, 8(4), 512–518.

Pierson, Paul. (1996). The New Politics of the Welfare State. *World Politics*, 48(2), 143–179.

(2000). Increasing returns, path dependence, and the study of politics. *American Political Science Review*, 94(2), 251–267.

Pinedo Bravo, Enith. (2012). *El acceso de los indígenas al Congreso de la República: Una mirada desde el diseño del sistema electoral y del principio de igualdad*. Lima: Jurado Nacional de Elecciones.

Piscopo, Jennifer. (2010). *Setting agendas for women: Substantive representation and bill introduction in Argentina and Mexico*.PhD dissertation, University of California San Diego.

(2013). *The changing face of Latin American politics: Perspectives on gender quota diffusion and women's political empowerment*. Paper presented at the Latin American Studies Association, Washington, DC.

(2015). States as gender equality activists: The evolution of quota laws in Latin America. *Latin American Politics and Society* 57, 3 (Fall).

Piscopo, Jennifer, & Thomas, Gwyn. (2012). *New approaches to studying institutional norms in Latin America*. Paper presented at the 2012 Latin American Studies Association Meeting, San Francisco.

Pitkin, Hanna Fenichel. (1967). *The concept of representation*. Berkeley: University of California Press.

Pizarro Leongómez, Eduardo. (2001). Colombia: Renovación o colapso del sistema de partidos? In Manuel Alcántara Sáez & Juan Manuel Ibeas Miguel (Eds.), *Colombia ante los retos del siglo XXI: Desarollo, democracia y paz* (pp. 99–126). Salamanca: Ediciones Universidad de Salamanca.

(2002). Giants with feet of clay: Political parties in Colombia. In Scott Mainwaring, Ana María Bejarano & Eduardo Pizarro Leongómez (Eds.), *The crisis of democratic representation in the Andes* (pp. 78–99). Stanford, CA: Stanford University Press.

¿Por qué se indignaron los negros? (2014). *Revista Semana*. Retrieved from www
.semana.com/nacion/articulo/las-dudas-contra-los-parlamentarios-electos-
afrodescendientes/380379-3

Postero, Nancy. (2006). *Now we are citizens: Indigenous politics in postmulticultural
Bolivia*. Stanford, CA: Stanford University Press.

(2010). Morales's MAS government: Building indigenous popular hegemony in
Bolivia. *Latin American Perspectives*, 37(3), 18–34.

Powell, G. Bingham. (2000). *Elections as instruments of democracy: Majoritarian and
proportional visions*. New Haven, CT: Yale University Press.

Power, Timothy J, & Zucco, Cesar. (2012). Elite preferences in a consolidating democracy: the Brazilian legislative surveys, 1990–2009. *Latin American Politics and
Society*, 54(4), 1–27.

Prewitt, Kenneth. (2005). Racial classification in America: Where do we go from here?
Daedalus, 134(1), 5–17.

Przeworski, Adam, Stokes, Susan C., & Manin, Bernard. (1999). *Democracy, accountability, and representation*. Cambridge: Cambridge University Press.

Quotaproject. (2011). Global database. Retrieved from www.quotaproject.org

Rabushka, Alvin, & Shepsle, Kenneth A. (1972). *Politics in plural societies: A theory of
democratic instability*. Columbus, OH: Merrill.

Rahier, Jean Muteba (Ed.). (2012). *Black social movements in Latin America: From
monocultural mestizaje to multiculturalism*. New York: Palgrave Macmillan.

Ranger, Terence. (1983). The Invention of Tradition in Colonial Africa. In Eric
Hobsbawm & Terence Ranger (Eds.), *The invention of tradition* (pp. 211–262).
New York: Cambridge University Press.

Rappaport, Joanne, & Dover, Robert V. H. (1996). The construction of difference by
native legislators: Assessing the impact of the Colombian Constitution of 1991.
Journal of Latin American Anthropology, 1(2), 22–45.

Regalsky, Pablo. (2010). Political process and the reconfiguration of the state in Bolivia.
Latin American Perspectives, 37(3), 35–50.

Rehfeld, Andrew. (2005). *The concept of constituency: Political representation, democratic legitimacy, and institutional design*. New York: Cambridge University Press.

(2006). Towards a general theory of political representation. *Journal of Politics*,
68(1), 1–21.

(2009a). On quotas and qualifications for office. In Ian Shapiro, Susan C. Stokes,
Elisabeth Jean Wood, & Alexander S. Kirshner (Eds.), *Political representation* (pp.
236–268). New York: Cambridge University Press.

(2009b). Representation rethought: on trustees, delegates, and gyroscopes in the
study of political representation and democracy. *American Political Science Review*,
103(02), 214–230.

Rehfeld, Andrew, & Schwartzberg, Melissa. (2013). Designing electoral systems: Normative tradeoff and institutional innovations. In Mala Htun &
G. Bingham Powell, Jr. (Eds.), *Political science, electoral rules, and democratic governance*. Washington, DC: American Political Science Association.

Reichmann, Rebecca. (1999). Introduction. In Rebecca Reichmann (Ed.), *Race in contemporary Brazil: From indifference to inequality* (pp. 1–36). University Park: The
Pennsylvania State University Press.

Reingold, Beth. (2000). *Representing women: Sex, gender, and legislative behavior in
Arizona and California*. Chapel Hill: University of North Carolina Press.

(2008). Women as office holders: Linking descriptive and substantive representation. In Lisa Baldez, Karen Beckwith, & Christina Wolbrecht (Eds.), *Political women and American democracy* (pp. 128–147). New York: Cambridge University Press.

Report of the Fourth World Conference on Women, New York. (1996). Retrieved from www.un.org/womenwatch/daw/beijing/pdf/Beijing full report E.pdf

República de Bolívia. (2009). *Constitution of the Republic of Bolivia.*

República de Colombia. (1993). *Ley 70 de 1993. Diario Oficial No. 41.013, de 31 de agosto de 1993. Por la cual se desarrolla el artículo transitorio 55 de la Constitución Política.*

República de Colombia. (2001). *Ley 649 de 2001. Diario Oficial No. 44.371, del 28 de marzo de 2001.*

Restrepo, Eduardo. (2004). Ethnicization of blackness in Colombia: Toward de-racializing theoretical and political imagination. *Cultural Studies*, 18(5), 698–715.

Reyes Gonzáles, Guillermo Francisco. (2007). *Resultados del desempeño electoral afrocolombiano Estudios sobre la participación política de la población afrodescendiente: La experiencia en Colombia.* San José: Inter-American Institute of Human Rights (IIDH).

Reynolds, Andrew. (2005). Reserved seats in national legislatures: A research note. *Legislative Studies Quarterly*, 30(2), 301–310.

(2011). *Designing democracy in a dangerous world.* Oxford: Oxford University Press.

Rice, Roberta, & Van Cott, Donna Lee. (2006). The emergence and performance of indigenous peoples' parties in South America: A subnational statistical analysis. *Comparative Political Studies*, 39(6), 709–732.

Riker, William H. (1992). The justification of bicameralism. *International Political Science Review*, 12(1), 101–116.

Roca, Jose Luis. (2008). Regionalism revisited. In John Crabtree & Laurence Whitehead (Eds.), *Unresolved tensions: Bolivia past and present* (pp. 65–82). Pittsburgh: University of Pittsburgh Press.

Rocca, Michael S., & Sanchez, Gabriel R. (2008). The effect of race and ethnicity on bill sponsorship and cosponsorship in Congress. *American Politics Research*, 36(1), 130–152.

Rogowski, Jon, Sinclair, Betsy, & Fowler, James. (2010). *The social bases of legislative behavior.* Paper presented at the 68th Annual MPSA National Conference, Chicago.

Rojas Birry, Francisco. (1991). *Ponencia: Los derechos de los grupos étnicos.* Bogotá: Asamblea Nacional Constituyente, Comisión Primera.

Rosaldo, Michelle Zimbalist. (1974). Woman, culture, and society: A theoretical overview. In Michelle Zimbalist Rosaldo & Louise Lamphere (Eds.), *Woman, culture and society* (pp. 17–42). Stanford, CA: Stanford University Press.

Rosser, Sue V. (2004). *The science glass ceiling: Academic women scientists and the struggle to succeed.* London: Routledge.

Rousseau, Stephanie. (2011). Indigenous and feminist movements at the constituent assembly in Bolivia: Locating the representation of indigenous women. *Latin American Research Review*, 46(2), 5–28.

Salmón, Elizabeth. (2011). Entre las promesas de consulta previa y la continuidad de la protesta social: Las ambigüedades de la participación política indígena en el Perú. In Beatriz Cajías de la Vega (Ed.), *Participación política indígena y políticas públicas para pueblos indígenas en América Latina* (pp. 279–311). La Paz: Fundación Konrad Adenauer.

Samuels, David, & Snyder, Richard. (2001). The value of a vote: Malapportionment in comparative perspective. *British Journal of Political Science*, 31(3), 651–671.

Sanbonmatsu, Kira. (2006). State elections: Where do women run? Where do women win? In Susan J. Carroll & Richard L. Fox (Eds.), *Gender and elections: Shaping the future of American politics* (pp. 189–214). New York: Cambridge University Press.

Sánchez, Beatriz Eugenia. (2001). El reto del multiculturalismo jurídico. La justicia de la sociedad mayor y la justicia indígena. In Boaventura de Sousa Santos & Mauricio García Villegas (Eds.), *El caleidoscopio de las justicias en Colombia. Análisis socio-jurídico. Tomo II* (pp. 75–87). Bogotá: Siglo del Hombre Editores.

Sandberg, Sheryl. (2013). *Lean in: Women, work, and the will to lead.* New York: Random House.

Sawyer, Mark Q. (2006). *Racial politics in post-revolutionary Cuba.* New York: Cambridge University Press.

Scherlis, Gerardo. (2013). *Parties and ballot access in Latin America.* Paper presented at the Political Legitimacy and the Paradox of Regulation, Leiden.

Schlesinger, Joseph. (1984). On the theory of party organization. *Journal of Politics*, 46(2), 369–400.

Schmidt, Gregory D. (2003). *The implementation of gender quotas in Peru: Legal reform, discourses and impacts.* Paper presented at the International IDEA Workshop, The Implementation of Quotas: Latin American Experiences, Lima, Peru, February.

Schmidt, Ronald, Sr., Hero, Rodney E, Aoki, Andrew L, & Alex-Assensoh, Yvette M. (2010). *Newcomers, outsiders, and insiders: Immigrants and American racial politics in the early twenty-first century.* Ann Arbor: University of Michigan Press.

Schwartzman, Luisa Farah. (2008). Who are the blacks? The question of racial classification in Brazilian affirmative action policies in higher education. *Cahiers de la Recherche sur l'Éducation et les Savoirs*, 7, 1–17.

(2009). Seeing like citizens: Unofficial understandings official racial categories in a Brazilian university. *Journal of Latin American Studies*, 41(2), 221–250.

Schwartzman, Simon. (2008a). *A medida da lei de cotas para o ensino superior.* Retrieved from www.schwartzman.org.br/simon/cotas2008.pdf

(2008b). A questão da inclusão social na Universidade Brasileira. In Maria do Carmo de Lacerda Peixoto & Antônia Vitória Aranha (Eds.), *Universidade pública e inclusão social: experiência e imaginação* (pp. 23–43). Belo Horizonte: Editora UFMG.

(2009). Student quotas in Brazil: The policy debate. *International Higher Education*, 56(Summer), 11–13.

(2013). Affirmative action in higher education in Brazil: São Paulo's turn. *The World View.* Retrieved from www.insidehighered.com/blogs/world-view/affirmative-action-higher-education-brazil-são-paulo's-turn

Schwindt-Bayer, Leslie A. (2006). Still supermadres? Gender and the policy priorities of Latin American legislators. *American Journal of Political Science*, 50(3), 570–585.

(2009). Making quotas work: The effect of gender quota laws on the election of women. *Legislative Studies Quarterly*, 34(1), 5–28.

(2010). *Political power and women's representation in Latin America.* New York: Oxford University Press.

Scott, James C. (1998). *Seeing like a state: How certain schemes to improve the human condition have failed.* New Haven, CT: Yale University Press.

Scott, Joan Wallach. (2004). French universalism in the nineties. *Differences: A Journal of Feminist Cultural Studies,* 15(2), 32–53.

Seed, Patricia. (1982). Social dimensions of race: Mexico City, 1753. *The Hispanic American Historical Review,* 62(4), 569–606.

Sen, Amartya. (2001). The many faces of gender inequality. *Frontline,* 18(22). Retrieved from www.frontline.in/static/html/fl1822/18220040.htm.

SERNAM. (2008). *Estudio de opinión pública: Paridad, medidas de acción afirmativa, mujer y política.* Santiago, Chile: Servicio Nacional de la Mujer.

Sheriff, Robin. (2001). *Dreaming equality: Color, race, and racism in urban Brazil.* New Brunswick, NJ: Rutgers University Press.

Shugart, Matthew Soberg. (2013). Why ballot structure matters. In Mala Htun & G. Bingham Powell (Eds.), *Political science, electoral rules, and democratic governance.* Washington, DC: American Political Science Association.

Shugart, Matthew Soberg, Moreno, Erika, & Fajardo, Luis. (2007). Deepening democracy by renovating political practices: The struggle for electoral reform in Colombia. In Christopher Welna & Gustavo Gallón (Eds.), *Peace, democracy and human rights in Colombia* (pp. 202–266). Notre Dame, IN: University of Notre Dame Press.

Silva, Graziella Moraes, & Paixão, Marcelo. (2014). Mixed and unequal: New perspectives on Brazilian ethnoracial relations. In Edward Telles (Ed.), *Pigmentocracies: Ethnicity, race, and color in Latin America* (pp. 172–217). Chapel Hill: University of North Carolina Press.

Silva, Nelson do Valle. (1985). Updating the cost of not being white in Brazil. In Pierre-Michel Fontaine (Ed.), *Race, class and power in Brazil* (pp. 42–55). Los Angeles: Center for Afro-American Studies, University of California.

Skidmore, Thomas. (1993). Bi-racial USA vs. multi-racial Brazil: Is the contrast still valid? *Journal of Latin American Studies,* 25(2), 373–386.

Skidmore, Thomas E. (1993). *Black into white: Race and nationality in Brazilian thought.* Durham: Duke University Press.

Skocpol, Theda. (1992). *Protecting soldiers and mothers: The political origins of social policy in the United States.* Cambridge, MA: Harvard University Press.

Skocpol, Theda, Ganz, Marshall, & Munson, Ziad. (2000). A nation of organizers: The institutional origins of civic voluntarism in the United States. *American Political Science Review,* 94(3), 527–546.

Skrentny, John. (2002). *The minority rights revolution.* Cambridge, MA: Harvard University Press.

Smith, Richard Chase. (1982). Liberal ideology and indigenous communities in post-independence Peru. *Journal of International Affairs,* 36(1), 73–82.

Soberanis, Catalina. (2011). Participación política indígena y políticas públicas para pueblos indígenas en Guatemala. In Beatriz Cajías de la Vega (Ed.), *Participación política indígena y políticas públicas para pueblos indígenas en América Latina* (pp. 215–235). La Paz: Fundación Konrad Adenauer.

Spiller, Pablo T., & Tommasi, Mariano. (2007). *The institutional foundations of public policy: A transaction theory and an application to Argentina.* New York: Cambridge University Press.

Stavenhagen, Rodolfo. (2002). Indigenous peoples and the state in Latin America: An ongoing debate. In Rachel Sieder (Ed.), *Multiculturalism in Latin America: Indigenous rights, diversity, and democracy* (pp. 24–44). London: Palgrave.

Streeck, Wolfgang, & Thelen, Kathleen. (2005a). Introduction: Institutional change in advanced political economies. In *Beyond continuity: Institutional change in advanced political economies* (pp. 1–39). New York: Oxford University Press.

& Thelen, Kathleen (Eds.). (2005b). *Beyond continuity: Explorations in the dynamics of advanced political economies.* New York: Oxford University Press.

Strolovitch, Dara Z. (2007). *Affirmative advocacy: Race, class, and gender in interest group politics.* Chicago: University of Chicago Press.

Sturm, Susan. (2006). Architecture of inclusion: Advancing workplace equity in higher education. *Harvard Journal of Law & Gender, 29,* 247.

Sulmont, David, & Callirgos, Juan Carlos (2014). ¿El pais de todas las sangres? Race and Ethnicity in Contemporary Peru. In Edward Telles (Ed.), *Pigmentocracies: Race, ethnicity, and color in Latin America* (pp. 126–171). Chapel Hill: University of North Carolina Press.

Suplicy, Marta. (1996). Novos paradigmas nas esferas de poder. *Revista Estudos Femi-nistas,* 4(1), 126–137.

Swers, Michele L. (2002). *The difference women make: The policy impact of women in Congress.* Chicago: University of Chicago Press.

Tannenbaum, Frank. (1946). *Slave and citizen: The classic comparative study of race relations in the Americas.* Boston: Beacon Press.

Taylor, Charles. (1992). The politics of recognition. In Charles Taylor & Amy Gutmann (Eds.), *Multiculturalism and 'the politics of recognition'* (pp. 25–73). Princeton, NJ: Princeton University Press.

Taylor, Steven. (2010). Ballot design (and voter knowledge) matters. Retrieved from http://fruitsandvotes.com/?p=3868 – footnote_3_3868

Telles, Edward. (2004). *Race in another America: The significance of skin color in Brazi.* Princeton, NJ: Princeton University Press.

(2014a). The project on ethnicity and race in Latin America (PERLA): Hard data and what is at stake. In Edward Telles (Ed.), *Pigmentocracies: Ethnicity, race, and color in Latin America.* Chapel Hill: University of North Carolina Press.

(Ed.). (2014b). *Pigmentocracies: Ethnicity, race, and color in Latin America.* Chapel Hill: University of North Carolina Press.

Telles, Edward, & Flores, René D. (2014). A comparative analysis of ethnicity and race in Latin America based on PERLA findings. In Edward Telles (Ed.), *Pigmentocracies: Ethnicity, race, and color in Latin America* (pp. 218–236). Chapel Hill: University of North Carolina Press.

Telles, Oscar. (2012, November 6). Debatedores defendem reforma política que favoreça eleição de negros, *Câmara Notícias.* Retrieved from www2.camara.leg.br/camaranoticias/noticias/POLITICA/429500-DEBATEDORES-DEFENDEM-REFORMA-POLITICA-QUE-FAVORECA-ELEICAO-DE-NEGROS.html

Thomas, Sue. (1994). *How women legislate.* New York: Oxford University Press.

Toranzo, Carlos. (2008). Let the mestizos stand up and be counted. In John Crabtree & Laurence Whitehead (Eds.), *Unresolved tensions: Bolivia past and present* (pp. 35–50). Pittsburgh: University of Pittsburgh Press.

Torres, Javier. (2008). Perú: Los límites de la participación política de la población indígena en el Perú. *Población indígena: derechos y participación aportes al debate multicultural desde la perspectiva nacional y regional. Memoria de las sesiones públicas realizadas en el Congreso de la República del Perú los días 2, 9, 23 y 30 de marzo de 2007.* Lima: Fundación Konrad Adenauer.

Towns, Ann. (2010). *Women and states: Norms and hierarchies in international society.* New York: Cambridge University Press.

Tremblay, Manon. (2006). The substantive representation of women and PR: Some reflections on the role of surrogate representation and critical mass. *Politics & Gender*, 2(4), 502–511.

Tripp, Aili Mari. (2006). Uganda: Agents of change for women's advancement? In Gretchen Bauer & Hannah Evelyn Britton (Eds.), *Women in African Parliaments* (pp. 111–132). Boulder: Lynne Rienner.

Tsebelis, George, & Money, Jeannette. (1997). *Bicameralism.* New York: Cambridge University Press.

Ungar Bleier, Elisabeth, & Arévalo, Carlos Arturo. (2004). Crisis o reordenación institucional? Partidos y sistema de partidos en Colombia hoy. *Partidos políticos en la región andina: Entre la crisis y el cambio* (pp. 51–69). Stockholm: International Institute for Democracy and Electoral Assistance.

United Nations. (2001). *Declaration: World Conference against Racism, Racial Discrimination, Xenophobia and Related Intolerance.* Retrieved from www .un.org/WCAR/durban.pdf.

United Nations Development Programme. (1995). *Human Development Report.* New York: Oxford Univerity Press.

Urbinati, Nadia. (2006). *Representative democracy: Principles and genealogy.* Chicago: University of Chicago Press.

Urbinati, Nadia, & Warren, Mark. (2008). The concept of representation in contemporary democratic theory. *Annual Review of Political Science*, 11, 387–412.

Urrea, Fernando, López, Carlos Viáfara, & Vigoya, Mara Viveros. (2014). From whitened miscegenation to tri-ethnic multiculturalism: Race and Ethnicity in Colombia. In Edward Telles (Ed.), *Pigmentocracies: Ethnicity, race, and color in Latin America* (pp. 81–125). Chapel Hill: University of North Carolina Press.

Vail, Leroy (Ed.). (1989). *The creation of tribalism in Southern Africa.* Berkeley: University of California Press.

Valdés, Teresa, & Gomariz, Enrique. (1995). *Mujeres latinoamericanas en cifras. Tomo comparativo.* Santiago: Facultad Latinoamericana de Ciencias Sociales (FLACSO).

Valenzuela, J. Samuel. 1985. *Democratización Vía Reforma: La expansión del sufragio en Chile.* Buenos Aires: Ediciones del IDES.

Van Cott, Donna Lee. (2000). *The friendly liquidation of the past: The politics of diversity in Latin America.* Pittsburgh: The University of Pittsburgh Press.

(2005). *From movements to parties in Latin America: The evolution of ethnic politics.* New York: Cambridge University Press.

Vega, Silvia. (2005). La cuota electoral en Ecuador: Nadando a contra-corriente en un horizonte esperanzador. In Magdalena León (Ed.), *Nadando contra la corriente: mujeres y cuotas políticas en los países andinos* (pp. 169–206). Bogotá: UNIFEM, United Nations Population Fund..

Villamizar, Mateo. (2014). Qué pasó con las circunscripciones especiales? *Congreso Visible*. Retrieved from: http://congresovisible.org/agora/post/y-que-paso-con-las-circunscripciones-especiales/6294/

Villamizar, Mateo, Duque, Cristina, & Martínez, Paulina. (2014). ¿Jaque a la Circunscripción Afro? *Congreso Visible*. Retrieved from http://congresovisible.org/agora/post/jaque-a-la-circunscripcion-afro/6570/

Villanueva Montalvo, Aída. (2012). En torno a la representación especial indígena en el Perú: Percepción de líderes indígenas y características del modelo peruano. *Debates en Sociología*, 37, 43–76.

Vincent, Louise. (2004). Quotas: Changing the way things look without changing the way things are. *The Journal of Legislative Studies*, 10(1), 71–96.

Volden, Craig, Weisman, Alan, & Wittmer, Dana. (2010). *The legislative effectiveness of women in congress*. Working paper (04-2010), Center for the Study of Democratic Institutions, Vanderbilt University.

Wade, Peter. (1993). *Blackness and race mixture: The dynamics of racial identity in Colombia*. Baltimore: The Johns Hopkins University Press.

(1995). The cultural politics of blackness in Colombia. *American Ethnologist*, 22(2), 342–358.

(1997). *Race and ethnicity in Latin America*. London: Pluto Press.

(2002). Introduction: The Colombian Pacific in perspective. *Journal of Latin American Anthropology*, 7(2), 2–33.

(2009). Defining blackness in Colombia. *Journal de la Société des Américanistes*, 95(1), 165–184.

(2011). Multiculturalismo y racismo. *Revista Colombiana de Antropología*, 47(2), 15–35.

Wampler, Brian. (2010). *Participatory budgeting in Brazil: Contestation, cooperation, and accountability*. University Park: Penn State University Press.

Wang, Vibeke. (2013). Women changing policy outcomes: Learning from pro-women legislation in the Ugandan Parliament. *Women's Studies International Forum*, 41(2), 113–121.

Webber, Jeffery. (2010). Carlos Mesa and the divided Bolivia 2003–2005. *Latin American Perspectives*, 37(3), 51–70.

Weissberg, Robert. (1978). Collective vs. dyadic representation in Congress. *American Political Science Review*, 72(2), 535–547.

Weldon, S Laurel. (2002). Beyond bodies: Institutional sources of representation for women in democratic policymaking. *Journal of Politics*, 64(4), 1153–1174.

(2006). Inclusion, solidarity, and social movements: The global movement against gender violence. *Perspectives on Politics*, 4(1), 55–74.

(2008). Intersectionality. In Gary Goertz & Amy Mazur (Eds.), *Politics, gender, and concepts: Theory and methodology* (pp. 193–218). New York: Cambridge University Press.

(2011). *When protest makes policy: How social movements represent disadvantaged groups*. Ann Arbor: University of Michigan Press.

Wilkinson, Steven I. and Kitschelt, Herbert (2007). Citizen-politician linkages: An introduction. In Herbert Kitschelt & Steven I. Wilkinson (Eds.), *Patrons, clients, and policies: Patterns of democratic accountability and political competition* (pp. 1–46). Cambridge: Cambridge University Press.

Williams, Melissa S. (1998). *Voice, trust, and memory: Marginalized groups and the failings of liberal representation.* Princeton, NJ: Princeton University Press.

World Bank. (2011). *World development report 2012: Gender equality and development.* Washington, DC: World Bank Publications.

World Economic Forum. (2013). *The Global Gender Gap Report.* Geneva: World Economic Forum.

Yashar, Deborah J. (2005). *Contesting citizenship in Latin America: The rise of indigenous movements and the postliberal challenge.* New York: Cambridge University Press.

Young, Iris Marion. (1994). Gender as seriality: Thinking about women as a social collective. *Signs, 19*(3), 713–738.

(2000). *Inclusion and democracy.* New York: Oxford University Press.

Zavaleta, Diego. (2008). Oversimplifying identities: The debate about what is *indígena* and what is *mestizo*. In John Crabtree & Laurence Whitehead (Eds.), *Unresolved tensions: Bolivia past and present* (pp. 51–60). Pittsburgh: University of Pittsburgh Press.

Zetterberg, Pär. (2008). The downside of gender quotas? Institutional constraints on women in Mexican state legislatures. *Parliamentary Affairs, 61*(3), 442–460.

Zoninsein, Jonas. (2004). Minorias étnicas e a economia política do desenvolvimento: Um novo papel para universidades públicas como gerenciadores da ação afirmativa no Brasil? *Econômica, 6*(1), 105–121.

Index